# CREDIT ANALYSIS

How to measure and manage credit risk

# CREDIT ANALYSIS

## HOW TO MEASURE AND MANAGE CREDIT RISK

John Coleshaw

WOODHEAD-FAULKNER

NEW YORK LONDON TORONTO SYDNEY TOKYO

Published by Woodhead-Faulkner Limited,
Simon & Schuster International Group,
Fitzwilliam House, 32 Trumpington Street,
Cambridge CB2 1QY, England

First published 1989



*British Library Cataloguing in Publication Data*

Coleshaw, John
Credit analysis: how to measure and manage credit risk.
1. Business firms. Credit management
I. Title
658.8′8

ISBN 0-85941-458-2

Designed by Geoff Green
Typeset by Goodfellow & Egan Phototypesetting Ltd, Cambridge
Printed in Great Britain by BPCC Wheatons Ltd, Exeter

# CONTENTS

# ACKNOWLEDGEMENTS

The author would like to thank the following for their kind and valuable assistance:

ERNST & YOUNG
Adamson, S.
Bloom, A.
Gibson, M.
Mills, Mrs M.
Pallen, D.

BARCLAYS BANK PLC
Arden, D. S.
Blyth, I.
Jones, J. I.
Turle, D. R. G.

DUN & BRADSTREET INTERNATIONAL
Kazmierska, Mrs K.
Mitchinson, P.

EXPORT CREDIT GUARANTEE DEPARTMENT
Bossom, M.

H & H FACTORS LTD
Bayford, T.
Keep, N.
Onslow, J.

ICC COMPANY INFORMATION SERVICES LTD
Parry-Evans, G.

TRADE INDEMNITY PLC
Brunner, D.
McCarton, C.
Friend, J.

Views advanced in this book are not necessarily representative of those persons who have provided assistance or of their organisations unless explicitly stated.

# INTRODUCTION

In most countries throughout the civilised world, there exists an elite group of experts. They sit in quiet offices, surrounded by filing cabinets and computers. Their job has gained universal recognition for its value to national security. It has been romanticised on film and in books. I refer to the 'intelligence services', and in particular to their job of information gathering.

The purpose of this activity is to keep under constant surveillance anything and everything which could pose a threat to national security. Information, opinions, monitoring radio transmissions, satellite scanning, all play their part in this process. Nor is it solely threatening information that is checked. An accurate profile of a country's attitudes, political condition and economic fortune can have a profound influence on its future development and stability.

On a smaller scale, but no less important, is the need to protect your company from threat. This can come in many forms – the introduction of a new product, a new manufacturing process, changes in management in your major competitors, supplier problems caused by a shortage of supply of components. The most obvious and painful of threats is the loss of a customer, and the money he owes you, because of insolvency. All this information needs to be gathered, collated and evaluated, and the relevant managers need to be advised, in case it has some impact on current plans or schedules.

This may not be the first time that credit assessment, a major component of the credit management function, has been compared in such a fashion. But how many trading organisations have emulated the example of the Foreign Office, or Department of State? How many corporate 'intelligence officers' exist, complete with backup team and the resources necessary for constant surveillance?

There are some practical problems in setting up such a function. When does it become necessary to set up an 'intelligence unit'? What information is needed? Where can it be found? How can it be interpreted? How can it be organised to enable it to operate efficiently? These are the central questions which, during the following chapters, I hope will be answered.

*Credit Analysis* will cover all aspects of the measurement and management of credit risk. In this context it means obtaining, assessing and reviewing customer information, whether it be on a domestic or an export customer. Also covered will be crisis management and customer failure.

Computers and scoring techniques are becoming increasingly well regarded for their value in credit risk management. Both subjects will be covered, and some practical suggestions on making the most use of them will be given.

*Credit Analysis* is intended as a convenient source of information, reference material and ideas, on making the most of your customers while minimising the risk of bad debts. In the process it will examine the balance sheet; profit and loss account; financial ratios; insolvency; credit risk protection – each of which is a subject in its own right, and on which definitive textbooks are already available.

Thus the material chosen for this book has been based on practicality and simplicity. Chapters 1 to 3 deal with defining and discussing the features which influence credit risk, and how to gather this information. Chapters 4 to 6 look at ways of analysing it. Three case studies are included for the reader to see the theory put into practice. The remaining chapters explore key areas which have a bearing on the management of credit risk. Concluding each chapter is a summary of its main points, so that the casual reader can glean the maximum idea of its content without having to read all the text.

Though this book's title uses the word 'credit', that does not imply that its contents should be neatly and quickly packaged as a specialist area to be read only by credit personnel. When all is said and done, credit, sales, marketing and to some extent production personnel have one common feature – they all have contact with *customers*. Each discipline must concentrate on its own particular field in its own particular way, but there are areas of overlap.

This is especially so in the case of banking activity. Though not referred to specifically as credit management, lending money involves many of the techniques described in this book. Credit analysis was first used by money lenders in Roman times. Corporate credit managers and bank managers share many features in the way they go about their respective jobs, though there are also differences. These will be described as we go along.

The sales/credit relationship (to which Chapter 7 is devoted) investigates one of the more delicate areas of corporate credit management. Friction can arise if it is felt that the priorities of one are imposed on the other. Sadly this occurrence has fuelled an occasional undercurrent of enmity between the two parties, which has greatly devalued its possible benefits. As an example of this devaluation, many credit controllers fail to make full use of the salesperson as a prime source of customer information. One objective of this book is to show how sales and credit personnel can help each other more, and also help the salesperson to be more 'credit aware'.

Business of any kind is a risky venture, and those who succeed are the ones whose risks paid off for them. The process of taking risks is a fascinating subject in its own right. Instinct, acumen, luck, timing, expertise and knowledge all have a part to play. Often, in credit risk management, these do not come into play. There is usually insufficient time available to concentrate fully on the risks that are being taken, because of the constant need to keep the cash flowing in. However, if the value of consequent bad debts remains at or below an 'acceptable' level it is sometimes possible to be lulled into a false sense of security that risk management is effective. This security is often shattered by the occurrence of a large bad debt which, with the benefit of hindsight, could have been reduced or avoided. Chapter 8 offers some suggestions on how to prioritise risk management effort so that scarce resources can be most effectively applied.

Throughout the book, attention will be paid to credit risk associated with exporting. The polarisation of trade within Europe, North America and Australasia will increasingly mean that many export risks will be no different from domestic risks. However, that still leaves a large number of less-developed countries who represent both opportunity and greater credit risk. Credit analysis includes sections on measuring country risk and the many ways it can be minimised which will be of use to small and large exporter alike.

I have already referred to the job of the 'credit controller' and 'salesperson'. These titles will appear quite often in some parts of the book, and I would like to note that for the sake of uniformity they will be referred to in the masculine gender, though they may equally be feminine.

Finally I hope that the broad and practical treatment of the subject will provide valuable reading for those directly involved in credit risk assessment and management, and useful background for others who have contact with a company's greatest asset, their customers.

# CHAPTER 1

# CREDIT MANAGEMENT IN PERSPECTIVE

The origins of credit management go back to Roman times, where moneylenders would set up a bench in the local forum, and ply for trade. It was in this period that the term 'credit' emerged. Loosely translated it means he/she believes. The moneylender would say this to his clients as they came and asked him for a loan.

Another word to originate from this period is 'bankruptcy'. A moneylender who made a mistake in believing his customer was able to repay, sometimes found himself unable to continue in business. To signify this event, his bench was snapped in half.

Ancient Chinese moneylenders used an ingenious method of minimising the risk of non-payment. If a borrower was incapable of repaying the loan, or died before repayment was due, credit could be extended into the afterlife. Obviously belief in life after death is, or was, strong in China.

Thus the discipline of credit analysis and management was borne, albeit with some interesting variations in attitude. Instead of simple belief in the ability for a borrower to pay, a little investigation was needed:

1. Does the client really need the loan?
2. Does he own property?
3. What is his income?
4. How many animals does he own?
5. How many sons are there to help with the daily chores, and would they inherit the family property?
6. Can he meet the repayment?

If these simple tests proved positive a loan could be made. Failure to do so would result in confiscation of property or animals.

There has been little change in the principles of credit. What has changed out of all proportion is the amount of credit granted. First to grapple with the implications of this was, as one would expect, the banking community.

## 1.1 Credit management in banking

Ever since the snapping of the first bench, banks have evolved methods to control their credit risk. It is a core activity comprising four distinct stages:

1 Appraisal: Work done to collate information on the borrower. Banks tend to offer credit or loans of relatively high amounts over longer periods of time. It follows that a careful study of the prospect is necessary. From the borrower's point of view, it is perhaps not so unreasonable for him to be asked for a high volume of information.
2 Judgement: Based on the appraisal. Elaborate measures are taken to make sure a qualified person makes the decision. All banks have a hierarchy of authority for granting loans and credit, stretching from a clerk right through to a high-powered committee at head office. Corporate lending decisions rely on human judgement, but there is an increasing move towards automated scoring systems for dealing with personal loans.
3 Monitoring: The continuing review of the borrower's situation. Regular updates of a customer's finances and cash flow can be required, along with meetings and visits to get to know them.
4 Control: Actions taken to minimise the risk. Many companies find themselves reliant on the bank for survival. As such, by extending or restricting overdraft levels and honouring cheques, the bank is in a prime position to decide whether a company survives. Strenuous efforts are made to support customers, and often special departments exist to nurse them through the hard times.

The skilful execution of credit skills is central to a bank's reputation and profitability. With so much lent at any one time, even a small percentage of bad debt can run into many hundreds of millions of pounds. Equally important is the reputation for recognising the pressures of business life, and lending sufficient sums to sustain this.

Judging by the huge sales and profit figures posted by the High Street banks and other corporate lenders, their marketing and credit management are very successful. What is their secret? The answer is – security.

In the UK, the banking community is like a benign cartel. With only a handful of options open to the entrepreneur to get funds, he has no choice but to conform to the conditions of the moneylender. One of those conditions is that lending is secured by some form of collateral.

Securitised lending is the hallmark of British banking. This method is used to underwrite many doubtful risks which otherwise would not have been possible. There are countless thriving companies today who can thank the bank for supporting them in their early days. All would have been required to give security – a charge on assets, mortgage on property.

In contrast the US banking system, which has a far greater number of players, will lend more on cash flow generated from the loan. With increased competition in the banking sector, lenders cannot necessarily dictate the terms of their loans. The incidence of bank failure is also much higher.

The competitive element to banking is therefore closely linked to attitudes and practices. Just because there is a relatively small number of banks in the

UK does not imply absence of competition. This is most noticeable in the efforts made to attract new businesses. Every clearing bank has a special package offering higher loans, reduced interest in the first few years, ancillary services to help the business expand, and other benefits. Short-term high-risk lending, with minimal security, is a very profitable activity.

The competition is just as great for attracting the business of larger companies. Creditworthiness tends to assume less importance. Bank services and types of lending assume a much wider variety. Large companies can require large sums, not for day-to-day operations but for expansion plans, acquisitions and mergers. Sometimes funds are needed for major restructuring. In these circumstances banks will often act in consortia, sharing the risk and profit accordingly. Credit assessment may then be based more on confidence than on creditworthiness. 'If big bank "X" is prepared to contribute this amount to the consortium, the customer must be a good risk'.

Another important bank activity is the endorsing of Acceptance Credits. A Bill of Exchange, normally with a tenor (credit period) of three months, is drawn on a bank. When the bank accepts it, it becomes a prime bill available for immediate discount in the money market. At maturity the bill amount is repaid to the bank or a further bill issued. It is an effective and economical way of financing working capital requirements.

Whether lending money in a consortium or by acceptance credits, the banks will need to do some credit evaluation. However, with larger customers there are more restrictions in the information that can be obtained. The clout to insist on seeing management accounts, cash flow statements, does not exist. The bank is thus dependent on readily available information. Since many large companies are publicly quoted, this is easy to obtain.

To summarise, credit granting in the banking environment may seem to be well protected by security. But this in no way makes the task easier. The competition between banks is fierce. A bank cannot be seen to be a 'fair weather friend'. Great effort is placed on helping customers overcome their difficulties. Considerable credit expertise underpins these activities.

## 1.2 Corporate credit management

For a very long time companies entrusted credit management (as we now call it) to a combination of the accounts and sales departments. The former would collect money, the latter make commercial trading decisions. In smaller companies this continues to be an accepted practice.

There comes a stage in all growing companies where it becomes necessary to establish a more formal credit function. Usually this is because the expanding sales ledger cannot be adequately managed in conjunction with other accounting duties. Thus the credit department is established to fulfil a cash collection role.

At around this stage many companies also suffer their first serious bad debt.

They find, during the post-mortem, that warning signs were there to be seen. Alternatively the signs were seen but optimistically underrated. Either way, with the benefit of hindsight it becomes clear that some form of credit assessment expertise, independent from sales and marketing, is highly desirable. So the collection activities of the credit department are expanded to include credit analysis.

This is the painful way to realise that an expert credit department is necessary. Most companies take a more sensible view and establish such a department before the event.

Since banks sell money, the bank manager must take every precaution to control any credit risk. Corporate credit grantors, on the other hand, exist in an environment where goods, not money, are sold. Their role is thus regarded as secondary to selling.

Selling goods is an intoxicating job. Immediate success can be claimed if good salesmanship results in an order. In the early stages of a company's life, a reputation has to be built and new customers found. This can only be done by increasing one's presence in the market by good marketing and selling.

Good salesmanship also involves the intelligent use of customer information. To know the nature of the customer, his strengths and weaknesses, allows the right products to be sold and strengthens the negotiating position. Regular visits will enhance this knowledge. It follows that if anything untoward was happening, the salesman would spot it.

In these circumstances it is well worth having a second opinion, from an expert who can stand back and objectively assess a customer. That person is the credit analyst (who is often also the credit manager).

Suddenly there is an extra link in the customer trading chain. Someone who may not look as favourably on a sales order. Someone who may be vested with the authority to prevent that order being met. So begins a relationship laden with pitfalls – the sales function operates the accelerator pedal while the credit function has a foot over the brakes.

## 1.3 The profit motive

To maximise profit is a key objective of the credit department. Profit is increased if cash is collected quickly, because purchases and expenses can be funded from income rather than by overdraft. No profit at all can be registered until receipt of payment.

However, it would be wrong if credit staff were to lean too heavily on their strategic role as profit makers. The actual profit target they are chasing has been set by . . .

. . . the sales department, whose negotiating ability enabled goods to be sold at the highest margin possible and . . .

. . . the production department, who manufactured (or possibly acquired goods) at the lowest feasible price.

How is it possible to measure just how much profit has been maximised by the credit department? A large number of computations must be made before any such conclusion can be drawn. On the other hand the sales and production departments thrive on margins – it is part of their job to do so.

## 1.4 The role of the credit department

Quite simply, the role of the credit department is to collect money quickly. There is no ambiguity in this objective. The skills and organisation needed to do this function are on a par with any other department in a company. But what about credit analysis?

Credit analysis is not a precise science. Its influence on company profitability is very difficult to quantify. No credit controller has a crystal ball which unfailingly predicts insolvencies long before they occur. No credit controller can contend with total conviction that his decision is the most obvious and correct one in the circumstances. Few credit controllers have the time to devote to credit analysis that they should. Is this a solid enough foundation on which to judge the value of the credit department, other than as a cash collector?

For those who may regard this as too simplistic a view, and that it totally undermines the role and authority of the credit controller who takes prudent steps to minimise the chance of his company suffering a bad debt, then I make no apologies. This is because it is not the sole responsibility of the credit department to minimise bad debts – it is a joint responsibility taken with the sales and marketing departments. Here is a possible job description for a credit department:

> The job of the credit department is to collect money quickly; to monitor customers and promptly identify those representing a credit risk; to provide advice and coordinate action to minimise that risk and maximise sales.

Note the absence of any reference to bad debts and profits. By default everyone connected with customers is working to maximise profit and minimise bad debts. So what else does the credit department do apart from collect money?

1 It keeps the customer base under review, and is constantly alert for possible danger areas and, in the process, areas of opportunity.
2 It initiates damage-limitation measures and uses its expertise to coordinate the necessary repairs.

These two measures project both the positive and the negative aspects of credit management. The latter also draws attention to the pivotal role the credit controller should play to gain the cooperation of all departments in minimising an identified risk – a very skilful and important one.

## 1.5 The benefits of credit analysis

These lie fairly and squarely within the two measures above. Well-organised credit analysis can enable effective monitoring of the customer base and spotting the major strengths and weaknesses. Looking at the main benefits in turn:

### *Benefit 1*

Credit analysis concentrates the minds of all involved (sales/marketing/credit) on the merits or otherwise of doing business with the customer.

What, I hear you ask, have the sales and marketing departments got to do with credit analysis? The answer is that a prime essential for many companies is for them to know their customers. During the salesperson's initial call (and many later calls for that matter), his job is to listen and learn so that he can present and sell his products in a way which is most relevant to the customer. Much of what he hears is potentially of as much use to the credit as it is to the sales department.

There is a high correlation between sales and credit features which, if looked at together, will give the best possible picture of the customer's progress. However, to get to this level of interdepartmental cooperation requires a clear understanding of the features most likely to influence the credit risk (covered in Chapter 2). Specially designed for this purpose is a customer description language which from now on I shall call 'customer-speak'.

So called because it embraces elements of all the disciplines involved with customers, 'customer-speak' does not involve any complex ideas, nor does it require specialist knowledge to understand. Many people will already speak it, without realising. 'Customer-speak' is essentially the practical description of commonsense sales and credit features/policy related to customer trading. It should be a language of sufficient breadth that, if certain features are not known, as is increasingly the case with financial information, it is still possible to reach a worthwhile conclusion on the merits of trading with any given customer.

In short 'customer-speak', when used in credit analysis, is a way for all parties to be on the same wavelength. This is of most use when dealing with the marginal case. Marginal cases all too often are semicombative in nature, emotional trials of strength which require resolution at board level, to nobody's credit (excuse the pun). Decisions that are taken for the good of the company are much better than those for the aggrandisement of the credit or sales departments.

### *Benefit 2*

Credit analysis is the examination of customer information to assess the chances of a bad debt occurring. Based on this assessment, resources can be allocated to keep the relevant customer under review so that any increase in the risk can be promptly spotted and appropriate joint action taken.

Bad debts are a fact of life. Though it is quite possible to identify the potential failure, it is notoriously difficult to predict when the event will occur. To some extent the constant monitoring of payments ('the finger on the pulse') is a good way of spotting trouble. However, the pulse is by no means the only test of fitness, and often poor payment is the result of problems of delivery or quality. This is why review activity is so important.

A review system which does not entirely rely on payment experience is often regarded as being too time-consuming and expensive in terms of people and information expenses. By clearly defining the criteria influencing risk, this need not be so. More on this in later chapters.

### *Benefit 3*

Credit analysis can be used to spot opportunities and find future major accounts.

One essential prerequisite of healthy sales and profit growth is to make sure the maximum trading is done with customers doing well. From the company's view it is possible that more can be gained by the credit department spotting opportunities than by spotting potential bad debts!

Looked at from a different angle, it is more likely that a major customer will be lost to the competition than through insolvency. This then poses a question – who will take his place in such an event?

In an atmosphere of mutual customer objectives, and using the customer description language 'customer-speak', it should be possible for the sales department to turn to their credit colleagues and say: 'We may be about to lose a major account, can we have your suggestions on who might be good replacements?' The implications of this statement are as follows:

1 The opinion of the credit department is respected.
2 The decision will be made jointly and for the good of the company.
3 There is an appreciation that the credit department is not there solely as a prophet of doom.
4 If the sales department has good alternatives lined up to take the place of a major account, it strengthens their hand in negotiating the most profitable contracts.

This degree of honesty and cooperation is very rare, and it is up to credit departments around the world to develop a relationship with their colleagues to make it happen, because it will do wonders for the respect and position of the credit controller.

Trends in the world of credit information mean the credit controller will be equal to this task. Customer information can now be obtained in minutes rather than days, using computer communications. There is also an increasing use of industry norm ratios with which an individual balance sheet can be compared. This eases the task of spotting high and low performers. There is no reason that the credit department cannot become a fount of customer knowledge from which other departments can benefit.

### *Benefit 4*

Credit analysis is necessary to confirm the correct particulars of the customer.

It is by no means uncommon for company buyers to be unaware of the true name of their company, always referring to it by a trading style. Just as easy is the failure to get sufficient details from a telephone order for goods to be invoiced properly. These pitfalls are deepened by the number of daily sales orders received. Distribution companies, for instance, need to be very careful to get the correct order details. In legal terms all that is being done is clarifying exactly who is entering into a sales contract.

Yet for some reason this aspect is ignored. Sales department continually seem unable to get the precise details right every time, which is why in most large companies, or at least those who have a computer database of customer details, it falls on the credit department to make certain of the integrity of information held.

The need for accuracy is at its greatest when opening new customer credit accounts. A quick check of their formal name, invoicing address and if possible their credit rating is all that is required. Trade and bank references can be sought, though their value (in particular the former) is questionable, as we shall discuss in greater detail in Chapter 3.

### *Benefit 5*

The analysis of country risk is important if the most appropriate payment and shipping methods are to be used.

Exporters are faced with a variety of choices to meet a whole variety of different situations. While many companies operate some form of standard policy on payment terms, for instance all exports by confirmed irrevocable letter of credit only, in practice the need to beat the competition to an order will require more flexibility. Here an awareness and analysis of country conditions is paramount.

How much foreign currency is available? How long are the payment delays operated by the central bank? How reliable is the private banking system? How politically stable is the country? All these questions are relevant.

## CHAPTER SUMMARY

1 Credit management began in Roman times, when ill-founded belief in a customer's ability to pay resulted in the moneylender's bench being broken.

2 Over the centuries it has been developed by the banking community.

3 There are three main determinants of credit level:
   (a) customer creditworthiness;
   (b) security offered as collateral;
   (c) competition;

4 There are four main stages of credit management:
   (a) appraisal of the risk;
   (b) credit judgement based on appraisal;
   (c) monitoring of risk;
   (d) control of risk.

5 Measuring and managing credit risk should be done as part of a *co-ordinated group effort*, made by all departments involved with customers, to minimise bad debts and maximise profits. The more this message can be impressed the greater the success at reducing shipment errors, shipments to customers on stop, etc.

6 If the credit department is sufficiently alert to the opportunities and the risks inherent in trading with their customers, their positive contribution will enhance their position within the corporate structure.

7 The benefits of credit analysis are as follows:
   (a) it can be used to establish a common language so that the sales, marketing and credit departments can reach a mutual understanding about the merits of trading with a customer;
   (b) it helps to judge the level of scarce credit resources to be devoted to a risky customer;
   (c) it enables opportunities to be spotted, which in the longer term may be of even greater use than (b);
   (d) it ensures the correct customer details are held on file and quoted in contractual documents;
   (e) it establishes the country risk of exporting to less-developed countries.

# CHAPTER 2

# FEATURES INFLUENCING RISK

In this chapter we look at the features which determine our view on customer risk. The first and most obvious is the customer profile, as this is directly linked with a credit granting decision.

Also examined are the risks associated with industries and countries. Every customer is influenced by the market he trades in and, if overseas, his country. As you will see, the features to look out for fall into two main categories:

1. General industrial or country characteristics, such as the nature of products, level of competition, political stability, climate.
2. Financial characteristics, such as sales and profit growth, liquidity, GDP, foreign currency reserves.

There is a third group of characteristics which influence risk – the benefits of doing business with a customer, industry or country. These will be covered in the first section.

## 2.1 Customer characteristics

Chapter 1 introduced a customer description language which describes the merits of trading with a customer. Called 'customer-speak' it allows all parties to be on the same 'wavelength' when discussing a customer. To meet this objective would involve compiling a series of sales and credit features which are easy to understand and interpret and are broadly available for every customer. Above all, in order to help joint discussions and decisions between sales and credit disciplines, these features should not be too specialised or complex.

This chapter is devoted to describing the key elements of a technique which I call *attribute analysis*. It has eighteen components, which relate to every important aspect of the customer. In Chapter 5 they will be used in a straightforward model for customer scoring. It will also serve as the basis for the 'customer-speak' language.

Before looking at these attributes in more detail, it is worth drawing attention to a phrase above with which you may have some doubts – 'these features should not be too specialised or complex'.

To credit analysts who have studied in depth and have a wealth of experience on the subject, I would qualify the statement by saying that your expertise involves a sub-language which can be used to great benefit in coming to a thorough and in-depth conclusion on the creditworthiness of a customer. It is also one which we shall look at in Chapter 6.

Modern financial analysis encompasses some very sophisticated ideas and varied ratios. For instance take the cumulative profitability ratio, priority debt-service ability or normalised working capital level – each has a particular significance, and occasionally you may encounter a case where they are adverse enough to suggest limiting trade.

But if you used this as justification for doing so to a sales colleague, he may not be quite as prepared to accept the fact, first because he does not understand complex financial analysis and second the figures are all history anyway.

The perceived creditworthiness of a customer, as judged by a balance sheet, is not the sole criterion for judging the level of trade. There is an assessment technique used by banks, called CAMPARI, which shows that other features besides financial are important:

Character – a view of the people, products and history.
Ability – to repay.
Margin – the reward of trading.
Purpose – the reason for the loan request.
Amount – the value sought, and its suitability.
Repayment – feasibility of the schedule.
Insurance – security available or needed.

Here we have a range of considerations or attributes which combine to form the basis of the lending decision. Five of these seven attributes are linked to the accounts and finances of the prospective borrower, the two exceptions being character and margin.

With character we move into the realms of subjectivity, because it involves judging aspects which are not specifically quantified on the balance sheet. Likewise, the margin is a partially subjective measure of how acceptable the expected profit of the loan may be.

Banks are very fortunate – they can insist on seeing some form of recent financial information before lending any money – quite rightly so if the amount involved is high or repayment is to be over a long period.

The credit controller is not in the same position. Many credit decisions will be made on the most cursory of information – especially if the amount involved is low with payment terms less than or equal to sixty days. Rarely is the true and up-to-date financial position available. Asked to grant credit in excess of a low amount, the credit controller will be forced to look at non-financial features. This is an activity for which 'attribute analysis' is, in part, designed.

## 2.2 An overview of attribute analysis

The main considerations involved in making credit decisions are divided into three distinct groups with six features in each:

Customer attributes

- Outward impressions
- Product description
- Demand for product
- Strength of competition
- End-customer profile
- Management ability

Priority attributes

- Profit margin acceptability
- Goods/services required
- Market attraction
- Market competition
- Security
- Replaceability

Credit and financial attributes

- Trading experience
- Credit references
- Growth of equity and profit
- Balance sheet strength
- Gearing
- Capitalisation

The main characteristics of attribute analysis are as follows:

1 The attributes are placed into *three* distinct categories. This is a very significant variant on the more traditional approach of there being just two main categories – sales and credit.

The credit attributes are the most obvious and easily recognised of the three groups, comprising four very basic financial measurements, and also the familiar trade experience and credit references. Rather than balance these features with a single group called 'sales' attributes, they have been split into two groups, customer and priority.

The customer attributes, as you might expect, cover all the elements which describe the activities and potential of the customer. Since they have a direct influence on the sort of products you will be selling to them, it is reasonable to assume such information could be furnished by the sales and marketing departments.

Priority attributes concentrate on the benefits of doing business with a customer, and are intended to act as a balance to the other groups.

Every customer, even the largest or most well known, will have his strengths *and* weaknesses. This can make it very difficult to reach a balanced credit decision. The priority attributes are designed to reflect obvious corporate

*Table 2.1* Components of customer attributes

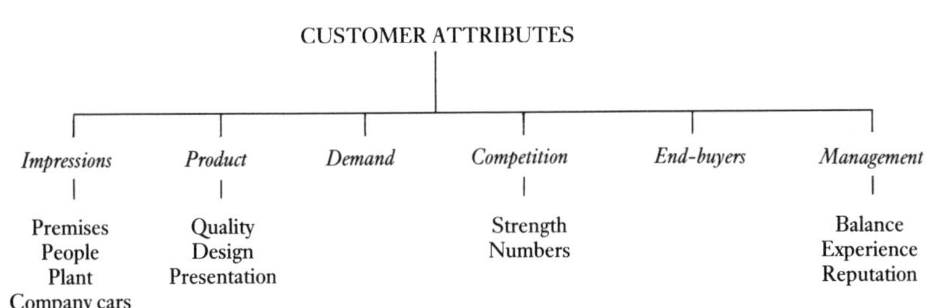


objectives, some of which can be measured in an objective way. For instance the acceptability of profit margin, or attraction of the market, could well be linked to policy determined at board level.

2 The attributes closely conform to the intuitive processes of credit decision-taking. Here we meet for the first time in this book the ubiquitous 'gut-feel', a term used to describe intuitive decision-making. 'Gut-feel' is the recognition that some feature exists which cannot be properly explained, but which is important enough to resolve a problem (one way or the other). Maybe it is astute guesswork; perhaps some heaven-sent ability to foretell the future? The biggest problem with the 'gut-feel' is that the special 'something' is never quantified, and therefore cannot be reused.

If all the processes which go to make a 'gut-feel' decision could somehow be trapped, and stored in a bottle, then you are talking about a potent weapon with which to make credit decisions! Without such a weapon however, you might find that attribute analysis is a worthy substitute – a method for allowing the analyst to put into context his innermost feelings on the case in question.

3 The attributes are comprehensive. Every conceivable nuance of a trading situation (though not necessarily with lending) should fall within these attributes. The structure of the attributes could be regarded like a tree, as in Table 2.1.

4 There is a degree of balance to the group. The sales and marketing departments should have a significant contribution to make in credit decisions. I have used the term 'degree' because, when looked at in a list as above, the credit attributes constitute only 33 per cent of the whole. It is very important for credit controllers to remember this, especially if they are vested with the

authority to set the maximum level of trading on a customer. However it is equally important to note that each of the attributes can vary in its significance, and there is no question that some of the credit attributes are very important.

5 Except for the financial measurements, all the attributes are elements of information which should be easy to compile from within the organisation. Looking in turn at the three groups, priority attributes can all be measured without obtaining third-party information. The same can be said of customer attributes if the salesforce is able to visit all (or most of its) customers at some time, and compile a call report. Trading experience and references can also be built up and obtained without difficulty.

Comprehensive financial data is getting harder to obtain due to a general relaxation in requirements for statutory disclosure. This heightens the need to develop analytical methods which rely less on balance sheet information.

6 The attributes make a very good outline for a visit report. More and more customer visits are being made by credit staff. It is an essential part of good risk management to see the riskiest prospects in person. While doing so, every one of the customer and credit attributes should be assessed.

## 2.3 Attribute analysis – the difficulties

Credit Analysis has so far concentrated on information which is objective, like balance sheet figures. A ratio is a ratio – no arguments. Sure it is possible to argue over the interpretation of ratios, but all the same, the figures are there to be seen. CAMPARI is a prime example of a system which is still heavily based on subjective information.

Attribute analysis is based mainly on subjective measurement. In order to make it most effective requires the interdepartmental understanding already discussed in Chapter 1. This is why I have also used the term 'customer-speak' – it is a language that has to be learned through experience. It is no good thinking that the worthwhile elements of this language are going to be automatically understood the moment the technique is tried out. Attribute analysis needs time to evolve, to settle down, so that all who have contact with it can adjust to the technique.

Another difficulty is the breadth of coverage of some of the attributes. A second glance at the tree-structure in Table 2.1, which suggests several different aspects to the outward impressions attribute, show that some features have to be considered and a subjective overview taken.

To help this process, I will describe, in a subjective way, my interpretation of the meaning and relevance of each attribute. However, you should bear in mind that different trading conditions can put different slants on the relevance and meaning of each attribute. I shall describe them from the viewpoint that you are the supplier, dealing with a customer who is a manufacturer.

## 2.4 The attributes explained in detail

### *2.4.1 Customer attributes*

The salesman, given his opportunities to visit the customer, is best placed to assess these attributes. What follows has been written with this in mind, though it is equally applicable to credit staff on a visit.

1 Outward impressions
Here we are concerned with our thoughts and feelings. This depends on how well you know the customer. At the most basic level, contact by letter or on the phone will occur at some stage with every customer:

(a) What does his stationery look like?
(b) How prompt are his answers to questions or replies to your letters?
(c) How professional or informed appears the customer?
(d) How interested does he sound in your products?

It does not take much contact to begin to get a feeling of what the customer is like. Of course companies spend much time getting their image right, which is reflected in material things. However, it does not necessarily matter how glossy the image, if you feel that you are dealing with idiots, or slowcoaches, or clock-watchers. These attitudes are a give-away that something is not quite right with the customer.

However, material things do have a bearing, and the visit gives an ideal opportunity to back up one's impressions of the people. Consider the following items:

(a) The state of the premises and plant, especially with a company which has occupied them for some time, is a good guideline to the general profitability of that customer.
(b) The quantities awaiting delivery in the storeroom or stockroom will give an idea of the current and future cash flow.
(c) The degree of activity in the manufacturing area is a sign of current order levels and sales potential.
(d) The company cars will suggest the attitudes of the management. A flash car parked outside a crumbling building filled with unhappy-looking people is always suspicious.

2 Product description
Centred purely on the product, this is a description of its attractiveness and design. Do not confuse this attribute with product demand, which is a different consideration altogether.

Products have to work, or do something, and obviously the construction of the product is important. The method of construction is an excellent guide to possible problems the customer could face:

(a) Does the process rely heavily on expensive energy?
(b) How much skilled labour is required and is it available in the area?
(c) Are there any unions involved?

Comparing the product with others of a similar type is the best way of judging its design and general attractiveness, unless you have specialised knowledge of the product, in which case a more professional opinion of its worth can be made.

However, there is one aspect of a product which is missing – quality. The quality of the product depends on the market in which the product will be sold. There are just as many opportunities to sell poor quality, and as a result cheaper goods, as there are high quality goods. It is the end customer who is ultimately the judge of quality.

3 Product demand

This is primarily concerned with market capacity and its general direction. One or other of two main questions needs to be answered, if any conclusion is to be drawn on this attribute:

Is there a gap in the market?
OR
Is there room in the market?

In the first question, the use of the word gap implies that there is something appreciably different about a product which will attract its own demand. The same applies if you are dealing with a brand new product, perhaps for an unestablished market.

More likely, however, you will be looking at a standard product destined to join an ever-growing multitude of similar products. Here the question of room in the market requires more exact definition:

(a) Is the product to be sold locally or nationally?
(b) What is the likely demand depending upon the areas above?
(c) Is the market growing or contracting?
(d) Is it seasonal in nature?
(e) Is your customer's marketing strategy suited to its task?

4 Strength of competition

The competitive conditions are closely linked to Product Demand, with the important difference that this attribute deals with the composition and capabilities of other companies in the market rather than the customer you are trading with.

Each market tends to assume its own profile, with the existence of:

(a) Market leaders, who are big and strong.

(b) The mid-range and competent members often with good penetration within their own geographic region.
(c) The minnows who eke out a meagre and difficult existence, running the large risk of either being eaten up by one of the bigger fish, or dying unnoticed.
(d) Market innovators, some of whom are also the market leaders, others who are small and trying hard to find a lucrative gap in the market.

The balance of this profile determines the strength of competition. The most interesting part of judging this strength is that, with any luck, you will deal with some of the other players in the market, and a very accurate measurement is possible.

In fact these last three attributes are very relevant to the process of sales targeting and it is in the interests of both the sales and credit departments that all efforts are made to assess them. Many company failures have come about as a result of poor marketing in an area of very heavy competition and static demand.

5 End buyers

The end customer destined to use your goods, albeit after modification by your immediate customer, is very important. The trouble is that you do not necessarily know who he is.

In trading situations there is often a high degree of trust that a creditworthy end buyer has been found, or that your customer is able to handle the difficulties of trading with his own customers. However, this attribute directly addresses the famous 'domino effect' – the chain reaction which can create, and also wipe out, an entire group of companies.

Closer examination of trading patterns may reveal that a huge number of these chains exist – the large factory in a town creating opportunities for many other small companies in the surrounding area, and so on. During periods of recession the awareness of this pattern is an important part of minimising credit risk.

6 Management ability

Without doubt the most important customer attribute, this is also the most difficult to assess. At the root of all company successes and failures is the quality of management. Just about any disaster that can befall a customer could be attributed in one way or another to a management shortfall. However, what are the main points to watch for, and how is it possible to assess the management?

(a) Market knowledge:

All managers/directors have served an apprenticeship in their chosen fields, and as a result acquire some form of reputation. The more sales and marketing knowledge you have of the market, the better the chance of getting to know the good and bad managers.

(b) Management balance and experience:
A common feature of new companies is their lack of balance, often brought about by a lack of experience. Good ideas have to be backed up with good organisation and money, and ideally every management team should contain all these qualities. If any one of them is missing then there is a weakness, and the most common weak link is lack of financial control.

A quick look at a company letterhead will give an idea of the directors – the more the better. The larger the company, the more directors there may be, but this is no guarantee of balance. Try to get an idea of how sales or financially oriented the customer is.

(c) Management style:
Again dependent on size, this is a useful indicator of risk. Constant referrals to a higher authority are a sign of insecurity and inability to delegate. It is also a sign of the purse strings being tightly controlled because of slow cash flow or heavy short-term borrowing.

Impressions on management style can be gained during a sales or credit visit, though it is possible to glean some insight from the press, or the annual company report (if you can get a copy of it, and if you can then believe all that is said in it).

(d) Dictatorships:
This management feature is worthy of specific mention. History tends to reveal dictators as 'impressive failures', and this is often the case in business.

How they can be identified is another matter, because it is very difficult. Casual comments from employees, or rumours in the market, are two possible avenues. If the company name is also the name of the founder, this might suggest some degree of dictatorship.

### *2.4.2 Priority attributes*

These are concerned with attaching some value or benefit of trading with a customer. It is well worth doing so, because on occasions, customers can be quite literally, 'more trouble than they are worth'.

1 Profit margin acceptability
It is assumed that all trading is done for profit, but that does not necessarily imply financial gain. Loss leaders are an obvious example. It may be expedient to accept a small loss on one product line if you are already making a good profit on another with the same customer.

Hence the word 'acceptability'. The degree of acceptability will most probably be linked to volume – the larger the volume the lower the acceptable margin. However, the degree can also be preset by management decision, in the same way as volume discounts or rebates are. It is this policy aspect to the margin which should make it easier to quantify.

2 Goods/services required
Though at face value it is beneficial to be honoured with an order, there is slightly more to it than that:

(a) Are the products in stock?
(b) Is there a long manufacturing lead time?
(c) Is there a shortage of supply meaning there is an order back-log?
(d) Is someone available to do the service?
(e) Is there some strategic value in supplying the goods?
(f) Does the production process require significant exceptional expense – perhaps it is a special order, or a product which has to be individually tailored to the customer's needs?
(g) Are there any company circumstances which have a special bearing on the order, i.e. to keep a production line going, or to maintain a trading presence in a country?

These are the main considerations surrounding this attribute. The larger the range of products and activities, the more important it can be.

3 Market attraction
This is an attribute which introduces another strategic element, 'is this where your company wants to be?'

Again of more significance the wider your range of company products, it has a direct bearing on the risk of trading, and is also the subject of marketing policy. Markets carry with them their own risk profile, and it may be expedient to accept a higher level if it falls in line with corporate strategy.

Country can be substituted for market attraction.

4 Market competition
The degree of difficulty in getting an order is often a compelling reason for doing business. Or so it may seem to the ambitious salesman. However, what if the customer does not pay, or pays so slowly that the acceptability dwindles to nothing?

In reality any order which is worthwhile will involve beating competent competition. It follows that if a significant sales coup is contemplated, a quick cross-check is made on the credit and customer attributes.

Sometimes an order in the face of stiff competition is more important than is the margin acceptability. Perhaps it opens the door to much greater things, or inconveniently restricts your competitor.

5 Security
The vast majority of business is done on standard terms, or within a band of acceptable credit periods. However, obtaining additional security is an excellent way to reduce risk, provided the security itself is acceptable.

Many companies increase the security of their terms by operating a retention of title condition, which allows for ownership of goods to pass only when payment is received. In exporting, there are many different ways to control the security of payment, the letter of credit or (less so) the bill of exchange being the best options.

For domestic trading situations, additional security usually takes the form of a third-party guarantee, perhaps from a parent or associated company, or the wealthy owner, or maybe even a bank. This security varies in its value according to the creditworthiness of the guarantor, who should always be investigated. The best payment securities are cash with order, a pro-forma invoice, or cash on delivery.

6 Replaceability

How easy or difficult it is to replace a customer has a bearing on the risk. Large or major customers are very difficult to replace, and this will influence your views on many of the priority attributes. Likewise customers who purchase a special product line or who have been known for a long time.

At the other end of the scale small customers are much easier to replace, and the consequent trading risks often that much lower.

### *2.4.3 Credit and financial attributes*

These relate to the financial position and credit record of the customer. For small orders or low-level business, the assessment of these attributes will be quite sufficient to judge the level of trade. It is possible to glean informed third-party comment on them, rather than rely on internal sources as with the other groups of attributes (though this is not meant to imply that internal sources are any less valuable).

1 Trading experience

With existing customers it is routine credit department procedure to keep some record and monitor customer's payment experience.

But the payment record itself is not the only element of this attribute. The histories of problems, invoice queries, proof-of-delivery requests and payment cooperation all contribute in a major way to the general trading experience. In fact many credit controllers will probably find that dealing with disputes and their knock-on effects is a bigger barrier to getting paid on time than the perceived payment ability of the customer.

Few customers pay their bills exactly on due date. They may wait until the end of the month, or the next computer run of their purchase ledger system, or the first chasing action by the credit department. Assessment of the experience must allow for these popular circumstances.

2 Credit references

These tend to be of most relevance when the customer is unknown, or where his trading pattern has significantly altered, either by sharply increasing or worsening. Every customer will have a track record with other companies and this is a good indicator of their capability to pay you.

3 Growth of equity and profit
In what direction is your customer travelling? This is measured best by looking at the results of trading and the level of assets and liabilities of the customer.

Lenders are particularly interested in this aspect – companies who are 'going somewhere' or can prove some worthwhile achievement are more likely to represent a good long-term prospect. In selling terms it makes sense to concentrate efforts on those same customers.

4 Balance sheet strength
The balance sheet measures the stability or solidity which underlie the performance of a company. Success can only really be built on solid foundations, and these can be reviewed by looking at this attribute.

Judging the strength of a balance sheet is no mean task, in view of the many variables within it. Some aspects will look favourable, others less so. Which ones should receive greatest attention? Some suggestions on a simple but effective measurement of strength will be given in Chapters 4 and 5. As a rule the strength is measured by reviewing a combination of general features.

5 Gearing
This is the term which describes how reliant a company is on the goodwill of other lenders. This usually means the bank, parent/associated companies, or both.

When a company starts business it almost invariably does so on the back of some borrowed money, and this state of affairs continues for the rest of its corporate life. However, the level of borrowing can reach a point where the business would not survive without it, and this is when credit risk gets much higher. Most company failures occur because of long-unpaid taxes, or the bank, not satisfied with the future prospects, withdrawing support.

6 Capitalisation
As with life, what you get out of a company depends upon what you put in. In corporate terms this input is called capital, and it can be measured by the value of share capital the owners have staked in their company.

The greater the share capital, the easier it is to borrow money, and to show to the world that the owners are committed to their business. However, other forms of capital exist, like money borrowed over a long period (more than one year), and profits retained in the business, and the measure of how satisfactory the capital level is made by comparing it with the profits, as will be seen when we look at financial ratios.

### *2.4.4 Attribute analysis in perspective*

Many bad trading decisions are made because of haphazard analysis, or over-reliance on a few good points, while neglecting the bad. The greatest benefit of attribute analysis is that it allows customer assessment to be organised in a comprehensive and logical manner and that the combination of sales and credit information, tempered by corporate policy, will result in the most consistent credit decisions. However, the conclusion of the analytical process will only be as good as the ability of the analysts.

## 2.5 Industry features influencing risk

Now that we have a framework on which to describe each main risk feature, it can be applied in the industrial context.

Industry attributes

- Type
- Product description
- Demand for product
- Strength of competition
- Customer profile
- Management ability

Financial attributes

- Payment patterns
- Bad debt history
- Growth of sales and profit
- Liquidity
- Gearing
- Return on shareholders' funds

There is a similarity between industry and customer attributes. Financial attributes remain almost the same, with adjustments to reflect the payment patterns of the industry, its bad debt history and its attractiveness to investors.

### *2.5.1 Type*

The three industry types are manufacturing, distribution and services. Each will have its own profile based on a wide range of measures.

### *2.5.2 Product description*

Different types of product, and the way they are manufactured or supplied, will influence the stability of an industry.

Products relying on components supplied from overseas may find themselves vulnerable to external pressures outside their control. Computer manufacturers are a prime example of this. The main source of supply for one of the most essential memory components is Japan. Japanese manufacturers therefore dictate both the supply and the price. This has resulted in shortages of components and higher prices.

The method of production determines the quality and continuity of supply. Automated production lines and industrial robots are steadily overtaking manual production processes. Labour-intensive production is more prone to interruption because of worker unrest. Also manufacturing costs tend to rise at a higher rate – wage bills rise faster than the cost of components. This is why many labour-intensive products are sent for assembly to Far-Eastern countries with low wage rates.

Alterations in production techniques can cause fluctuations in the stability of an industry. For instance, farming has become more intensive, and machines are assuming an ever-greater importance. The down side is that the quality of land is reducing, and expensive chemicals are required to keep it in shape.

The agricultural industry is also prone to unexpected climatic conditions. Poor summer weather affects harvests, hurricanes can wipe out an entire crop.

Government regulations can affect the cost of goods. The cost of furniture in the UK is set to rise as new regulations on fire retardation come into force. More expensive foams are now required, putting up production costs. Car prices are rising in those countries requiring more stringent exhaust emission controls. The cost of petrol production is rising now that unleaded fuel is being more actively promoted.

### *2.5.3 Product demand*

A key industrial feature is the rate at which demand is increasing or decreasing. This will influence the number of new businesses entering the market, and the degree of penetration of overseas goods.

The prime determinant of demand is the general economic condition of a country. A booming economy increases demand, recessions having the opposite effect. The eighties have seen a general trend of economic growth in the developed nations. However, this may lead to overcapacity in the market, which in turn can cause deflation and high interest rates.

Many industries are subject to the whims of the consumer. Clothing and fashion goods can alter from year to year. Those not catering to the latest fashion can find survival difficult. The food business is undergoing a change due to the increased health-consciousness of the consumer. The demand for whole foods, organic vegetables and additive-free products is creating new opportunities for the industry.

### 2.5.4 *Strength of competition*

As industrial activity expands, so too will the strength of competition. However, it will influence industries in differnt ways, according to their type.

Manufacturers are most prone to international competition. This is especially so in those with higher labour costs. Consumer electricals, cars, footware, electronics and computers, are sectors suffering from Far Eastern competition. Some of it is fair, but there are occasions where government intervention has been necessary to stop products being 'dumped' at an unreasonably low price. Import restrictions and protectionism are constantly under consideration. Some Japanese goods have long been subject to a quota, hence the trend for the major Japanese companies establishing manufacturing facilities in Europe. The steel community has also gone through a similar period.

The arrival of the 'single market' in 1992 will see the removal of existing trading obstacles and difficulties and competition increasing. Expansion of European markets is being heralded as a golden opportunity. However, there are fears that this will adversely influence competitive conditions for non-European manufacturers. There are now concerns that world trade will diminish as a result of retaliation by the US and Far Eastern countries, whose trade to Europe may be restricted.

### 2.5.5 *Customer profile*

We have already mentioned the three types of industry, and their different characteristics.

The amount of capital investment required will have a strong bearing on the make-up of the industry. Car manufacturing is heavily capital intensive, therefore it is limited to a small number of companies. Computer services is a high growth industry with low capital outlay, therefore its numbers are expanding. The composition of an industry is a pointer towards several important features. Industries with a high number of new companies is less creditworthy, and credit policy has to be adjusted accordingly.

### 2.5.6 *Management ability*

As with a customer, industrial strength is influenced by the management ability within it.

Personnel management, alteration of trade practices and acceptance of new technology are all controlled by management. The newspaper industry has been held back for years, partly as a result of management being unable to persuade staff to change working practices. The building sector is notorious for its high incidence of insolvency. One reason is that the many small subcontractors, providing a variety of building services, are managed by people practiced in the art of decorating, plastering, carpentry and plumbing. None of these arts is a good qualification for being able to manage the financial side of the business.

### *2.5.7 Payment patterns*

There is a wide variety of payment patterns. Companies trading in many different markets, and the banks who lend to all sectors, will be aware of these variations. Payment patterns determine the length of credit given, hence the credit exposure risk.

Food and retail companies are more fortunate, since they operate on cash terms, or credit periods below thirty days (much less for perishable foods). Most industries trade on thirty- to sixty-day terms. At the bottom of the league are commercial services, such as barristers and solicitors who tolerate credit periods in excess of 60 days.

Payment patterns in the building industry are further complicated by the nature of the work. A plumber may install a water system in a block of flats, but it could be some months later before the water is finally connected, allowing the plumbing to be fully tested. If the plumber was a subcontractor, he may not receive payment until the main contractor receives his. A retention (normally ten per cent) will be made until completion of the building project and successful testing of the work. A proper credit period is difficult to manage in these circumstances, and instead a system of 'pay-when-paid' has developed.

A form of discount is commonplace in the fuel distribution sector. Fuel is invoiced at full price, with an attractive rebate being offered if full payment is received. In the agricultural supply business, credit can be extended over a growing season, the farmer not paying for his fertiliser until the crop has been grown. Many different types of distributor get extended credit for stocking-up periods, during summer or over the Christmas months.

### *2.5.8 Bad debt history*

Industry risk is most forcibly illustrated by the incidence of bad debts. Table 2.2 shows the incidence of bad debts across a selection of industries, over the years 1980–1988, in which the credit insurance company Trade Indemnity PLC were involved on behalf of their policyholders.

### *2.5.9 Growth of sales and profit*

Looking at industry groups as a whole, there is a link between sales/profit growth and general economic activity. It is rare for industry sales to decline, though this has been the case with oil and gas, because of the corresponding decline in world fuel prices.

*Table 2.2* Company Failures 1980–1988 as registered at Trade Indemnity

| Year | 1980 | 1981 | 1982 | 1983 | 1984 | 1985 | 1986 | 1987 | 1988 |
|---|---|---|---|---|---|---|---|---|---|
| Retail, wholesale and distribution | 450 | 571 | 779 | 996 | 1,006 | 871 | 702 | 489 | 439 |
| Building and construction | 455 | 457 | 598 | 777 | 839 | 992 | 815 | 674 | 576 |
| Textiles and clothing | 379 | 407 | 494 | 489 | 452 | 401 | 308 | 256 | 230 |
| Engineering and metals | 449 | 481 | 775 | 967 | 911 | 771 | 714 | 524 | 462 |
| Furniture and upholstery | 267 | 313 | 436 | 370 | 371 | 315 | 267 | 195 | 150 |
| Food and agriculture | 108 | 145 | 183 | 247 | 216 | 201 | 218 | 153 | 115 |
| Chemicals | — | — | — | 103 | 99 | 80 | 79 | 64 | 67 |
| Services | — | — | — | 267 | 253 | 320 | 244 | 153 | 151 |
| Total | 2,108 | 2,374 | 3,265 | 4,216 | 4,147 | 3,951 | 3,347 | 2,508 | 2,190 |

(*Source:* Quarterly Economic Review, Winter 1989, Trade Indemnity PLC)

*Table 2.3* Growth of Sales and Profit, 1986/1987

| Activities | Annual sales growth % | Rank 1986/87 | Annual profit growth % | Rank 1986/87 |
|---|---|---|---|---|
| Commercial services | 37 | 1 | 27 | 7 |
| Ceramics & glass industry | 18 | 2 | 23 | 10 |
| Industrial services | 16 | 3 | 50 | 1 |
| Textile & footware manufacturers | 16 | 4 | 41 | 2 |
| Consumer services | 15 | 5 | 20 | 14 |
| Retail industry | 14 | 6 | 21 | 13 |
| Construction industry | 13 | 7 | 22 | 11 |
| Paper, printing & packaging industry | 12 | 8 | 35 | 3 |
| Food & drink distributors | 12 | 9 | 25 | 9 |
| Drinks industry | 11 | 10 | 13 | 21 |
| Transport industry – distributors | 11 | | 16 | 16 |
| Electronics industry | 11 | 12 | 13 | 19 |
| Timber & furniture industry | 10 | 13 | 12 | 22 |
| Electrical industry | 9 | 14 | 1 | 25 |
| Consumer goods manufacturers | 9 | 15 | 30 | 6 |
| Industrial equipment manufacturers | 9 | 16 | 21 | 12 |
| Transport industry – manufacturers | 9 | 17 | 35 | 4 |
| Publishing industry | 8 | 18 | 16 | 17 |
| Engineering equipment manufacturers | 8 | 19 | 31 | 5 |
| Building materials industry | 7 | 20 | 25 | 8 |
| Metals industry | 6 | 21 | 16 | 15 |
| Engineering components manufacturers | 6 | 22 | 9 | 23 |
| Transport industry – services | 5 | 23 | 8 | 24 |
| Engineering services industry | 5 | 24 | −4 | 26 |
| Chemical & plastics industry | 4 | 25 | 13 | 20 |
| Food manufacturers | 3 | 26 | 15 | 18 |
| Oil & gas | −22 | 27 | −19 | 27 |

(*Source:* 'Industrial Performance Analysis', 1988/89 Edition, ICC Business Publications Ltd)

*Table 2.4* Liquidity as measured by the Current Ratio, 1986/1987

| Activities | Current ratio 1986/87 |
|---|---|
| Engineering component manufacturers | 1.7 |
| Textile & footware manufacturers | 1.6 |
| Ceramics & glass industry | 1.5 |
| Industrial equipment manufacturers | 1.5 |
| Chemical & plastics industry | 1.5 |
| Consumer goods manufacturers | 1.5 |
| Engineering equipment manufacturers | 1.5 |
| Electrical industry | 1.5 |
| Transport industry – manufacturers | 1.5 |
| Metals industry | 1.4 |
| Timber and furniture industry | 1.4 |
| Construction industry | 1.3 |
| Electronics industry | 1.3 |
| Building materials industry | 1.3 |
| Paper printing & packaging industry | 1.3 |
| Food manufacturers | 1.3 |
| Engineering services industry | 1.3 |
| Industrial services | 1.2 |
| Transport industry – distributors | 1.2 |
| Publishing industry | 1.2 |
| Commercial services | 1.1 |
| Drinks industry | 1.0 |
| Consumer services | 1.0 |
| Retail industry | 1.0 |
| Transport industry – services | 0.8 |
| Food & drink distributors | 0.8 |
| Oil & gas | 0.7 |

(*Source:* 'Industrial Performance Analysis', 1988/89 Edition, ICC Business Publications Ltd)

The industries to look out for are those whose profit growth exceeds sales. This is a sign of healthy demand, capacity within the industry, and better management ability. Table 2.3 shows the main industrial groups and their growth in sales and profit for the year 1986/1987.

### *2.5.10 Liquidity*

There is a strong link between type of industry and liquidity. Distributors and service companies keep a lower level of stock. The food business, with its short payment terms, is one of the least liquid industries. Their methods of computerised stock control mean they can identify exactly which product lines are in heaviest demand, and gear their purchasing decisions accordingly.

Manufacturers are the most liquid, since a higher proportion of stock is held to meet demand.

*Table 2.5* Gearing Ratio, 1986/1987

| Activities | Gearing ratio 1986/87 |
|---|---|
| Drinks industry | 0.4 |
| Retail industry | 0.4 |
| Textile & footwear manufacturers | 0.5 |
| Electronics industry | 0.6 |
| Ceramics & glass industry | 0.6 |
| Food manufacturers | 0.6 |
| Food & drink distributors | 0.6 |
| Timber & furniture industry | 0.7 |
| Industrial equipment manufacturers | 0.7 |
| Metals industry | 0.8 |
| Consumer goods manufacturers | 0.8 |
| Construction industry | 0.8 |
| Engineering component manufacturers | 0.8 |
| Paper, printing & packaging industry | 0.8 |
| Chemical & plastics industry | 0.8 |
| Electrical industry | 0.9 |
| Consumer services | 0.9 |
| Building materials industry | 0.9 |
| Commercial services | 0.9 |
| Engineering equipment manufacturers | 1.0 |
| Transport industry – distributors | 1.0 |
| Industrial services | 1.1 |
| Transport industry – manufacturers | 1.2 |
| Publishing industry | 1.3 |
| Engineering services industry | 1.6 |
| Transport industry – services | 2.4 |
| Oil & gas | 4.0 |

(*Source:* 'Industrial Performance Analysis', 1988/89 Edition, ICC Business Publications Ltd)

Table 2.4. shows liquidity, as measured by current assets as a proportion of current liabilities, for the year 1986/87.

### *2.5.11 Gearing*

Since high gearing is the major cause of company failure, it follows that industries with higher gearing are more vulnerable. Banks carefully monitor their market exposures using gearing/borrowing ratios.

Table 2.5 shows gearing as measured by total debt as a proportion to net worth (share capital plus retained earnings), for the year 1986/87.

### *2.5.12 Return on shareholders' funds*

This final industry feature measures profit as a percentage of shareholders' funds (share capital plus retained earnings less intangible assets). Investment in

*Table 2.6* Return on Shareholders' Funds, 1986/87

| Activities | Return on shareholders' funds 1986/87 |
|---|---|
| Oil & gas | 60.5 |
| Commercial services | 60.2 |
| Industrial services | 36.4 |
| Food & drink distributors | 32.7 |
| Electronics industry | 30.4 |
| Chemical & plastics industry | 29.1 |
| Paper printing & packaging industry | 28.0 |
| Building materials industry | 25.9 |
| Retail industry | 25.4 |
| Textile & footwear manufacturers | 24.3 |
| Food manufacturers | 24.3 |
| Construction industry | 23.9 |
| Ceramics & glass industry | 23.7 |
| Timber & furniture industry | 22.9 |
| Publishing industry | 21.7 |
| Industrial equipment manufacturers | 21.6 |
| Consumer goods manufacturers | 21.2 |
| Consumer services | 20.9 |
| Transport industry – services | 20.8 |
| Electrical industry | 20.0 |
| Engineering component manufacturers | 19.4 |
| Transport industry – distributors | 18.5 |
| Engineering equipment manufacturers | 17.7 |
| Drinks industry | 17.0 |
| Transport industry – manufacturers | 16.1 |
| Metals industry | 14.5 |
| Engineering services industry | 10.2 |

(*Source:* 'Industrial Performance Analysis', 1988/89 Edition, ICC Business Publications Ltd)

an industry is determined by the rewards that can be gained by investors. Industries which can easily attract investors are more likely to be able to generate funds for expansion and modernisation.

Table 2.6 lists the main industries, in order of attractiveness, for the year 1986/87.

## 2.6 COUNTRY FEATURES INFLUENCING RISK

Country attributes

- Country classification
- Natural assets
- Economic and industrial structure
- Local customs
- Political stability

*Table 2.7* Exports by Value 1987

| Country | £ million |
|---|---|
| USA | 1,101.4 |
| Germany, Federal Republic of | 949.4 |
| France | 778.2 |
| Netherlands | 585.6 |
| Italy | 414.6 |
| Belgium & Luxembourg | 385.8 |
| Ireland, Republic of | 383.2 |
| Sweden | 232.2 |
| Spain | 216.4 |
| Saudi Arabia | 197.8 |
| Canada | 193.8 |
| Switzerland | 183.6 |
| Japan | 149.5 |
| Denmark | 123.1 |
| Australia | 122.4 |
| Norway | 122.1 |
| India | 109.0 |
| Hong Kong | 101.3 |
| South Africa | 94.9 |
| Finland | 79.7 |
| Portugal | 70.0 |
| Singapore | 60.3 |
| Israel | 52.4 |
| Turkey | 51.3 |
| USSR | 49.2 |

(*Source:* EETC)

Financial attributes

- Balance of payments
- Gold and currency reserves
- Growth of GDP and GNP
- Inflation
- Debt structure

Exporting may be strategically important to sell goods which could not be sold domestically. Or the profit could be very attractive. Perhaps close links have been established over many years with an agent in another country. These are just some of the motivations for selling overseas.

Associated risks are many. The risks of customer insolvency or default are still of prime importance, but now we have an extra dimension – country risk. A brief scan round the countries of the world serves only to emphasise that risk:

1 Middle East war zone.
2 Brazilian inflation and debt crisis.
3 Hong Kong reverting to China.
4 Political instability in the Philippines.
5 Vast debt burden of Third World nations.

*Table 2.8A* OECD Consensus Country Classifications

| Category I Countries | |
|---|---|
| American Samoa | Irish Republic |
| American Virgin Islands | Israel |
| Andorra | Japan |
| Australia | Kuwait |
| Austria | Libya |
| Bahrain | Liechenstein |
| Belgium | Luxembourg |
| Bermuda | Mayotte |
| Brunei | Monaco |
| Canada | Nauru |
| Canary Islands | Netherlands |
| Ceuta Mellila | New Caledonia |
| Czechoslovakia | New Zealand |
| Denmark | Norway |
| Faroe Islands | Puerto Rico |
| Finland | Qatar |
| France | Ross Dependency |
| French Antarctic Territories | San Marino |
| French Guyana | Saudi Arabia |
| French Polynesia | Spain |
| German Democratic Republic | St Pierre et Miquelon |
| | Sweden |
| German Federal Republic | Switzerland |
| Gibraltar | United Arab Emirates |
| Greece | United States |
| Greenland | USSR |
| Guadeloupe | Vatican |
| Guam | Wallis & Fatuna |
| Iceland | |

(*Source:* Export Credit Guarantee Department)

At first sight it could be assumed that exporting is not for the faint-hearted. In practice however much of the risks of exporting can be mitigated, either with some form of export insurance, or by use of secured payment terms like the Letter of Credit. Table 2.7 shows the major countries to which UK goods are exported, for 1987.

Clearly, looking at this list, the developed nations are the major export markets. These countries represent less risk. Since many of them are in the European Economic Community, it could be argued that trade with them will no longer be regarded as exporting, once there is a 'single market' in 1992.

As with customer and industry risk, the main considerations have been split between general and financial features. Here, there are five of each.

### *2.6.1 Country classification*

We are concerned here with the extent of country risk, rather than any particular country feature. Country risk varies from minimal with developed

*Table 2.8B* OECD Consensus Country Classifications

| Category II Countries | |
|---|---|
| Albania | Macao |
| Algeria | Madeira |
| Anguilla | Malaysia |
| Antigua & Barbuda | Malta |
| Argentina | Mauritius |
| Azores | Mexico |
| Bahamas | Mongolia |
| Barbados | Monserrat |
| Belize | Morocco |
| Botswana | Namibia |
| Brazil | Netherlands Antilles |
| British Antarctic Territories | Nigeria |
| British Indian Ocean Territory | Niue |
| British Virgin Islands | Oman |
| Bulgaria | Panama |
| Cayman Islands | Papua – New Guinea |
| Chile | Paraguay |
| Columbia | Peru |
| Cook Islands | Poland |
| Costa Rica | Portugal |
| Cuba | Romania |
| Cyprus | Seychelles |
| Dominican Republic | Singapore |
| Ecuador | South Africa |
| Falkland Islands & | St Helena & Dependencies |
| Dependencies | St Kitts – Nevis |
| Fiji | St Lucia |
| Gabon | Surinam |
| Guatemala | Syria |
| Hong Kong | Taiwan |
| Hungary | Trinidad & Tobago |
| Iran | Trust Territory of the Pacific Islands (US) |
| Iraq | Tunisia |
| Ivory Coast | Turkey |
| Jamaica | Turks & Caicos Islands |
| Jordan | Uruguay |
| Kiribati | Venezuela |
| Korea (North) | West Indian Associated States |
| Korea (South) | Yugoslavia |
| Lebanon | |

(*Source:* Export Credit Guarantee Department)

nations, to very high with some Third World countries. In 1970 the major nations (OECD members) decided to categorise countries. They reached what is now known as the 'Consensus'. Countries were split into three categories: I, II and III. Table 2.8 A–C shows those categories.

This classification is used to determine the length of credit which can be allowed (five years for Class I, ten years for Class III), and the interest rates charged by exporters for these periods.

*Table 2.8C* OECD Consensus Country Classifications

| Category III Countries | |
|---|---|
| Afghanistan | Madagascar |
| Angola | Malawi |
| Bangladesh | Maldives |
| Benin | Mali |
| Bhutan | Mauritania |
| Bolivia | Mozambique |
| Burkina Faso | Nepal |
| Burma | Nicaragua |
| Burundi | Niger |
| Cameroon | Pakistan |
| Cape Verde Islands | Philippines |
| Central African Republic | Pitcairn Islands |
| Chad | Rwanda |
| China | St Vincent & The Grenadines |
| Comoro Islands | Sao Tome & Principe |
| Congo | Senegal |
| Djibouti | Sierra Leone |
| Dominica | Soloman Islands |
| Egypt | Somalia |
| El Salvador | Sri Lanka |
| Ethiopia | Sudan |
| Gambia | Swaziland |
| Ghana | Tanzania |
| Grenada | Thailand |
| Guinea | Togo |
| Guinea – Bissau | Tokelau |
| Guinea – Equatorial | Tonga |
| Guyana | Tuvalu |
| Haiti | Uganda |
| Honduras | Vanuatu |
| India | Vietnam |
| Indonesia | Western Samoa |
| Kampuchea | Yemen Arab Republic (Sanaa) |
| Kenya | Yemen People's Democratic Republic (Aden) |
| Laos | Zaire |
| Lesotho | Zambia |
| Liberia | |

(*Source:* Export Credit Guarantee Department)

The classification is also a broad description of risk. Category I denotes relatively rich countries; Category II intermediate developing countries; Category III relatively poor nations. Significantly only two of the major importers of UK goods, Hong Kong and South Africa, are not in Category I.

### *2.6.2 Natural assets*

Every country has natural assets of some form of another, which can be subdivided into the following categories:

1 Raw materials and energy

Fortunate indeed are the countries rich in natural deposits of oil, coal, iron, copper, bauxite, etc., all being fundamental to the manufacture of goods. Most fortunate of all perhaps, are countries with gold deposits (since gold is a major 'currency' of the world), and oil producers.

Many of the Category III countries lack any substantial holding of natural resources. This reduces their ability to export and so earn foreign currency with which to pay for structural improvement. Others have an overdependence on their natural asset. For example Zambia relies on copper exports, Nigeria on oil. In both cases, downward fluctuations in world prices have seriously eroded their balance of payments.

2 Agriculture

The agricultural activity has a major influence on the development of a country. In the temperate zones of Europe, agricultural practices have become very sophisticated. Trading also has evolved so that deficits in one crop can be made good by international trade. Russia, though rich in fertile land, is not well enough organised to capitalise on this asset. Huge volumes of wheat are imported from the US to make up any crop shortfall.

3 Climate and geographic location

Countries in the tropical zones have suffered from a different problem. Growing conditions and the climate are so favourable that in some instances a country can be largely self-sufficient in food. A quick look at countries in Category III reveals an interesting phenomenon. Almost all are located in equatorial and tropical zones. The climate is one of their greatest natural assets, and many basic items, like tea, coffee and sugar emanate from these regions. Favourable climatic conditions open opportunities for tourism, which is a major source of income in some of these countries.

Unfortunate geographic location is a constant risk feature. Earthquake damage in Mexico and China, flood damage in Bangladesh, frost damage in Brazil, can in a short period of time temporarily ruin a country's economy, with international borrowing the only way out for those countries.

4 Workforce

Perhaps the greatest asset of a nation is its people. In the industrialised nations, the workforce tends to be well educated and cared for through welfare systems. In Third World countries, standards of welfare are much lower, as are those of education. As a result they are severely hampered in their ability to develop industrial based products.

### *2.6.3 Economic and industrial structure*

The economic structure of a country is closely linked to its natural features.

Countries in the West have developed a mixed free-market economy. Industry is owned by a mixture of the state and free enterprise, with market forces dictating levels of supply and demand.

Iron-Curtain countries operate on a state ownership basis, with all aspects of trading strictly controlled. These principles have tended to stunt the potential of those countries. Government buyers can be regarded as being better credit risks (provided there is political stability in the relevant country). At the time of writing there are moves to liberalise the economic and industrial patterns of the Communist bloc, with the intention of boosting production and increasing industrial efficiency. This has led to the emergence of trading direct with 'private' companies (not supported by the state). It is now possible that such companies can become insolvent (examples have already been found in Poland). Liberalisation in the Soviet Union may increase difficulties of direct trade.

There is no fixed pattern to the types of economic and industrial structure in Third World countries. Those once part of the Commonwealth, or under the influence of other Western nations, are on the whole better developed. Industries established during colonisation often provide a source of income, the contributing companies being owned by large Western multinationals. The existence of dictatorship does not necessarily imply that a thriving economy is not possible. Kenya in the 1970s is an example of this.

### *2.6.4 Local customs*

'When in Rome, do as the Romans do.' This is a key motto towards successful trading overseas and minimising country risk. Knowledge of local customs, practice and legal systems is important. In some countries it is advisable to offer incentives to the potential purchaser. In others it is wholly inappropriate to do so.

Knowledge of and an association with the professions within a country will help avoid some of the legal pitfalls of trading. The best way to trade in an overseas country is to employ an agent familiar with local customs (in some you must have an agent). However, agency agreements can be restrictive and more expensive – careful consideration is required before appointing an agent.

### *2.6.5 Political stability*

A whole range of trading risks has evolved as a result of losses sustained through political action. The duty of a government is to protect and promote the interests of its people. In the developed nations this tends to be done based on democracy and tolerance. As a result governments are more stable and have a longer time in office to make their policies work.

Less developed countries and the so-called Third World have a long way to go before reaching the stage of development of the West. Democracy is often replaced by autocracy, dictatorships and military regimes. A change in government is the result of a coup, assassination, or sometimes full-scale civil war. If there are insufficient natural assets for income to be generated from exporting, such governments have serious difficulty in raising the money required to make the people happier and more prosperous.

It is in this context that country risk is highest. The heavy hand of government control will be on every element of trading. Imports are strictly controlled, foreign currency carefully allocated by a central bank.

### *2.6.6 Balance of payments*

The most basic 'housekeeping' function of every government is to earn sufficient from exports to pay for imported goods. There are few countries in the world which maintain a balance of payments surplus on a consistent basis – Japan and West Germany being the two most notable examples. The main problems associated with the balance of payment are the following:

1 Deficit with high level of economic activity
Internal inflation and low interest rates cause prices to be too high to compete overseas, and money flows out to earn higher interest elsewhere. Remedial action includes boosting productivity, lowering prices, high interest rates and lower currency value. Finland is a nation which, in the late 1980s, is experiencing these problems.

2 Deficit with low level of economic activity
A monetary crisis caused by excessive government support to industry and an overvalued currency. Cure is to minimise government aid and devalue currency. The smaller Third World nations are particularly prone to this – Liberia, Cote d'Ivoire and Ecuador being current examples. Such countries find it necessary to rely on advice from the International Monetary Fund as a condition for continued financial support.

3 Surplus with high level of economic activity
Currency undervalued causing exports to appear cheap to foreign countries, while imports appear expensive. This is the result of a booming economy and can cause embarrassment with trading partners anxious to export as much as possible into that economy. The remedy is to revalue currency, allow a greater level of imports and even increase aid to foreign countries. West Germany is the prime example. Japan, in an attempt to reduce its similar problems, is investing heavily in manufacturing facilities throughout Europe.

4 Surplus with low level of economic activity
A slack economy with high interest rates attracts money from overseas. Remedy is to lower interest rates to stimulate the economy and equalise the level of overseas money invested. No nations can be described in this way at this time.

### 2.6.7 *Gold and foreign currency reserves*

A country's ability to meet its import commitments is determined by its holdings of currency reserves. Apart from the risk of customer insolvency, the so-called transfer risk is the most common cause of payment default. Governments with heavy balance of payments deficits and high repayment commitments on overseas loans will have a very limited supply of foreign currency. The central bank will then exercise heavy control over when and to whom foreign currency can be paid.

Gold reserves are a form of last-ditch security, for use in settling debts due to other countries or suppliers. Gold continues to be an internationally acceptable form of currency for use where the debt cannot be repaid in the relevant currency.

### 2.6.8 *Growth of GDP and GNP*

The growth of a country is measured by the gross domestic product (GDP, the sum of all internal trading and economic activity) and gross national product (GNP, being GDP together with all export activity). Ideally both figures should increase, suggesting success of industrial policies, and a reasonably priced exchange rate.

### 2.6.9 *Inflation*

In a healthy economy, it is natural for prices to rise from one year to the next. Ideally this rise should be very small, but many features can make it higher. Higher interest rates, wages and imported raw materials lead to higher prices and thus inflation.

Inflation can be a natural event, or deliberately induced by government action. Economic expansion financed by borrowings rather than production will increase inflation. Some governments have tried to reduce their domestic and international debt burden by simply printing more money, without any increase in productivity. This leads to hyperinflation.

### 2.6.10 *Debt structure*

A country's debt structure will consist of national and international borrowing, the latter having the greater impact on country solvency. There has long been a belief that a country cannot go into 'receivership', and that any loan will ultimately be repayed. Many Third World countries have capitalised on this belief and borrowed amounts well above what can be reasonably repayed out of their own economy. They have relied on organisations like the IMF and World Bank to finance schemes to improve their economy, such as irrigation systems and power generation facilities.

The international banking community have now become more wary of 'Third World' lending, and are writing off many loans made to countries unable to service their repayments.

Servicing of external debt is best financed from export earnings. Countries with a poor exporting record can suffer from having to repay external debt from internal means, which means diverting it from pressing domestic social or economic needs. Debt servicing is often measured as a percentage of export earnings. A figure below 30 per cent can be regarded as satisfactory. A figure in excess of 75 per cent implies that further borrowing will be required to meet existing repayments.

## Chapter summary

1 Risk analysis requires an understanding of the features which influence risk. They can be grouped into three categories:
   - (a) customer/industry/country features;
   - (b) financial features;
   - (c) priority features (the relevance of the risk to your own organisation).

2 Consistent analysis requires the use of a common and well-structured language, but to define this language requires patience and experimentation with a range of circumstances.

3 Complex financial analysis has a part to play in the process, but in the end it is the simple measures of risk which are the most accurate.

4 Attribute analysis requires a large quantity of subjective judgement, but also serves a very much more useful purpose than the 'gut-feel'.

5 Attribute analysis establishes a core of features which could affect the trading:
   - (a) customer attributes, which describe:
     - (i) the outward impressions given by the customer;
     - (ii) his product;
     - (iii) demand for that product;
     - (iv) the competition he faces;
     - (v) who his customers are; and, most important of all;
     - (vi) the quality of his management.
   - (b) industry attributes:
     - (i) industry type;
     - (ii) product description;
     - (iii) demand for product;
     - (iv) strength of competition;
     - (v) customer profile;
     - (vi) management ability.

(c) country attributes:
  (i) country classification;
  (ii) natural assets;
  (iii) economic and industrial structure;
  (iv) local customs;
  (v) political stability.
(d) priority attributes, to measure what benefits there are in trading with a customer. These describe:
  (i) profit margin;
  (ii) ease of manufacture of the products the customer wants;
  (iii) attraction of his market;
  (iv) degree of competition in obtaining each order;
  (v) terms and security;
  (vi) how easy it is to replace the customer.
(e) credit and financial attributes, describing:
  (i) experience of payments and disputes;
  (ii) credit references;
  (iii) growth of equity and profitability;
  (iv) the strength of his balance sheet;
  (v) reliance on borrowed money;
  (vi) level of capital put into the business by its directors.
(f) industry financial attributes:
  (i) payment patterns;
  (ii) bad debt history;
  (iii) growth of sales and profit;
  (iv) liquidity;
  (v) gearing;
  (vi) return on shareholders' funds.
(g) country financial attributes:
  (i) balance of payments;
  (ii) gold and currency reserves;
  (iii) growth of GDP and GNP;
  (iv) inflation;
  (v) debt structure.

# CHAPTER 3

# INFORMATION GATHERING AND INTERPRETATION

Chapter 2 looked at a comprehensive range of features which influence credit risk. This chapter describes how the information can be gathered, gives guidelines on interpretation, and considers factors relating to this activity. Before discussing the various sources, it is necessary to put in proper perspective the need for customer information.

Attitudes to this need vary widely. Some companies are so thankful for receiving an order that goods are shipped or services delivered without delay, and before any sort of investigation can be made. This 'head in the sand' approach can work very well, especially if by good fortune the level of sales loss through bad debts is small – a position which can easily occur in times of a booming economy with a low incidence of bad debt. Equally this attitude can come very seriously unstuck.

Another common attitude is to relax information gathering on large and well-known companies, on the expectation that such organisations are immune to insolvency. There are many companies who can confirm that one of their largest customers has failed over the last five years, and that paying more attention to keeping information on that customer up to date might have enabled them to take action to minimise their exposure, or even avoid it altogether.

Expense plays a major part in determining the type of information sought. The investment of a few pounds at an early stage could save many thousands of pounds later. Credit agencies do not necessarily help if they ask for a large subscription contract to be agreed in advance.

One of the main messages of this book is that early credit investigation on customers saves money. It helps to minimise bad debts and it helps to avoid getting into slow payment situations.

Credit analysis is a combination of several different routines, all requiring an adequate level of information and all directly related to saving money:

1 gathering the most useful information quickly;
2 expertly analysing that information;
3 comparing the finances of a customer with the industry norm;
4 constantly reviewing information to spot the potential failure *and* success;

5 feeding important information on sales targets, markets, suppliers and competitors to colleagues in different departments.

By doing these routines the credit department can truly claim to be a valuable source of 'customer intelligence'.

Note again, in the list above, the inclusion of the need to identify success. Scanning information for bad points is a big part of the credit grantor's role, but even more use can be made of it if the good points are noticed as well. This saves money by enabling the sales function to concentrate their time on the good customers, by giving them regular appraisals of those customers appearing to be making very good progress.

So to the sources of information. There is a degree of significance to their order, taking into account availability, usefulness and cost:

1 Internal information: gathered from sources within one's own organisation;
2 Trading experience: which accumulates over the period of trading;
3 Credit clubs: industry groups and contacts with colleagues within one's own industry;
4 The media: including the financial press, trading and industrial journals;
5 Customer visits;
6 Information from the customer;
7 Credit reports;
8 Financial statements and annual accounts;
9 Rating books;
10 Reference books;
11 Bank references;
12 Trade references;
13 Overseas information sources.

As we shall see later, a large volume of information can be readily obtained at very little cost. The order has not been established on the quality of the information since this is very difficult to comment upon. Any one source could yield a single gem which, even on its own, could strongly influence the type of decision taken.

## 3.1 Internal information

In Chapter 3 we looked at the eighteen attributes which are the basis of both 'customer-speak' and attribute analysis. Six of them related to general customer information, and it was suggested that this information should be readily available from a salesperson's initial 'call report'.

Taking a general viewpoint, there is everything to be gained from learning as much as possible about a customer during visits and phone calls. The resultant information helps to decide the products to be sold; it is absolutely essential in customer negotiations; feedback can be obtained of a product's strength and development potential; it can be added to a store of information on a market sector; indicators of the customer's future prospects and current financial status can be obtained.

There is so much to be gained from seeking this information that it seems common sense to establish a formal or semi-formal system for recording and distributing it to everyone associated with dealing with that customer, including of course the credit department. Imagine the quality and depth of customer intelligence which could be built up, to enable the timely allocation of scarce resources in exactly the right areas.

Yet in the corporate environment no such attention has been paid to this matter – or if it has it rarely seems to percolate down to the credit manager until it is too late and a credit problem of one sort or another has come to light.

There are a few hurdles which get in the way of this worthy ideal. The two most popular phrases heard on this subject are: 'we haven't the time to go into that great a depth of investigation on customers'; and 'we can't expect the overworked salesperson to devote that much attention to writing reports'.

Both these points are related – an assumption is being made that there are more important things to spend time on than record and collate customer information. This can be answered in two ways:

1 If a customer description language has been established then it is not necessary to spend hours on a lengthy report. Rather than the salesperson writing a long report so that it contains what he believes is useful, using 'customer-speak' all that is required is to concentrate on the six simple attributes:

(a) outward impressions;
(b) product description;
(c) product demand;
(d) market competition;
(e) end buyers;
(f) management ability.

We will talk in Chapter 5 of a simple scoring system (the scores being backed up by brief justifying comments), which will suffice as good customer information and can be compiled in a matter of minutes.

2 How much time is spent dealing with problems which could have been avoided? 'Prevention is better than cure', and the time taken in keeping up-to-date knowledge on a customer can often be saved in other ways. For instance salespeople chasing after orders on uncreditworthy customers, and time spent in chasing money from them, could be channelled into dealing with good customers if only the means to identify them at an early stage existed.

There is another important consideration linked to internal information. How accurate and objective is it?

This aspect has already been covered in Chapter 2. The goal of any company is to increase profitable sales. In the long run, it is more important for a salesperson to be realistic about the attributes of his customers, than present an overly optimistic view. The relationship between sales and credit is very much more solid and successful if both are completely honest with each other.

Perhaps one of the greatest benefits of internal information is that it costs nothing and can be obtained on every customer who is visited, or with whom there is close contact. There is however one associated problem. It is not always possible to see every customer. Those in mail-order distribution and similar circumstances will, by definition, probably not be able to get any salesperson's input.

Finally on this section, the process of talking and getting information from each other is very educational. It promotes a better understanding of the pressures and considerations involved in selling, marketing and credit management. It is for this and the other reasons above that I soundly repeat my own view that the most important source of customer information is from within.

## 3.2 Trading experience

Many may regard this as the most important source of information. There are some compelling reasons for this point of view:

1. Trading experience is as up-to-date as you can get – a 'finger on the pulse'.
2. It is available for all customers who are currently trading.
3. Information of this type can be easily generated by the computer and its sales ledger software. Some of the most important computer tabulations show the aged debt, and some go further in computing the average period it is taking for invoices to be paid.
4. Normal collection routines are based around a customer's payment performance. Chasing letters and ultimately suspension of trade are directly connected to the experience.
5. Trading experience is a good guide on the most appropriate trading level. A financially overstretched customer can be easily identified and closely monitored as part of the collection activity.

Nevertheless, there are a few circumstances which distort the experience patterns.

The most difficult to deal with are the persistent late payers, or those who consider it acceptable practice to delay payment as long as possible. In all probability there are no real problems with cash flow, nor is there any intention of not paying at all. Many customers fall into this category, and it is an integral part of the cash collector's job to recognise the symptoms and act accordingly.

Another distortion is the customer dispute. Poor invoicing, incorrect pricing, early delivery and proof of delivery are situations which all too often occur, and the brunt of the consequent problems often falls on the cash collector.

The eradication of such problems is or should be a very high priority in any company. As much as 10 per cent of accounts receivable can be tied up in such disputes. However, there is another reason why they should be minimised. The customer dispute is the single most useful smokescreen a customer can raise, to disguise the fact that he is in financial trouble.

It is then that the company information network and 'customer-speak' comes into their own. If details are held on the customer's business, his product, market and management, the smokescreen is much more likely to be adopted by those with less favourable attributes. This is a prime example where information can be *corroborated* to help take the most appropriate action.

Thus trading experience should be judged not by the exact time it takes a customer to pay his invoices, but by the total amount of time it takes to get him to pay. The less time, the more acceptable the experience.

There is an anomaly about trading experience to which larger companies are most prone – collection efficiency and product necessity. Large companies, who by their nature are major suppliers of raw materials and who have an efficient collection system, are usually right at the top of the list of payment priorities with many of their customers. This causes the illusion that a customer is trading satisfactorily because he always pays on time, whereas the customer may be in all kinds of trouble, which would be made even worse if he got on the wrong side of his major supplier. Once again 'customer-speak' is an essential if a full and accurate profile is to be kept on such a customer, and it emphasises the danger of being over-reliant on trading experience, especially on larger customers.

Finally, like internal information, trading experience is freely and readily available.

## 3.3 Credit clubs

There is an increasing trend in the formation of and active participation in credit clubs. At one time they were regarded by some as a sort of unofficial cartel. Members would plot against the unfortunate few customers who had a bad credit record and who therefore merited going on some kind of blacklist. This is certainly not the case, the club being used for a mutually beneficial exchange of information and experiences.

Customer trading experience is discussed in these clubs. To each member, here is an excellent chance of getting valuable third party opinions on potential or existing customers. It often becomes clear that a handful of problematical customers continually appear on the list for discussion. This serves the useful function of confirming that such customers fall into the 'persistent problems but no serious financial problems' category.

Provided club members enter responsibly into the club spirit, the information is usually accurate and reliable. No member will last long if he abuses the club by giving false information intended to give his company a trading advantage.

Another benefit of credit clubs is that it gives an opportunity to discuss broader issues, like credit terms, or retention of title. Potential pitfalls can be avoided if the experience of others can be called upon for sound advice.

It is often the case that good business relations are established with other members, which extends to the odd phone call if an urgent and accurate piece of trading experience is needed. Some clubs actively encourage the broadening of their knowledge by inviting speakers to talk on topical subjects, i.e. the value of credit insurance, the effectiveness of the current insolvency laws, etc. The credit club is therefore a good source of customer information, and has other side benefits.

## 3.4 The Press

The sight of the *Financial Times* is commonplace in the credit department, and it is well recognised as an up-to-date source of information. But for many companies, its greatest use is not for customer information, but for market surveys and general background details. Many of the articles feature companies of the larger variety; nationally known public companies and their interim/final reports; huge takeover battles; share issues and prospectuses.

To get adequate coverage of the smaller companies, the ones which credit managers tend to be more worried about, is more difficult. A good source is the local paper, but to get these papers on customers who may be spread all over the country is not really practicable. A better idea is to subscribe to trade journals which cover a wide range of companies in their own particular industry sector. Also these journals can give useful background information on products, trends and people.

There are several specialist publications which provide useful information. For example the *London Gazette* and *Stubb's Gazette* list companies involved in legal action or bankruptcy/liquidation.

## 3.5 Customer visits

A visit is a golden opportunity to find out more about your customer. It is a means of discovering background details on the facts of which you are already aware. It is a means of filling gaps of knowledge not covered by the information already held. It enables valuable contact to be made with customer managers, possibly directors, and sometimes even the people with responsibility for paying your invoices. A customer visit, especially the first, should always be made in the company of a salesperson, and the process enables him to learn more about the customer, and more about you and the credit considerations linked to the case.

There is much to be gained from this activity, and it is worth looking in more detail at each aspect.

### *3.5.1 Background information*

If there is time before the visit, find out as much as possible about the customer from as many information sources as is practical. Construct a company profile, which will probably contain the following:

1. sales and profit performance;
2. capital and equity in the business;
3. sources of borrowed funds, and security taken by the lenders. These can be split between short and longer term borrowings and should also take into account inter-company funds;
4. working capital availability and liquidity;
5. collection performance;
6. stock turnover;
7. products sold and the market factors surrounding them.

All these are elements or sub-components of the, by now I hope familiar, 'customer-speak'.

### *3.5.2 Gap filling*

Find out about the customer attributes not covered in above:

1. of greatest importance is information on the management, who they are and how they work;
2. the companies the customer deals with;
3. competitive conditions they have to face;
4. future plans on both product development and marketing;
5. ask for a tour round the premises, so that outward impressions can be formed on manufacturing efficiency, stock turnover and the general morale in the company.

If little or no information was available before the visit, then the task of filling gaps will include all the points covered in 3.5(1) above.

### *3.5.3 Customer contact*

Make sure the salesperson arranges for the right person to be seen. Meetings with buyers are not very satisfactory from the credit point of view. Better to see if possible a board member who is much more likely to be able to answer the range of questions above. The best person is the finance director or controller as he will be in charge of the purchase ledger, and to have such a contact can be immensely valuable if problems in collecting money are encountered. It follows that a brief introduction to the purchase ledger controller for your invoices is equally valuable.

It may seem rather ambitious to expect a senior member of the customer to spend a few hours answering the above questions, and the groundwork necessary to reach this position lies in the hands of the salesperson.

### *3.5.4 The salesperson's role in the credit visit*

First it is his task to sell your company's products to the extent that the customer is keen to buy them. If there are problems in allowing a trading level sufficient to cover the order, then a visit by a credit manager should be presented as a positive suggestion of the commitment your company is prepared to invest in supplying the customer. In effect you are meeting his needs with the right product, at the right price, and on the right credit terms. A credit visit should always be presented as a normal function of the supplier's credit department – part of a routine which many customers have been happy to accept.

Customer visits mainly arise in these circumstances because the customer is small or has only recently started in business. Such companies recognise the need to establish their credibility, and this is the motivation for them to submit to a credit visit. Hopefully they are proud and confident about their trading prospects and are prepared to show others that this is so.

However, there is a different and altogether more difficult type of credit customer visit. This is where problems have been encountered, usually as a result of a poor payment record, and where there are reservations on the long-term viability of the customer. The so-called 'crisis visit' is covered in Chapter 7.

Try and make visits to as many customers as possible – it is an opportunity to strengthen a relationship which will not only benefit the credit department, but will do no harm to sales prospects.

## 3.6 Information from the customer

The best informed person on the creditworthiness of a customer is the customer himself. However, getting him to give you this information is quite a different matter.

In corporate credit, standard information to be requested (on a Credit Account Application Form) is the names of bank and trade referees. Financial statements are not included in this list, because companies are generally reluctant to divulge information to outside parties. Insistence on seeing some figures can often lead to the customer taking his business elsewhere. There is a paradox to this situation. Customers who are very touchy about giving further information, especially if their accounts are not up to date at Companies Registry, and their payment record is poor, should be monitored most closely. Those willing to divulge information tend to do so in the knowledge that it is reasonable in content. Thus the benefit of customer-originated information is not so much for its content, but for judging the reaction of the customer.

In banking, the position is very different. The average company is under no illusion that, in order to borrow money, they are going to have to reveal information to the bank. This will include a balance sheet and management accounts, and a cash flow statement. With new companies, who have no antecedent financial information, a business plan will be required. All this information will be required, no matter which bank is asked, for very good reason. Banks lend amounts well in excess of the average creditor, over longer periods.

## 3.7 Credit reports and credit agencies

This section not only covers the reports available, but also looks at the many types of services supplied by credit agencies.

Since the mid-1800s an industry has evolved which gathers a range of customer information to sell in report form to business. The largest, and longest established, is Dun & Bradstreet, who now have offices in every major country in the world.

The development of the credit agency sector remained for many decades the province of a small group of companies. However, the ever-increasing use of credit in many business transactions, and the emergence of credit management as a distinct corporate function, has ensured that the number of credit agencies has grown in the last twenty years. So too has the product range they can provide. Most notable of recent developments is the introduction of 'on-line' services which enable credit reports to be ordered and transmitted to the user in a matter of minutes, using a desktop microcomputer connected by phone line to the credit agency's information data base.

At the heart of the services of the credit agencies are their standard credit reports.

### *3.7.1 Credit reports*

In essence they should contain details sufficient for an indication of a customer's creditworthiness to be assessed. In practice, however, credit reports can contain only that information which is publicly available, or which can be obtained direct from the customer.

In recent times the amount of generally available information has been decreasing, it being thought that the provision of such information is an excessive burden, particularly for smaller companies. Credit management, and its difficult task of setting the most appropriate customer trading level, is the poorer as a result. It also emphasises the importance of correlating information in an alternative way, hence the relevance of language systems such as 'customer-speak'.

There follows a list of the ideal content of a credit report, including an explanation of its significance to the trading decision:

1 full name and address;
2 legal status and ownership;
3 length of time in business;
4 activities and industrial sector;
5 financial information;
6 payment experience;
7 details of any legal actions;
8 background information;
9 credit ratings and opinions.

1 Full name and address: Trading with customers involves entering into a legal contract. It follows that it is absolutely vital that the correct customer name be used. The name will always be that registered, either in a registry of business names or registries used for tax purposes. In the UK this means the Register of Companies based in Cardiff, or the VAT authorities who issue a number against the name of every company which is liable to pay the tax. It should be added here that this information can be obtained from the customer's letterhead, and it is desirable to get such a letterhead before entering into trading. Responding to new orders on the strength of just a telex is not to be recommended.

Other names can be shown in the report, such as trading styles and business divisions. These names should not alone be used on any invoices to the customer.

The address given will be that registered along with the name, at a companies registry. It is a common practice worldwide for companies to attach a brass plate, with their full name and address, outside their registered office. It is to this address which official documents, like for instance legal summonses, should be addressed.

However, it is not necessarily the case that invoices should also be directed there. Many larger companies have special locations where invoices and monthly invoice statements are processed, and also where goods should be delivered. This sort of information must be made available by the customer at order stage; however, some credit agencies will include such details.

2 Legal status and ownership: This describes the ownership of a company, the extent of ownership, and ultimately determines your rights as a creditor if the customer fails.

The various type of legal form are:

(a) Proprietorship of partnership: one or a group of people have formed a business, using in part their own capital to do so. They undertake full personal responsibility for the conduct of all aspects of their business, and in return 'draw' sufficient funds (hopefully for them!) in the form of personal income. The commitment of a proprietor/partner can thus be reasonably assumed to be at the highest possible level.

This is most relevant should their enterprise fail, or go into bankruptcy. In the event they are personally liable to all their creditors to repay money owed, perhaps out of the proceeds of the bankruptcy or, if not, out of their own personal assets.

From a credit point of view the commitment in the business by its owners is a positive and favourable feature. However, such companies are not often obliged to register or provide financial information about their companies, in part because it may not be possible to separate their business and personal affairs.

(b) Private limited company: identified by the term 'Limited' which appears after its name. Two or more people, or companies, have formed a company by issuing and purchasing shares in the new business. The amount of shares they can purchase could be as little as just £2.00 in the UK, called share capital. The resultant company becomes a 'person', or legal entity in its own right, and the extent of commitment of its owners is limited solely to the share capital they have invested in the business. The description of the company as being 'private' means that shares are not traded publicly in a stock market though this does not prevent interested parties in making private arrangements to buy shares in such a company.

The two main credit implications are first, the financial responsibility of the shareholders, in the event of insolvency, is limited to the value of their shares. It follows that the higher the level of shares issued and paid up, the greater the confidence in the business of the shareholders. Second, formally registered companies are usually required to lodge information about themselves, including details of their financial accounts, and charges/mortgages/debentures and other forms of security linked with funds which have been borrowed. A comprehensive credit report may well include such details.

In many instances, shareholders of companies are businesses in their own right, and the subject company is thus a 'subsidiary'. If their shareholding exceeds 50 per cent then they naturally have a controlling interest in their subsidiary and are regarded as the 'parent' company. Many of the largest companies are called 'holding companies', because they have a majority interest in a number of subsidiaries. Full name and address details of the parent/

holding company will be included in the credit report, and it is always prudent to obtain information on them if there is any doubt about the creditworthiness of the subject company.

The most debatable practice linked to the corporate ownership of companies is the so-called 'tax-loss company'. Here, a rather unsuccessful company which is trading at a loss can be purchased in order for the parent to reduce their tax burden, on the pretext that some of their income has to be siphoned off to support their ailing subsidiary. Companies whose continued existence is purely for accounting purposes such as this are very poor credit risks. Close attention should be paid to their products to see whether there is sufficient potential for them to continue trading.

(c) Public limited company: identified by the initials 'PLC' after the name. As its title suggests, this is the most well-known type of company. The shareholders risk losing their money should insolvency occur in the same way as for a private limited company, except that with public companies there are potentially a large number of shareholders. This is because these shares can be openly traded in a stock exchange. Their price is determined by market forces and the general comparative performance of the company concerned.

In the UK a company has to satisfy stringent solvency conditions before it becomes eligible for 'flotation' in the stock market. This is an added comfort to the credit grantor when assessing such companies. Of even more use is the constant monitoring of the share price. A public company in trouble can always be detected by a downward movement in share prices. If this downward movement becomes too severe, a stock exchange can be empowered to suspend trading on the market – a very positive indicator of impending failure.

There are two features to watch out for with public companies. First, there is the ever-present threat of a 'dawn raid' – action taken by a 'predator' to acquire a controlling interest in a company. At a stroke the entire prospects of a company can change, sometimes to the good, sometimes to the bad. Second, even the most robust and successful company can suffer from a lapse in confidence, either in the market or the company itself, even though the original lapse may be based on tenuous grounds.

One word of caution. The appearance of PLC after a company's name is by no means an automatic suggestion that a company is totally creditworthy. A credit report should always contain a sufficient range of information for a fuller judgement to be made.

3 Length of time in business: The most accurate figure is based on the date the company started trading. This may not be the same as the time it was incorporated, since many companies begin life as a proprietorship and move on to register as private limited companies as the business grows in size.

There is a 'honeymoon' period after which, if a company survives, it can be regarded as a fully established concern. However, the period is by no means universally agreed, varying from two to eight years. The writer's preference is for a three-year period, during which time most companies should mature in terms of their product, image and organisation. After this period, financial information may become available on which to make a more informed judgement on the robustness of a newish business.

4 Activities and industrial sector: Of obvious importance is the correct classification of the main activities of your customer. This has two components:

(a) Activity type: manufacturer, distributor, wholesaler, services, or a mixture of the preceding types. The activity type, as we shall see in the next chapter, can have a significant impact on the shape of the balance sheet.
(b) Industrial sector: the relevant branch of industry in which the customer trades, sometimes called SIC (Standard Industrial Classification), which is a coding system originating from the London Stock Exchange. There are hundreds of these codes (numbers between 0000 and 9900). The SIC code structure is cumbersome and difficult to use. There are so many different classifications, some with little difference between them, that it can make it difficult to decide which is the most appropriate code. Additionally, the SIC system as it stands does not specifically cover some of the emerging high-technology activities which merit individual recognition.

Knowing the correct sector type can be very useful. Some are growing in size, with a large proportion of new companies (electronics); some are static in size, with many members (engineering); some are very risky (building and construction); some have very short trading terms (food wholesale and retail); some have very small profit margins (computer dealers). Each sector has its own characteristics which must always be taken into account when making any sort of credit judgement.

There is one further sort of activity of note – the extent to which the subject company exports its goods, and if so where. A good credit report should include these details, especially if they are available in the company's annual report. Given the pitfalls discussed in Chapter 2, companies with a high proportion of sales to Third World countries run additional risks, especially if their trading terms are not by letter of credit.

5 Financial information: If annual financial returns are available, a credit report should always disclose details on at least the latest trading year. Part of the job of a credit agency is to update regularly its information as it is lodged publicly. It is preferable to have figures for three consecutive years, as this allows a trend to be established for all the main balance sheet and profit and loss items.

Most agencies also provide, either in the report itself or other special financial profiles, an analysis of the main financial ratios which goes to provide a picture of performance and stability. A description of the most useful ratios will appear in the next chapter, and definitions of the main balance sheet items.

Financial information, however well covered in a credit report, is by no means the ideal indicator of the true position of the company. Annual returns are made only once a year, within between six months (with public limited companies) to ten months (with private limited companies). The accounts are a snapshot of the position on one day (the last day of the financial year) and by no means represent the current position. Balance sheets can be 'window dressed' or 'engineered' to present a biased impression.

6 Payment experience: This is sometimes referred to as 'dynamic information', simply because it is an up-to-date measure of a customer's ability to pay.

The process of obtaining this information varies. Dun & Bradstreet request many items of trading experience from their subscribers, and also obtain it from computer tapes of the subscriber's sales ledger (called the trade tapes scheme). The result is a service called 'DunsPAR' (payment analysis report) which provides a payment score between 100 (anticipate payment) to 10 (payment 120+ after due date) on around 300,000 companies, with the number ever increasing.

Other agencies rely solely on the former method. It is a time-consuming activity which relies heavily on the cooperation of subscribers and is very valuable to the credit grantor.

7 Details of legal actions: A last-resort means of obtaining payment is to take legal action against your customer. This puts on public record the fact that the customer has so far refused to honour his obligations. One function of credit agencies is to scan those records and add the details to their customer records and credit reports.

The existence of this 'black mark' against a company is not necessarily all it seems. There could be perfectly valid reasons for withholding payment, and the plaintiff is not guaranteed a success in the courts. Therefore the presence of this information, especially if it is a one-off case or if the action was taken some time ago, need not necessarily be viewed in too adverse a light. However, the occurrence of several court actions, over a reasonable period of time, is a clear sign of uncreditworthiness.

8 Background information: There are many other items of information which can be discovered in credit reports. As a rule, the more expensive the report, the greater the level of background information. Here are some of the main items:

(a) Antecedent details: brief career records of the directors of a company, very useful for judging the balance, experience and age of the management.

(b) Product details and brand names.

(c) Territories of trading.

(d) Details of recent acquisitions: an item of great significance. Though a sign of an expanding company, the acquisition of other companies has to be financed from somewhere. The graveyard of failed companies is littered by companies which took on more than they could cope with, or were over-ambitious. Pay attention to the amount of debt and profitability of such a company to see if the position has deteriorated.

(e) Extracts from the report of directors, which is part of the annual return. This gives useful insight into the present position and future plans of a company.

(f) Bankers: appear in most credit reports.

9 Credit ratings and opinions: The opinion of an unbiased credit analyst on the amount of credit that could be reasonably given, is very valuable. Some regard it as the single most important piece of information on a report.

When requesting a credit report, a figure can often be given for the agency to comment upon. Such opinions are given as guidance only and are without responsibility. They are usually quite cautious or conservative, but no less useful for it. A familiar recommendation is:

> 'The subscriber may wish to seek further guarantees or security.'

This is another way of saying the suggested trading level is too high. It is very rare that such guarantees are forthcoming, and it is not always possible to have any idea how strong the securities are were they to be successfully obtained.

The other form of credit opinion is the credit rating. Some agencies have pre-defined criteria for establishing the rating, often based on trading experience levels and the size of the balance sheet. Dun & Bradstreet use three different types of rating:

(a) The Duns rating: a broad credit level suggestion.

(b) The Seyd rating: a more sophisticated rating which adjusts the suggested credit level according to the length of experience with the customer.

(c) The USA Duns rating: a three-component rating which measures the size of the subject company, its credit record, and a suggestion of a credit level.

### *3.7.2 Types of credit report*

These fall into several categories:

1 A standard report: comprising most of the readily available information outlined above.

2 A comprehensive report: which provides much greater depth of infor-

mation, including a full analysis of up to three years' financial figures, if available.

3 A shortform report: a summary of the main customer features and financial figures.
4 A financial profile: which analyses the financial figures, sometimes comparing them to the norms which exist in their own industry sector.
5 A continuous service report: often comprising a standard report, but backed up by updates of fresh information as and when it is received by the agency.
6 A payment report: Dun & Bradstreet's DunsPAR report.
7 A special report: a very full and in-depth investigation prepared at the request of the subscriber. Usually prepared on larger companies where a good quantity of information is available, and including many background details and comment on financial figures and the customer's market. Such reports are expensive.
8 Overseas reports: standard/comprehensive reports which are usually obtained on behalf of the subscriber from a branch of the agency in the relevant country, an agent, or a corresponding agency. Overseas reports, as a rough guide, cost twice as much as a domestic report.

### *3.7.3 Methods of delivery*

All credit agencies have the ability to deliver reports by telex, facsimile or mail. Some charge more for reports required urgently, especially if they have no existing and up-to-date report available on the subject customer.

A new delivery method rapidly gaining in popularity is 'on-line' information. Many credit agencies store their customer information on a computer database. To provide an 'on-line' service requires arranging for the records on the database to be transmitted in a recognisable form across a phone line. From the subscriber's point of view, they need a computer to receive the information and a device for communicating with the main database called a modem, which is driven by special computer software.

'On-line' information can be obtained at any time of the day and can be received in a matter of minutes. The agency provides the subscriber with the following facilities:

1 to search the database for the records they need;
2 to order reports on companies not on the database;
3 to request different types of report;
4 one of the more sophisticated databases, held by ICC, gives the user scope to compare company figures with the industry norm, in either text or graphical form.

The subscriber's software will then enable the report to be read on screen, printed out, or stored on the computer's floppy or hard disk for retrieving later.

In the writer's opinion, 'on-line' delivery will soon become the major means of credit information delivery. It is easy and inexpensive to set up, user-friendly, and enables information to be stored on computer for easy access and recall. Most important of all, it is very fast.

### *3.7.4 Buying credit information*

There are two main methods of purchasing credit information:

1 Subscription: where the subscriber forecasts the number of credit reports he may need during the year, and makes an advance payment sufficient to cover that number. The cost per report reduces on a scale, the more reports are anticipated. The initial forecast can be made on a historic basis. If it turns out to be too low, then subscription can be topped up. If it was too high, then the agency will usually agree to carry over the balance of unused subscription to the following year. The main advantage of subscription is the discounts which can be obtained for, in effect, buying in bulk. The disadvantage is that a large sum of money has to be paid up front.
2 Individual report purchase: each one is paid for at or just after its order. This method is more simple to operate, and does not tie up any cash in advance. The cost of the report need not be more than buying in advance, and there is no problem about having to decide how many reports should be ordered in any given period.

## 3.8 Financial statements and annual accounts

These will be included, where available, in a credit report, and their analysis will be covered in the next chapter. However, it is possible to obtain this information from two main sources:

1 Companies registry, Cardiff: All private limited companies and public companies are compelled by law to lodge an annual return giving details of their accounts. At present the information is stored on microfiche. It can be obtained by visiting Companies Registry, or by ordering the microfiche from a credit agency or one of the many organisations which specialise in obtaining them for a client. The cost of a microfiche is small, and the only additional expenditure is to get a print of its content, if a special microfiche reader is not available. Having obtained one, it is then necessary to spend some time reading, analysing and calculating any ratios of the figures that you need. It is quite normal to be able to obtain a fiche within twenty-four hours of ordering.
2 The subject company itself: There is nothing to stop the credit grantor requesting accounts from the customer he is looking at. If it is a public company, then this should present no problems, since they will probably have a glossy publication with the figures and other details about the company. With the private limited company, it usually proves more difficult

| | TURNOVER | BALANCE SHEET | TOTAL NO. OF EMPLOYEES |
|---|---|---|---|
| SMALL | £2.0m | £0.975m | 50 |
| MEDIUM | £8.0m | £3.9m | 250 |

*Figure 3.1* Size categories for determining amount of information lodged at Companies House

in practice to get such figures. The attitude of customers towards providing information on themselves is a good sign of their financial strength. Companies which object to this reasonable request may have something to hide. There are EEC regulations which determine how much information need be disclosed in the accounts, based on falling within two of the three thresholds outlined in Figure 3.1.

Small companies need only submit an abbreviated balance sheet. Medium companies need only submit the above, plus a profit and loss account (though this need not include a turnover figure), and a directors' report. The figures may be abbreviated.

In practice it is the smaller company which gives the credit grantor most difficulty if a large trading level is required, and these regulations do nothing to ease the position. Some information, however slight, is better than nothing, and there are other 'customer-speak' items which can be considered.

Though referred to above as containing financial information, microfiches also hold a wide range of other information on customers. They fall into the following categories:

1 General information:
Articles and memoranda of association, the formal documents used to describe the constitution and activities of the company. Also included are details of the director's name, address and other companies of which he is a director, the value of shares registered, issued and paid up, and any other names used for the company (it is not uncommon for a company to change its name in the early days of trading, especially if the company was purchased from a specialist company formation firm which sells companies 'off-the-shelf').
2 Annual return:
Accounts and related documents.
3 Mortgage and charge documents:
These itemise any loans that are currently outstanding, or have been in the past, listing also the type of security held.

## 3.9 Rating books

The best example of this is the Dun & Bradstreet rating book. Available either in book or microfiche form, it gives a broad range of information, some of it in coded form, plus a credit rating. Information of this type is very useful to the credit grantor. Many hundreds of thousands of companies have been given a rating, and there is a good chance that any company trading more than about two years will be covered.

Making trading decisions on the strength of a rating is perfectly feasible. Credit insurance companies, for instance, are quite happy for policyholders to give credit limits solely linked to the D&B rating, without the need to get a full-blown report.

The rating information is another good way to get the correct trading style and address, plus details of parentage. However, this is an expensive form of information, most suited to companies which open an appreciable number of new credit accounts on a regular basis, especially where speed of response in opening the account is important.

## 3.10 Reference books

The credit grantor can, if he wants, build up a valuable library of reference information, covering a range of topics. Here are some recommended books:

### *3.10.1 Industrial ratios*

Two major publications are available, both of which contain ratios by SIC code, calculated from the analysis of many companies in each sector. Care is taken to ensure those companies used have a majority of their activities in that sector, and that the correct figures are used for the calculations. The two main publications are:

1 *Key Business Ratios*: published annually by Dun & Bradstreet, they condense the information of over 200,000 companies into the form of ratios.
2 *Industrial Performance Analysis*: published annually by the ICC group. Fewer companies are used in the calculations, the industrial sectors have been edited into major groups, and performance graphs of each sector are given.

Both cost a similar amount, but are different in nature. *Key Business Ratios* is a massive volume packed with numbers. *Industrial Performance Analysis* is formatted in a way which makes it easier to find the data you want, but you may not necessarily find the exact sector you want figures for, because of the grouping of the ratios.

### *3.10.2 Ownership of companies*

Given the many complex corporate entities, embodying many subsidiaries, holding companies, branches, etc., it is useful to be able, at a glance, to get a clear picture of exactly who you are dealing with. The aptly named *Who Owns Who*, volumes, produced by Dun & Bradstreet, give this information, and can be obtained for UK and overseas companies.

### *3.10.3 Marketing and general reference books*

Most notable in this category is the Kompass Directory. It concentrates more on information relevant to marketing, such as product types and logos, names of the managers/directors of each company, with brief financial information of sales and profits where available.

Another major publication in this category is the *Macmillans Unquoted Companies*. As its name suggests it deals only with private limited companies not quoted on the Stock Exchange. It covers the name and address, directors, owners, with financial highlights including several key ratios. There are many other similar directories, most of which can be viewed at any main library.

There is a more specialist type of reference book which is a spin-off of 'Industrial Performance Analysis'. Available on over 100 major industry groupings, they are called the *ICC Business Ratio Reports*. Also including ratio norms, a more detailed analysis of the sector is given, along with balance sheets and profit and loss accounts for all the companies (usually around 150 in number) used to compile the report. This information is very useful for maintaining accurate intelligence on the markets you trade in, and is a good financial information source. There is also a series of reports known as the Key Note Reports, which do a similar function.

## 3.11 BANK REFERENCES

An often used service which banks are prepared to give is a reference on their own customers. It is worth saying immediately that is not necessarily the case they will always give a glowing reference on companies with which they deal, however they do couch the terminology of the reference carefully.

The best reference is a single word – 'undoubted'. Such references are rare, and simply mean there is no problem whatsoever with dealing on credit with such a customer.

Next on the list is 'respectably constituted . . . and good for your figures and purpose'. This means the company is known well, there have been no problems with the relationship, and they are capable of meeting their obligations.

The mid-range reference is 'properly constituted . . . and good for your figures and purpose'. The implication here is that nothing adverse is known and the credit level appears reasonable.

The less favourable bank reports will conclude with the term '. . . would not enter into a commitment they could not see their way to fulfil'. In effect the bank cannot speak for any specific credit figure either because the client is not well known, or because the figure is higher than they can recommend, based on their trading knowledge of the customer. The term above is sometimes prefaced with '. . . figures are higher than normally seen . . .'.

The least favourable bank comment is '. . . funds appear fully committed'. This means what it says – working capital is very scarce. The implication is the company is not able to assume any further debt burden.

Another comment a bank will make is if any form of secured lending has been made, such as a mortgage or debenture, and which thus gives the bank a preferential right to those assets in the event the company fails.

### *3.11.1 How to request a bank report*

Banks will not provide a reference directly to the credit grantor, but do so via your own bank. This means the reference request must be sent to the customer's bank, with details of your own bank to whom the reply should be sent. It will normally take about a week to get a bank reference. If you have a good relationship with your bank, it may be possible to get one quicker if your bank phones the customer's bank.

When requesting a bank reference, always give a credit figure for them to comment on. This should be a realistic figure based on the expected level of future business. Asking for a comment on a much higher figure than necessary may well prove to be counter-productive – a qualified reference could be returned, whereas for a lower figure a more favourable recommendation could be given.

The suggested format for a bank report request would be:

'To the customer's bank
We would be grateful if you could supply a reference on:
Name and address of customer
Amount of credit on which an opinion is sought, including the credit terms.
Please forward your reply to:
Name and address of your bank
Yours faithfully . . .'

Another type of reference, which is used in some sectors, is an urgent request (made by phone using the lines of communication described above) for an opinion on whether a specific amount could be cleared for payment if presented immediately. This is a short-term form of reference aimed at discovering the immediate cash position, rather than a longer-term opinion in the more standard reference.

## 3.12 Trade references

Considering all the other sources of information, it should not be necessary to rely on this information. The obvious underlying reason is that a potential customer is hardly likely to give the name of someone who will give a bad reference. This feature is well recognised, and yet it still seems the norm to request details of referees when opening a new credit account.

The best trade reference to get is from a company not proffered as a referee. To do so is not as difficult as it may seem, if it is possible to visit the customer. The eagle-eyed salesperson can help here. If the name of the car dealer that supplies the company cars, or the caterer who supplies canteen food, or the manufacturer of the fork-lift trucks in the warehouse (and many other similar situations), can be identified then they may yield a more realistic picture of your customer's paying habits.

## 3.13 Overseas information sources

The prime source of information is the international credit report, mentioned above. There are other useful sources which give information on countries:

1 ABECOR reports: this is a service available from Barclays Bank. It is a concise review of a country's profile, including all the details already discussed in Chapter 2.
2 Economist Intelligence Unit reports: the EIU is a specialist in monitoring countries, and is considered an authoritative source of information on all aspects of a country's trading profile. Their services include individual country reports, available also on computer disk.
3 International Risk & Payment Review: this is a regular monthly Dun & Bradstreet publication. Using a wide variety of published data, and experience obtained from a panel of exporters, this gives a guide to payment transfer problems and country risk. A report on individual countries can also be specially prepared at a subscriber's request.
4 BOTB – British Overseas Trade Board: This is a government department (part of the Department of Trade and Industry), with responsibility for promoting exports. They provide a wide range of services which include export intelligence, status reports, market statistics and many other services of value to the exporter. These services are provided on a subscription basis.

## 3.14 Choosing information sources

With so many different avenues to turn to when compiling information on a customer, it is worth looking at ways to organise the gathering of data. Just how appropriate are the sources when coupled with the needs of the credit grantor?

### *3.14.1 Information and its suitability for different types of customers*

This is determined by the size and difficulty of assuming the trading risk. The smaller the risk, the less investigation is needed. It is prudent to obtain a more comprehensive range of information, the higher risk, or the higher the amount likely to be outstanding.

Figure 3.2 gives some idea of a workable and effective system.

| Size of Customer | Choice of Information Type |
|---|---|
| Small | Bank reference<br>Rating from a rating book<br>Trade references<br>Salesperson's 'call report'<br>Unquoted company directory<br>Trading experience |
| Medium | Standard credit report or company microfiche<br>Bank reference<br>'Call report'<br>Trading experience |
| Large or high risk | Comprehensive credit report<br>Bank reference<br>'Call report'<br>Trading experience |

*Figure 3.2* Categories determining the type of credit information held

The 'call report' is included on the assumption that the six customer attributes can be assessed from it. The actual monetary value which is attached to the categories small, medium and large will vary according to the range of credit risk assumed by a company. A small customer to a major multinational could well be a major customer to a newly formed business.

1 Small customers: many companies now operate a 'quick start' system where little or no credit checking is done before issuing a credit limit. Small customers often comprise a large proportion of the customer base (as much as 60 per cent). What is more important at this stage is to check the correct name and address, and this can be done either from a rating book, companies directory, or letterhead from the customer.

The 'quick start' procedure does not necessarily mean that credit checking will not be done, or no information gathered. This can be done shortly after the event, using the sources suggested in the table. Especially useful is trading experience – if a new customer immediately embarks on a track record of slow payment then immediate account closure is highly recommended. Bad debts arising from this group can justifiably be recognised as an unavoidable fact of life.

2 Medium customers: this is a very special group. Within it may be the major customers of the future, and the most likely candidates for a sizeable bad debt. The job of credit analysis is to identify both types.

Most medium customers by their nature will be well established (three years in business and longer) and of a size for them to have to lodge annual returns at Companies Registry. This makes the task of analysis that much easier, and the range of information available on them that much wider.

It is important to define clearly the threshold at which a small customer enters this group. If the initial trading level was set on a 'quick start' basis, then a fresh investigation using a wider range of sources is advisable.

3 Large customers: under the '80:20 rule' (80 per cent of business from 20 per cent of customers) a large volume of a company's assets are invested in this group. Credit and sales resources will also be well used in this area. With so much at stake it makes sense to spend a few hundred pounds every year keeping abreast of your major customer's fortunes. A good way of doing this is by using the 'continuous service' facilities offered by some credit agencies. This will ensure you are always up-to-date about their status.

The level of contact between credit and sales departments is also highest with this group, making it easier to maintain a working knowledge of all the main 'attributes'.

## Chapter summary

1 Customer information is used by credit grantors to obtain the following:
   (a) accurate customer analysis;
   (b) comparing customer performance with the norm;
   (c) customer monitoring;
   (d) keeping the rest of the company informed on all aspects of a customer.

2 The main sources are as follows:
   (a) internal information: readily available at no cost, provided there are suitable links with the sales and marketing department;
   (b) trading experience: freely available on all active customers, though not a source to be solely relied upon;
   (c) credit clubs: exchanges of information between credit grantors in the same industry sector;
   (d) the Press: an inexpensive and up-to-date form of information;
   (e) customer visit: an opportunity to meet and gain background data on a customer;

(f) information from the customer: always provided to banks, but less so to suppliers;
(g) credit reports: available in the following forms:
   (i) standard reports;
   (ii) comprehensive reports;
   (iii) shortform reports;
   (iv) financial profiles;
   (v) continuous service reports;
   (vi) payment reports;
   (vii) special reports;
   (viii) overseas reports.
(h) Credit reports will normally contain the following information:
   (i) full name and address;
   (ii) legal status and ownership;
   (iii) length of time in business;
   (iv) activities and industrial sector;
   (v) financial information;
   (vi) payment experience;
   (vii) details of any legal actions against the customer;
   (viii) background information;
   (ix) a credit rating or credit opinion.

3 Financial reports and annual returns: available from Companies Registry at low cost, or from the customer himself.
4 Rating books: expensive, but contain brief information on hundreds of thousands of names.
5 Reference books: inexpensive. Like rating books but without the rating. Available by industry groups.
6 Bank references: freely available, but have to be interpreted carefully.
7 Trade references: freely available, but biased in favour of the customer.
8 Overseas credit reports: expensive, but necessary if exporting.

CHAPTER 4

# FINANCIAL ANALYSIS

This chapter is devoted to analysing financial figures, or 'number-crunching' as it is sometimes called by analysts. It looks at some of the main constituents of the balance sheet and profit and loss account; ratios that can be calculated from them, and many other issues which have a bearing on financial analysis, such as accounting conventions; off-balance sheet figures and techniques for analysis.

The intention is to give a sound foundation to the science of financial analysis. I use the word 'science' deliberately, because, as you will see, there are several well-tried methods for achieving a thorough and useful analysis. The 'art' of credit management is how you use the results in the credit decision, and explain the significance to non-financial colleagues.

Financial figures are staple fodder for business managers, city analysts, credit grantors, auditors and many others. To some their publication is awaited with eager anticipation. Every number is analysed, ratios by the dozen are calculated, variances to forecast are studied in detail, and a general assessment is then used to help in many ways – perhaps to determine an investment decision, or a credit decision.

They are also used to make management decisions by the company that issues the figures. More often, however, management decisions are made with the knowledge of the true position, not the one that is presented to the general public. The real and up-to-date financial position of a company is contained in management accounts, cash flow statements and many other internal financial reports and forecasts. It is very rare for we, the public, to be able to see these. So we, the public, have to make do with studying an out-of-date document which has been tailored to give maximum satisfaction.

In the UK we are lucky – there tends to be only one set of accounts available. In Italy, for instance, and in some of the Far-Eastern countries, there can be as many as three sets, one for the bankers, one for the shareholders and the real one for managers. In Sweden, company taxation can be so severe that the profit and loss position is very heavily doctored to minimise this burden – which results in a reduction in the value of those figures to an outsider.

The purpose of the foregoing paragraphs is to put firmly into place the value of financial analysis. Figures should not be regarded as a definitive statement of a company's true position. They cannot and must not be viewed in isolation.

So what is the value of financial analysis? Why does it have such an important part to play in credit decisions? There are three key aspects which can be examined with the help of financial figures:

1 Comparison: with other companies either in the same sector, or perhaps of the same size;
2 Trends: can be identified over a period of years (assuming more than one set of figures is available);
3 Corroboration: of other features can be made. Movement in a company's fortunes, the attraction of their product, market features, end buyers and general management ability, will be reflected in the figures (customer attributes).

We will return in more detail to these aspects later in the chapter. First to the balance sheet and profit and loss account – what is each, and what are its main constituents?

## 4.1 The balance sheet

Figure 4.1 shows a typical balance sheet. It is listed with fixed and current assets appearing first, from which current and fixed liabilities are deducted. Another accepted layout convention is for the left side to list liabilities and equity, the right assets.

The two sides will always balance. In equation form A = C + E, where A is assets, C is claims (or liabilities) and E is equity (or shareholders' funds). Looking at each major balance sheet group in turn:

### *4.1.1 Fixed assets*

These are assets which have no role to play in the current trading activity of the company. The main items are:

1 Plant and machinery: used in the process of trading, but not available for resale. Their value is carefully calculated to take account of age. This is known as depreciation, where a fixed proportion of their value is deducted each year, to take into account the reduction in their resale value.
2 Land is a common fixed asset: it appreciates in value over time, though a figure for appreciation is not included in the accounts. It is generally valued at original cost, though from time to time it can be revalued to present a more accurate valuation. Revaluation is sometimes an adverse sign, the implication being that the balance sheet is in need of a boost. The value of leasehold can also be included in this category, and here it is possible to depreciate its value.
3 Long-term investments: those with a maturity more than twelve months in the future are a fixed asset, more commonly seen in larger companies. Those investments could be in treasury bonds and other medium- to

long-term paper or, if the subject is a parent company, it could refer to long-term loans to subsidiaries. In the former case the investment is secure. In the latter this may not be so. As a rule, if the parent displays a weak balance sheet, then its subsidiaries may be similarly afflicted, thus reducing the security of this item.

4 Goodwill and patents: two fixed asset items which sometimes crop up. These items belong to a category called 'intangibles'. Goodwill reflects the notional premium on the value of a business as a going concern, on the assumption it has a good reputation. Patents have no intrinsic value, except when they are sold along with the business to a new owner. These items should be disregarded if it is apparent, from the rest of the balance sheet and profit and loss account, that the subject company is either technically insolvent, or loss-making.

### *4.1.2 Current assets*

Trading activity and income generation involve the movement of current assets. They are assets which can be sold or realised within a period of twelve months. There are three major items:

1 Stock or inventory is first on the list. This item is the total of three components, raw materials, work in progress and finished goods. In some accounts the value of all three components is disclosed. The marketable value of stocks is really limited to that of finished goods, and if a breakdown is available it is useful to assess the balance of the three. If finished goods represent a comparatively low proportion of the overall value, there is possible evidence of inefficiency, or the goods may be complex to manufacture. Conversely a high level of finished goods may suggest slow moving stock. There is an element of uncertainty to the stock item, because it an unrealised asset, relying on the selling and cash collection effort of the company to convert it into cash.

2 Debtors or accounts receivable is the next stage in the trading cycle. They occur when finished goods have been sold and invoiced. Unlike the stock figure, this item is a reliable indicator of what might confidently be expected to be realised.

3 Cash and investments are funds, either available in a short-term account like a bank account, or quickly realisable investments (within twelve months), in either some form of investment paper or with group companies, or in an associate. There is an anomaly in interpreting the cash item. While it is heartening to see evidence of ready funds available to a business, it does pose the question – could not this cash be invested in the business to better effect? Perhaps it could be used to buy more raw materials, or pay more of its creditors, rather than reside in an account? The point here is that a low cash figure is quite acceptable, and high figures are uncommon.

4 Prepayments sometimes appear in the figures. All companies prepare financial statements at the end of a financial year. Sometimes money is paid for a service which falls after the year end. Take the fire insurance on a factory, for instance. Assume the annual policy is renewed three months before the year end. The value of nine months' insurance falls into the next financial year, and is thus shown as a prepayment on the balance sheet of the current year.

### *4.1.3 Fixed liabilities*

These are debts, or claims against the company, scheduled for repayment over several years. Like fixed assets, it is usual to regard long-term debt as being used to finance structural elements of the business, rather than settle the day-to-day expenses. As such there is an unofficial link between fixed assets and liabilities, the debt being used to finance the asset.

Because long-term debt is used to finance the structure of a business, it follows that the lenders have contributed directly to the long-term well-being of the borrower. For this reason such debts can be defined as debt capital items. The main components of this balance sheet group are as follows:

1 Long-term loans: money lent over a period of four or more years, usually by a bank or financial institution, though it could be from an associated company or parent. The cost of such loans is usually higher than with a short-term overdraft, but the compensation is that the loan sum is guaranteed to be available over the agreed period. The funds are often used to purchase fixed assets.
2 Medium-term loans: similar to the above, with repayment periods between one and four years.
3 Minority interest: represents the shareholding of the subject company in another company not under its control (i.e., the shareholding is less than 50 per cent).
4 Leasing obligations: rather than tie up company assets, major capital items such as machinery or company cars are often leased. The item is purchased on the company's behalf by a leasing company which then receives payment on a regular instalment basis, over a period of years. At the end of that period, the lessee may then assume ownership of the asset (finance leasing), or the asset will be returned to the lessor (operating leasing).

Long-term lenders will normally insist on security for their loans (unless the subject is very well known and financially secure). They will also be at the top of the list for repayment if the company becomes insolvent. Evidence of any of the following can be found in documents registered at Companies Registry, or in bank reports. They can take the following legally contractual forms:

1 Mortgages: on property, similar to the way individuals finance a house purchase.

2 Debentures: where the sum borrowed, time period and interest paid is fixed over several years.
3 Charges: which identify assets to which the lender has a legal right if the conditions of the loan are not met.

### *4.1.4 Current liabilities*

Debts which are currently owed and fall due within a twelve month period. Such debts will arise as a result of day-to-day trading activity, including the manufacturing process and related services. Again there is a link between current assets and liabilities, the latter debt arising as a result of the purchase of the former. However, there should always be an excess of current assets over current liabilities to take account of the added value of converting raw materials into the sale of a finished product.

The main items of current liability are:

1 Creditors: money owed to suppliers of raw materials and services.
2 Overdraft: the limit to which the current bank account can be overdrawn, to meet day-to-day expenses.
3 Short-term loans: this item could refer to money borrowed over twelve months, from banks or associated companies, and also the current portion of longer term loans.
4 Tax: the value of corporation tax owed.
5 Dividends: money to be paid to shareholders. This item normally arises with public companies. It is rare for private limited companies to pay dividends, preferring to retain the money for use within the company.
6 Accruals: payment for services rendered in the year running up to the financial year end. The most obvious example is the electricity bill, if the next quarterly payment falls a month or so after year end.

### *4.1.5 Equity or shareholders' funds*

This balance sheet group measures how much money has been invested in the company by its owners, and the success of the business in terms of retained earnings or profit. Its main components are:

1 Ordinary share capital: the value of shares that has been issued and fully paid by the shareholders. With private limited companies the value tends to be static from year to year. It will never reduce, but it can increase by issuing and paying up more share capital.

With public companies the position is different. Shareholders can be members of the public or financial institutions, who have a right to vote at shareholders' meetings on issues affecting the company. The value of the shares may vary according to the fortunes of the company. Shareholders would also hope to receive a dividend, though the subject company is not compelled to give them one, and if there were funds available for distribution, the dividend would go first to preferential shareholders (see below).

2 Preference share capital: these are shares issued with a specific dividend attached to them, payable at a specific time. Such shareholders do not have any voting rights in the way ordinary shareholders do. In many ways the preference share is more akin to a debt rather than equity item.
3 Retained earnings and reserves: earnings generated by trading activity will normally be used to fund further business. However, if a profit has been made then they can be retained as equity. Another form of retention is the reserve, held by a company to meet unexpected contingencies; possible future expense on asset replacement; maintaining dividend levels throughout good and bad years; providing the premium for redemption of preference shares or debentures.

As can be seen, the balance sheet reflects movements related to all the major structural and trading activities of a company, and describes its value, in terms of equity or, as it is also known, net worth. The picture it gives is a snapshot of the position on a single day, and an idea of assets which can be realised, and debts paid in the future.

To get an idea of what happened during the previous year, and to judge the performance rather than stability of the company, requires looking at the profit and loss account.

## 4.2 The profit and loss account

This shows the total revenue generated over the accounting period, from which is extracted expenses, to arrive at a profit figure.

A very important element of a company's financial figures, it is unfortunate that, certainly in the EEC, very little need be disclosed unless the company is a public one. Much information on the ability of management can be gained from studying the P&L account.

The P&L account flows in a specific order, starting with sales revenue, then reducing as costs and expenses are deducted one by one. The order is:

1 Turnover or sales revenue: the value of sales (usually including any forms of sales tax or VAT, as this item will be accounted for as an expense elsewhere). Sometimes this figure is broken down into the categories domestic and export.
2 Cost of goods sold: costs directly related to the manufacture of goods, including those for raw materials and labour. This figure is variable according to the level of sales, and is thus called 'variable costs'.
3 Gross profit: sales less cost of goods sold.
4 Selling and distribution costs: the costs of the sales force, promotional activities and distribution to the point of sales.

5 Administrative expenses: the general costs of administering the company. Along with item 4, these costs are called 'fixed', in that they will be incurred irrespective of the volume of sales. Another term for this is 'overheads'.
6 Profit/loss before tax and interest: gross profits less overheads, which could also result in a loss.
7 Profit/loss before tax: profit/loss after taking account of interest expenses incurred during the financial year.
8 Profit/loss after tax: profit after deducting taxes. Because of the taxation system, the tax may not relate to the activities during the current year, but to previous ones. With newer companies, or those making losses, tax can sometimes be credited to the account if a past overpayment had been made.
9 Retained profit for year: the amount of profit not distributed to shareholders, to be added to the equity of the company.

All the above items relate to matters arising from ordinary trading. Extraordinary events can also arise which may not fall within the normal income, cost and tax structure. Examples of these are losses incurred as a result of selling a subsidiary, or costs incurred from redundancies and business closure.

The balance sheet and profit and loss account are, for analytical purposes, the most important figures to use. However, there is another statement accompanying the accounts of larger companies, called the sources and application of funds. This restates many items in the foregoing account sections in terms of their impact on working capital, bank and cash balances. Sales and money borrowed are deemed a 'source' of funds, and the repayment of loans and the balance of stocks, debtors and creditors are the 'applications' to which the funds have been put. The net result will reflect an increase or decrease in the overdraft.

## 4.3 Ratios

Having described the main components of the balance sheet and profit and loss account, we can now move on to see how they are used. Ratios, or the relationship between the various figures, give us the means to construct a profile of the strengths and weaknesses of a company.

In this section a selection of ratios will be described, and grouped into various categories. No suggestions will be given on the 'ideal' ratio, because this varies enormously between industry groups. This will be done in Chapter 6, which looks at three case studies in an attempt to assess a reasonable credit level. However, it may first be worth making a few observations on the subject.

First, there is an almost infinite number of ratios which can be calculated. In the studies made by Altman, Taffler and Tisshaw while calculating the so-called 'Z score', a basket of seventy ratios was used, then tested to determine their impact on the solvency of a company (we will look at Z scoring in Chapter 5). In this book we will be concerned with a smaller group.

Second, no formal code exists which defines both the name and formula for any particular ratio. There are cases where ratios can be calculated in different ways, and have different names. Where relevant, different names and formulae will be shown.

Third, one reason that the previous point should be so is the imperfect availability of figures. As we know, the depth to which a set of accounts is available varies according to the size of companies. For practical reasons therefore, it is expedient to 'bend' a formula, if by doing so a reasonable result will be achieved in the place of none at all.

Fourth, there is nothing to stop anyone from compiling any ratio they want, if it serves a useful purpose. We will look at 'hybrid' ratios later in the chapter.

Finally, a circumspect attitude should be adopted towards ratios. They reflect a historic view of a company only. There are many other features which determine our attitude towards it. For this reason it makes sense to use the simplest, clearest, most comprehensive and easiest to calculate ratios.

So to the major ratio groups, giving first the name, then formula(e), then definition, followed by comments.

### *4.3.1 Liquidity measures/ratios*

This is possibly the most well-known group of ratios, mainly because uppermost in the mind of the credit grantor is his customer's ability to meet his credit obligations.

1 Working capital or Net current assets

$$\text{Current assets} - \text{Current liabilities}$$

Ideally this should be a positive figure, suggesting an excess of assets. A negative number is a sign of weakness, suggesting that even if all current assets were converted into cash, there would still be insufficient funds to meet current obligations. This state is described as 'technical insolvency' and is one of the most difficult to deal with when deciding a trading level.

2 Normalized working capital (hybrid)

Manufacturing companies $\dfrac{\text{Stock}}{100} \times 25 + \text{All other current assets} - \text{Current liabs}$

Retailing companies $\dfrac{\text{Stock}}{100} \times 75 + \text{All other current assets} - \text{Current liabs}$

Service companies $\dfrac{\text{Stock}}{100} \times 50 + \text{All other current assets} - \text{Current liabs}$

Where a full breakdown of the components of stock is not available, this hybrid calculation expresses working capital taking a realistic view of how much stock can be quickly realisable. The figure varies according to the type of company.

The techniques and suggestions of the percentages of stock available for sale are put forward by the analyst Alexander Bathory.

3 Current ratio or Working capital ratio

$$\frac{\text{Current assets}}{\text{Current liabilities}}$$

The working capital, calculated in ratio terms. This figure should at least be greater than 1:1 otherwise the comments on technical insolvency apply.

4 Quick ratio or Acid test ratio or Liquidity ratio

$$\frac{\text{Current assets less stock}}{\text{Current liabilities}} \text{ or } \frac{\text{Quick assets}}{\text{Current liabilities}}$$

The current ratio excluding stock from the equation. This is done to eliminate the uncertainty involved in how quickly stock can be sold, and the existence of raw materials and work-in-progress included in the stock figure. This is a more stringent ratio which again should be above 1:1, but in practice is often below that threshold. There is however a flaw in this ratio. It fails to take into account how quickly the debtors figure can be realised. This will vary according to the credit terms offered, the speed of collection and the efficiency of the cash collection system.

5 Normalized liquidity ratio (hybrid)

Manufacturing companies $$\frac{\text{Stock}}{100} \times 25 + \frac{\text{All other current assets}}{\text{Priority dept}}$$

Retailing companies $$\frac{\text{Stock}}{100} \times 75 + \frac{\text{All other current assets}}{\text{Priority dept}}$$

Service companies $$\frac{\text{Stock}}{100} \times 50 + \frac{\text{All other current assets}}{\text{Priority dept}}$$

Bathory's normalized equivalent to the quick ratio, taking into account the realisation of stock. Also computed in this formula is priority debt, or debt which may reasonably be expected to be called on first. Eighty per cent of creditors and taxation is a suggestion, though a viewpoint on priority should be established based on first-hand experience of companies within a given sector.

### *4.3.2 Operating measures/ratios*

These are concerned with operational features of the company, the speed at which raw materials are converted into cash, creditors' bills are settled and the efficiency of the business generally.

1 Debtors-to-sales ratio or Debt-turn

$$\frac{\text{Debtors}}{\text{Sales}} \text{ or } \frac{\text{Debtors}}{\text{Sales}} \times 100$$

Measures the proportion as a ratio or percentage of debtors to sales. The higher the figure, the longer it takes to convert debts, or outstanding invoices, into cash.

2 Days sales outstanding or DSO or Collection period

$$\frac{\text{Debtors}}{\text{Sales}} \times 365$$

A more attractive alternative to the above, because it quantifies how many days of sales is represented by the stated debtor figure. A figure of 365 is used to denote the number of days covered in the accounts – the financial year. If the period is shorter, perhaps when companies change their year end, then this figure should reflect the number of days covered (180 or 270 etc.).

3 Creditor ratio or Creditor turnover ratio

$$\frac{\text{Creditors}}{\text{Purchases}} \text{ or } \frac{\text{Creditors}}{\text{Sales}}$$

Again this can be expressed as a ratio or percentage. Two formulae have been shown. The first divides debtors with purchases, which is the more accurate method, using the purchase figure derived from the profit and loss account. However, the sales figure is a good alternative if the value of purchases is not available (it hardly ever is). The ratio measures the proportion of sales which must be allocated to meet creditor obligations.

4 Creditor period

$$\frac{\text{Creditors}}{\text{Sales}} \times 365$$

Like the DSO, it shows how many days of sales must be generated to meet creditors' bills. The lower the better.

5 Stock turnover ratio

$$\frac{\text{Stock}}{\text{Sales}} \text{ or } \frac{\text{Stock}}{\text{Sales}} \times 100 \text{ or } \frac{\text{Stock}}{\text{Cost of sales}}$$

This ratio is both useful and difficult to calculate accurately. Ideally the cost of sales (or cost of goods sold) is the best figure to use as this measures the actual value of stock used to generate the sales figure. In its absence, the sales figure is used instead. There are further problems – the breakdown of stock into its three components will affect the ratio. There may also be a difference as a result of sales tax being added to the sales figure, but not the stock.

Having emphasised the crudity of this ratio, it is still very useful to show how long the approximate 'shelf-life' of stock is – the shorter the better.

6 Stock turnover period

$$\frac{\text{Stock}}{\text{Sales}} \times 365$$

Measure in days the shelf-life of stock.

7 Efficiency ratio (hybrid)

Stock turnover period + Collection period

This measure is derived not from the figures, but from two other ratios. It describes the 'efficiency' of a company in converting raw materials into hard cash – a combination of manufacturing, selling, distribution and cash collection. The shorter the period, the better.

### *4.3.3 Capital structure measures/ratios*

Of fundamental importance to the survival prospects of a company is its capital structure. How much money has been put in the business by its owners, and how much borrowed, are perhaps from the credit grantor's point of view, the first questions asked. Lack of capital, or undercapitalisation, is the most common cause of company failure. A common description for ratios in this group is 'gearing' or 'leverage'.

1 Net worth or Net assets or Equity or Shareholders' funds

Total assets − Total liabilities

Perhaps the most basic measurement from a balance sheet is the 'paper value' – what would be left if all assets were sold and all liabilities paid off. This is such a basic calculation that several different names to describe it have emerged, all accurate or easily understandable. The author's preference is NET WORTH.

The net worth in reality is more of a psychological rather than a real measurement. The fact that there are more assets than liabilities is heartening to a credit grantor. But balance sheet asset value is really just 'paper' value. Market forces determine the true value, which for a company in bankruptcy is well below the paper valuation.

2 Capital employed

Net worth + Long-term liabilities

Capital employed is a statement of the value of funds which have been pledged to the structural development of the business (not to the day-to-day running of it). It is a measure of share capital, retained profits and long-term loans.

3 Debt-equity ratio or Borrowing ratio or Gearing ratio

$$\frac{\text{Current} + \text{Fixed liabilities}}{\text{Net worth}}$$

One of the most important indicators of financial risk, this ratio expresses all liabilities as a proportion of equity (or net worth). The higher the ratio, the worse the position, implying the company has borrowed heavily in relation to its own resources. The ability to borrow money itself can be determined by this ratio, as lenders are reluctant to advance a figure well above the money pledged by the owners.

4 Short-term debt-equity ratio or Short-term gearing ratio

$$\frac{\text{Current liabilities}}{\text{Net worth}}$$

This ratio is distinguished from the one above, because it measures the burden of just short-term debt as a proportion of net worth. By their nature, short-term liabilities fluctuate more widely than long-term ones, and there is less flexibility in the short period in which they must be repaid (within twelve months).

The purpose of this ratio is to examine, in conjunction with the debt–equity ratio, the 'shape' of debt obligations. For instance a high debt-equity ratio could be viewed in a more favourable light if a high proportion was long-term debt, and the converse also applies.

Of course if a company has no long-term liabilities the short-term debt–equity becomes the only practicable gearing ratio.

5 Debt ratio

$$\frac{\text{Total debt}}{\text{Total assets}}$$

This ratio measures how much of the company's assets have been financed by borrowed money. The lower the figure the better.

6 Bankers' ratio or Proprietorship ratio

$$\frac{\text{Net worth}}{\text{Capital employed}}$$

Measures the proportion of capital contributed by the owners, in relation to the total capital employed. So called the Bankers' Ratio because of its significance in determining a balanced level of permissible lending to clients by banks.

### 4.3.4 *Performance ratios*

Performance is measured in terms of sales and profit. All the ratios in this group use one or other of these figures. The greater the profit, the higher the level of efficiency within the business. Also money and capital are more likely to be invested in the company. Thus the higher the ratio, the better.

An important note: pre-tax profit as used in the ratios below, does not take into account the payment of interest. It is quite common for the profit figure before tax and interest to be used. However it is the author's view that, since an interest figure is not always available in accounts, it is at the analyst's discretion whether it be used. From a practical point of view, the payment of interest is a standard business expense which cannot be avoided if money is borrowed. It is thus more realistic, and stringent, if profit before tax and after interest is used.

1 Return on sales or Profit margin

$$\frac{\text{Pre-tax profit}}{\text{Sales}} \times 100$$

Pre-tax profit as a percentage of sales. Profit before tax is used to eliminate the unpredictable nature of tax, which is calculated taking into account more than one period/year of trade, and is charged in a variable way.

The profit margin is an obvious measure of business success, but can also be difficult to assess properly. Companies will take steps to reduce legitimately the burden of tax. Unavoidable and sometimes unpredictable industrial trends can also influence profit. Therefore the final figure may not be too accurate in determining the true profitability of an organisation.

2 Return on capital employed or ROCE or Prime ratio

$$\frac{\text{Pre-tax profit}}{\text{Capital employed}} \times 100$$

Measure how effectively business capital is being used to build a business.

3 Interest burden ratio or Interest cover ratio

$$\frac{\text{Pre-tax profit}}{\text{Interest}} \times 100 \text{ or } \frac{\text{Profit before tax and interest}}{\text{Interest}}$$

This is a ratio which should, if possible, be calculated before interest is paid. It expresses pre-tax profit as a percentage of interest paid. A figure of 100 per cent or less suggests a serious condition, where only just enough profit is being made to service debt, without having to dip into the reserves of the company.

4 Assets utilisation

$$\frac{\text{Sales}}{\text{Total assets}} \times 100$$

A measure of how effectively all assets, including plant, machinery, stocks and debtors are being used.

### *4.3.5 Growth*

The final, and arguably most significant group of ratios, are those which measure growth. Taking a simplistic but none the less commonsense view, if acceptable growth ratios are displayed by a company (unless of course it is a growth in losses), there is a greater chance of its survival, even though some of the other measures may be adverse.

Three measures of growth have been chosen for this group, in sales, pre-tax profit and net worth. All three are directly related to the success of a company, and should all be as high as possible. Growth ratios could be worked out for any item on the balance sheet and P&L account, but each would have to be looked at within the total framework of the figures, rather than discreet indicators in their own right.

1 Sales growth

$$\frac{\text{Sales (previous period)}}{\text{Sales (current period)} - \text{Sales (previous period)}} \times 100$$

2 Equity growth or Net worth growth

$$\frac{\text{Equity (previous period)}}{\text{Equity (current period)} - \text{Equity (previous period)}} \times 100$$

3 Profit growth

$$\frac{\text{Pre-tax profit (previous period)}}{\text{Pre-tax profit (current)} - \text{Pre-tax profit (previous)}} \times 100$$

### *4.3.6 Author's choice*

The twenty-two ratios above have been selected for their use and general popularity within the financial analyst community. There are many more, some used regularly, some useful hybrids. An example of this is employee ratios, which measure how effective a workforce is, though the results are better suited to company management than credit analysts. By now, therefore, we have ample equipment with which to tackle the job of analysing financial figures.

To conclude this section of the chapter, I would like to suggest a range of ratios which will help make a thorough assessment, while being based on figures which are easier to obtain and understand:

1 Liquidity
  (a) Current ratio
  (b) Quick ratio
2 Gearing
  (a) Debt–equity ratio
  (b) Short-term debt–equity ratio
3 Operations
  (a) Collection period (days)
  (b) Stock turnover period (days)
4 Performance
  (a) Profit margin
  (b) Return on capital employed
5 Growth
  (a) Growth in sales
  (b) Growth in equity
  (c) Growth in pre-tax profit
6 Measures
  (a) Total assets
  (b) Total liabilities
  (c) Working capital
  (d) Net worth
  (e) Capital employed

These ratios and measures will often recur in Chapter 11 devoted to credit analysis.

Earlier in the chapter we looked at the three main objectives which can be achieved through financial analysis, *COMPARISON*, *TREND ANALYSIS* and *CORROBORATION*. Now that the main tools of analysis have been defined, we can look in more detail at these three objectives.

## 4.4 Comparison

In the ratio definitions above, deliberate care was taken to avoid making some

*Table 4.1* Radio Variance between sectors

| Ratio | Highest | Lowest |
|---|---|---|
| Current | 1.7:1 | 0.7:1 |
| Quick | 1.1:1 | 0.4:1 |
| Debt–equity | 4.0:1 | 0.4:1 |
| Collection period | 167 days | 8 days |
| Stock turnover | 110 days | 4 days |
| Profit margin | 11.4% | 1.2% |
| Return on capital employed | 35.3% | 6.4% |

(*Source:* 'Industrial Performance Analysis' 1988/9)

sort of judgement on what is a good or bad ratio. The reason for this is quite simple – the figure will vary depending on the industry sector.

Analysing ratios on their own serves a useful purpose in pinpointing an individual company's strengths and weaknesses. *However, the job cannot be done properly without having some framework on which to compare the ratios.*

It cannot be stressed too highly how important it is to compare a ratio with its 'industry norm'. What may appear a good set of ratios on their own could turn out to be merely average or even poor after norm comparison – and vice versa. For many years now credit agencies have saved their client's time by providing the main ratios, ready calculated, but with nothing to compare them with. Some analysts may have grown used to this and have thus slipped into a routine of doing no further investigation. Others will have gained experience of the most common ratios for a given sector, from looking at many balance sheets, and do an instinctive form of comparative analysis.

Now that agencies hold financial information on data bases, it is possible for them to calculate norm ratios more easily, and there are services emerging, like the D&B Duns Financial Profile and Key Business Ratios, which are ideal for comparative analysis. Other agencies have also identified this need – especially Inter Company Comparisons (ICC) who for many years have published the book *Industrial Performance Analysis* and now include comparative information in many of their standard reports. In the author's view such information should be a standard, no-extra-cost feature of any report intended to help financial analysis. Table 4.1 emphasises the wide variance between sectors.

It is perhaps easiest to calculate the variance as a percentage:

$$\frac{\text{Company ratio} - \text{Norm ratio}}{\text{Norm ratio}} \times 100$$

A typical table of comparisons for a balance sheet may look like Table 4.2.

With variances it is important to remember the result should be interpreted differently according to which ratio is being assessed. Take stock turnover in Table 4.2. In the year 1985 there is a positive variance, which changes to a negative variance in the other two years. This shows a shift from an adverse to a

*Table 4.2* Ratio Comparison

| | Year | CA/CL | (CA−S)/CL | CL/NW | TL/NW | DSO | ROS | STOCK T/O |
|---|---|---|---|---|---|---|---|---|
| Company | 31/03/85 | 0.71 | 0.59 | 7.10 | 8.52 | 67 | 2.40 | 51 |
| Norm | 1985 | 1 | 0.90 | 0.80 | 0.88 | 67 | 3.50 | 31 |
| Variance % | | −29 | −34 | 788 | 868 | 0 | −31 | 65 |
| Company | 31/03/86 | 0.63 | 0.42 | 4.73 | 6.57 | 35 | 2 | 18 |
| Norm | 1986 | 1 | 0.90 | 0.88 | 1.08 | 65 | 4.30 | 28 |
| Variance % | | −37 | −53 | 438 | 508 | −46 | −53 | −36 |
| Company | 31/03/87 | 0.80 | 0.59 | 1.15 | 1.42 | 51 | 1.44 | 25 |
| Norm | 1987 | 1 | 0.90 | 0.85 | 1.20 | 65 | 4 | 29 |
| Variance % | | −20 | −34 | 35 | 18 | −22 | −64 | −14 |

*Table 4.3* Extract of financial figures on two companies

| | Customer A | Customer B |
|---|---|---|
| Working capital | 135,000 | 128,000 |
| Net worth | 117,000 | 110,000 |
| Sales | 5,000,000 | 5,300,000 |
| Current ratio (variance) | 1.2 (−30) | 1.8 (30) |
| Debt–equity ratio (variance) | 3.8 (−45) | 2.0 (−10) |
| Profit margin (variance) | 6% (0) | 3% (−50) |
| Trading (credit) limit | 50,000 | 75,000 |

more positive position – the shelf-life of stock is reducing, which is a good sign, even though a negative variance is shown. It may therefore be expedient to alter the formula for calculating the variance, by swopping the numbers as follows:

$$\frac{\text{Norm ratio} - \text{Company ratio}}{\text{Norm ratio}} \times 100$$

This approach could be adopted for the gearing and operating ratios above, since ideally they should be below the norm. By doing so, a positive ratio would suggest a favourable position with all the ratios above, and a negative variance an unfavourable position.

### *4.4.1 Comparative analysis and underwriting consistency*

Comparing ratios between the subject company and industry norm is not the only form of comparison. Equally important is comparing performance between other customers. The purpose is to achieve one of the most important elements of a credit underwriter's job – *consistency*.

Like customers should be given like trading limits. Every customer will have his own individual characteristics, strengths and weaknesses, but it should still be possible to match them with other customers. This is certainly a possibility between customers with similar working capital, net worth and sales figures. Take the example in Table 4.3.

Customers A and B are in similar industry sectors and their balance sheet measures are similar. There are differences in their ratios, as shown by the variances in brackets. Company A has a less favourable liquidity and gearing position, but a better profit margin. Customer B looks to have a more stable balance sheet, but lets himself down by the profit margin. The question is, should there be such a difference in the trading levels?

I know this is a contrived situation, showing only extracts of the full picture. However, it does give sufficient data to pose a problem in credit underwriting which can be resolved by comparative analysis between companies. In the author's view, an identical level credit level is justified for both companies. Whether it should be £50,000 or £75,000 depends on looking deeper into both cases.

The real benefit of company comparisons is to achieve underwriting consistency and avoid conflict. Conflict (and here I refer to conflict between an enthusiastic salesperson and a credit manager) can occur when a less favourable credit level is set. If it is possible to identify other similar examples which have been given the same (or nearly the same) credit limit, it is the best defence against the accusation of unfair treatment.

Over time, a credit manager noted for the consistency and predictability of his underwriting will be respected more. The occasional adverse trading decision will be accepted more readily. Underwriters who make the most effort to get a good depth of information on a customer will have a better chance of achieving this consistency.

The difficulty of company comparison has not been forgotten. How can one go about storing customer information in a way that it can be accurately retrieved for comparative underwriting? The answer is that microcomputers can help us with this task, and this is a subject which will be looked at in Chapter 11.

## 4.5 Trend analysis

Financial figures for a single year and compared to the industry norm are useful. However it is still only part of the picture. The figures, no matter how good or bad, should be compared to previous years in order to see whether there has been any improvement. The movement in the numbers gives a much better idea of the direction the company is going. It can emphasise both the strengths and the weaknesses of the balance sheet.

In order to interpret trends in the numbers themselves (not the ratios) a technique called 'common size analysis' can be employed to good effect. It reduces each balance sheet item into a percentage of either fixed assets or liabilities. Figure 4.1 is an example:

The common size percentages give a good indication of the 'shape' of the balance sheet. Some interesting observations are:

| Name: Coms (Northern) Ltd | | | | | | |
|---|---|---|---|---|---|---|
| Year: | 31/03/85 | 31/03/86 | 31/03/87 | | | |
| Months: | 12 | 12 | 12 | | | |
| Sales | 1,808,825 | 2,359,703 | 2,951,896 | | | |
| Ptprof | 22,820 | 0 | 0 | | | |
| *Fixed assets* | | | | *Common-size analysis* | | |
| Plant, machinery | 243,726 | 224,182 | 208,587 | 17 | 14 | 11 |
| Others | 0 | 0 | 0 | 0 | 0 | 0 |
| Total | 243,726 | 224,182 | 208,587 | 17 | 14 | 11 |
| *Current assets* | | | | | | |
| Stock | 558,512 | 628,539 | 351,357 | 39 | 40 | 19 |
| Debtors | 214,360 | 728,039 | 1,301,436 | 15 | 46 | 70 |
| Others | 403,358 | 0 | 626 | 28 | 0 | 0 |
| Total | 1,176,230 | 1,356,578 | 1,653,419 | 83 | 86 | 89 |
| *Fixed liabilities* | | | | | | |
| Loans | 0 | 0 | 0 | 0 | 0 | 0 |
| Others | 0 | 0 | 0 | 0 | 0 | 0 |
| Total | 0 | 0 | 0 | 0 | 0 | 0 |
| *Current liabilities* | | | | | | |
| Creditors | 408,185 | 351,806 | 760,633 | 45 | 35 | 53 |
| Overdraft | 55,579 | 86,962 | 58,920 | 6 | 9 | 4 |
| Others | 449,595 | 579,934 | 613,582 | 49 | 57 | 43 |
| Total | 913,359 | 1,018,702 | 1,433,135 | 100 | 100 | 100 |
| *Equity* | | | | | | |
| Shares | 50,000 | 50,000 | 50,000 | | | |
| Retained | 456,597 | 512,058 | 378,871 | | | |
| Total | 506,597 | 562,058 | 428,871 | | | |
| Total assets | 1,419,956 | 1,580,760 | 1,862,006 | | | |
| Total liabs | 913,359 | 1,018,702 | 1,433,135 | | | |

*Figure 4.1* Balance sheet and common-size analysis

1 89 per cent of assets are current – there is very little substance to the company in terms of land/machinery ownership.
2 There has been a significant increase in the percentage of debtors. Is this a sign of an inefficient cash collection system?
3 The creditor figure has more than doubled. This is a misleading conclusion. The common size percentage has only increased from 35 per cent to 53 per cent in the last two years.
4 The overdraft has reduced in total size by 33 per cent, but in common size

*Table 4.4* Ratio Trends

| Year | 1985 | | | 1986 | | | 1987 | | |
|---|---|---|---|---|---|---|---|---|---|
| Ratio | Comp | Sect | Var % | Comp | Sect | Var % | Comp | Sect | Var % |
| Current | 1.29 | 1.20 | 8 | 1.33 | 1.40 | −5 | 1.15 | 1.40 | −18 |
| Quick | 0.68 | 0.40 | 70 | 0.71 | 0.50 | 42 | 0.91 | 0.50 | 82 |
| Stdb/Eq | 1.80 | 1.84 | 2 | 1.81 | 1.70 | −6 | 3.34 | 1.08 | −209 |
| Debt/Eq | 1.80 | 4.93 | 63 | 1.81 | 3.70 | 51 | 3.34 | 3 | −11 |
| DSO | 43 | 54 | 20 | 113 | 67 | −69 | 161 | 67 | −140 |
| ROS | 1.26 | 2.40 | −48 | 0 | 1.80 | −100 | 0 | 1.45 | −100 |
| Stock T/O | 112 | 132 | 15 | 97 | 130 | 25 | 44 | 136 | 68 |

terms it is now less than half its previous size (9 per cent to 4 per cent in the last two years).

In 2 this technique has helped to identify easily what could be a disturbing trend in collection performance. In (c) and (d) it has helped avoid any misinterpretation in the changing trend of the figures involved.

Let us complete the trend analysis of these figures by looking at the ratios in Table 4.4.

We have three columns for each financial year, showing the COMPany ratio, the SECTor norm and the VARiance as a percentage, adjusted so that a positive variance is always favourable. Some more observations:

1 The adverse trend in DSO shown up by common size analysis is born out by both a declining ratio and an increasing variance (in the negative direction).
2 The gearing has worsened dramatically in the last year, and common size analysis has helped pinpoint the effect of the increase in creditors.
3 Stock turnover has steadily improved over the three years, and is now much better than the norm. A pity this is not mirrored in the collection performance.
4 Despite the slowdown in collection, the liquidity ratios are around the norm, while the quick ratio in 1987 is well above the norm. This effect highlights how misleading the quick ratio can be, by not taking into account the DSO (as we discussed in the relevant section above).

By a process of comparison and trend analysis, we have been able to build up a thorough picture of this example company. Liquidity and stock turnover strengths have been identified, also the collection and gearing weaknesses. While other companies having been making just sufficient profit to add to their net worth, our subject has failed to keep up. He is paying the penalty of heavy borrowing in relation to worth, a high proportion being creditors. Of greatest interest is the collection performance, which if improved could help generate profits and so bring the company onto a more 'average' path.

Our analysis work has given us a useful insight into the nature of the company. However, we are not yet ready to make a final judgement on the best level of credit to advance. This is the point at which credit analysis takes on a broader, more fascinating aspect. This is because our task now is to go beneath the surface of the figures, to corroborate them with other items of information at our disposal.

## 4.6 Corroboration

In Chapter 2 we identified six features influencing risk – six customer attributes which are central to describing the customer's products, markets and management. These attributes alone could be of such significance that, taking into account the priority attributes (the benefits of doing business with a customer, like profit; market penetration; difficulty of replacement), might persuade us to overcome any doubts we may have over the finances. Of course the opposite may be the case.

Corroboration involves piecing together all the different bits of known customer information, to arrive at the most suitable credit decision.

For the sake of example, the following information is known about the company:

1. Activities: distribution of cheap spare parts for commercial vehicle operators. Going since 1980.
2. Premises: rented corrugated iron shack at the side of a busy trunk road just outside major city.
3. Products: cheap but medium-quality clones of established spare part products.
4. Market demand: highest in winter, increasing as more road freight being transported in region.
5. Competition: no other similar distributors in the region, but all the main commercial vehicle distributors operate a comprehensive spare parts division.
6. End customers: proprietor/operators, with no more than two vehicles in their fleet, who operate on a shoestring.
7. Management: two highly experienced manager/owners, who used to be road hauliers; know the ropes and many of the people they trade with, personally.

All it takes is a few succinct comments, which could realistically have been obtained from a salesperson who visited the company regularly and knew the people there. An accurate and comprehensive profile of a company can be compiled for analysis. This sort of approach should be taken with all key and high-risk accounts.

We can now begin to match information.

1. The sales increase from 1986–87 could be attributed to the buoyant demand created by the scarcity of similar competition.

2 The slow collection is due to the managers being reluctant to pressure their customers for payment, partly to keep their custom, partly perhaps through sympathy for the difficulties encountered by small road hauliers which are well known to them.
3 The low fixed asset base is explained by the 'ramshackle' nature of their premises.
4 The profit margin, or lack of it in the last two years, suggests their goods being sold at the minimum possible mark-up.

Assume for a moment we did not have this attribute information. By analysing the figures in the way we have, we would be well equipped to ask the right questions at a credit visit. Or we can 'see-through' any glowing description proffered by a salesperson in justification for an excessive credit limit.

To round-off this chapter, there are a few other matters which need discussion.

## 4.7 Trading patterns

Most businesses encounter wide variations in the state of their finances, caused by trading patterns within their industry.

A prime example of this is *seasonality*. At Christmas, High Street traders will expect to sell a disproportionately high volume of stock. In August there is a huge rush for new cars. Agricultural distributors often extend their credit terms over the period between planting and harvest (crop credit). Electrical distributors buy a large proportion of stock during summer (summer stocking). Insurance companies find many of their policies are renewed at the end of the financial year.

These peaks have influenced all the areas of the balance sheet. In order to present the most realistic results, most companies gear their financial year to a time when trading is at its most normal.

We have already discussed industry characteristics. Different types of company can expect to have a different shape to their balance sheet. Distributors will have a low fixed asset base and high stock turnover. Manufacturers will have a higher proportion of fixed assets, a slower stock turnover, and a higher profit margin.

## 4.8 Accounting conventions

The production of a balance sheet is far from a random compilation of accounts details. The figures are produced using a series of accounting conventions:

1 The business entity convention: differentiates between the owners of a business and their personal affairs, and the business as a legal entity in its own right.
2 The going concern convention: it is assumed that a business will continue

in operations. The assets can then be valued taking this into account. Were the business to be dissolved, the value of assets would be different, consistent with selling them off, usually at a much lower price than in a going-concern position.

3 The accounting period convention: company accounts always cover a fixed period of time in the past, usually twelve months. No idea of future trends in the figures is given.
4 The monetary measure convention: only account items which have a monetary value can appear in a financial statement.
5 The historical cost convention: in most financial statements, the value of items is based on the historical, original cost of purchasing them. From this can be obtained the revenue generated, by comparing with the historical cost.
6 The materiality convention: There can be so many elements to compiling a balance sheet that a degree of commonsense is used. How do you account for the value of writing paper taken out of the stationery store – by going round all the people who use it to see how much has been used? This convention enables the total quantity of writing paper taken from the store to be accounted for, without going into further detail.
7 The consistency convention: all accounting methods used to value an item should remain consistent from year to year.
8 The prudence convention: it is more prudent to understate rather than overstate a figure.
9 The matching convention: requires that costs shown in the accounts match the revenue they were used to generate.
10 The duality convention: the essence of bookkeeping is that any increase in assets will mean an increase in liabilities, and vice versa.

## 4.9 Off-balance sheet figures

Not all the financial information relevant to a business is included in the balance sheet. It is therefore easy to ignore it as a feature to consider. However, there are some situations which analysts should look for, or be aware of, and which are usually noted on the notes accompanying the balance sheet:

1 Contingent liabilities: these take the form of:
   (a) cross-guarantees of subsidiaries, pledged as a security for money borrowed by them;
   (b) obligations that arise on the non-performance of a contract, which were guaranteed under a performance bond;
   (c) legal action pending;
   (d) guarantees given on goods sold.
2 Leases: are a form of long-term borrowing with an obligation to maintain a repayment schedule. However, many companies were able to account for

lease repayments in their profit and loss account without registering the true value of their obligations in the balance sheet. This has the simple effect of understating the gearing and increasing the net worth of the company concerned. Current legislation requires more formal disclosure in the balance sheet, both by the lessor and the lessee.

## 4.10 Forecasting

The next logical step after trend analysis is to forecast the possible balance sheet over a future period. Of course the day-to-day running of a business involves establishing a forecast, or business plan, then continuously measuring performance against it.

The application of advanced mathematics, using computer models, gives the analyst a chance to plot the progression of financial figures, and estimate what the future has in store. Such a computation also includes weightings on the importance of each item forecast, and an assessment of external features which could influence the outcome. This is a complex process involving disciplines which fall outside the limits of this book.

Bearing in mind the historical nature of publicly available accounts, an attempt to quantify the present has a very persuasive appeal. Methods of doing so should not be lightly dismissed. However, there are some fundamental problems in interpreting the value of a forecast:

1 One basic purpose of forecasting is to enable comparison of newly published figures with the existing forecast. What happens if there is a considerable adverse variance between the two? The answer is that no judgement on a company's performance can be made in isolation – it must be compared to other similar companies' figures, rather than a forecast.
2 A forecast is too insubstantial to be used as the basis for making a credit decision. Speculators in the stock markets of the world do and will continue to base their share dealings on the forecasts of quoted companies and stock market analysts. Credit management is a more conservative discipline which traditionally places greater emphasis on past track record.
3 Forecasting is not the only way to judge the likely outcome of a company's balance sheet. Astute observation of market and general economic trends can go a long way towards forming an opinion on the current fortunes of a customer.

## Chapter summary

1 Financial analysis is a very important part of credit analysis. It can be used to:
   (a) compare finances with the industry norm and other companies;
   (b) identify trends;
   (c) corroborate non-financial information.

2 Financial figures comprise:
   (a) the balance sheet: a snapshot of a company's resources and the resultant obligations. The balance sheet formula is

$$\text{Assets} - \text{Liabilities} = \text{Equity}$$

   (b) the profit and loss account: measures the accumulated revenue generated during the accounting period, and profit after taking into account costs and expenses;
   (c) the sources and application of funds: calculates the effect on working capital and the bank balance of the financial activity recorded in the balance sheet.

3 There are a vast number of ratios which can be calculated from the figures. No formal convention exists, but the following are generally recognised, and fall into specific groups:
   (a) Liquidity — Working capital measure; Current ratio; Quick ratio
   Measures the availability of working funds
   (b) Operating — Collection period; Creditor turnover; Stock turnover
   Measures company efficiency
   (c) Capital structure — Net worth measure; Capital employed measure; Debt–Equity ratio; Short-term debt–equity ratio; Debt ratio; Bankers ratio
   Measures the gearing, or indebtedness of a company to external lenders
   (d) Performance — Return on sales; Return on capital employed; Interest burden; Asset utilisation
   Measures how well capital and assets have been used to generate profit.
   (e) Growth — Sales growth; Equity growth; Pre-tax profit growth
   Determines the 'direction' in which a company is going.

4 Besides the standard ratios above, the following 'hybrid' ratios have been suggested:
   (a) normalized working capital: the speed at which stock can be sold varies between industry sectors. This ratio eliminates this effect in arriving at a working capital figure;

(b) normalized liquidity: as above but expressed in ratio terms;
(c) efficiency ratio: the period in days for raw materials to be converted into cash, which reflects on manufacturing, selling, distribution and cash collection efficiency.

5 In addition to calculating ratios, a technique called common size analysis is useful to understand the 'shape' of a balance sheet. It is done by showing each asset and liability as a percentage of total assets or liabilities.

6 Trading patterns within industry groups can significantly effect the structure of a balance sheet.

7 All balance sheets are constructed using a series of ten conventions:
(a) business entity;
(b) accounting periods;
(c) monetary measure;
(d) historical cost;
(e) going concern;
(f) matching;
(g) consistency;
(h) prudence;
(i) duality;
(j) materiality.

8 There is a series of professional accounting standards which regulate how a financial statement should be prepared.

9 Analysts should be alert to the existence of off-balance sheet figures, such as contingent liabilities and leasing commitments.

## CHAPTER 5

# MODEL BUILDING

We have looked at features influencing risk, the way we can get the information we need, and ways to manipulate it to glean valuable information. The next step is to piece together the jigsaw in order to make a credit decision. This is done by exercising human experience and judgement.

Human judgement, however, can be fallible and inconsistent. There is universal recognition of this failing, and no credit grantor can expect to make the right decision every time. What is less forgivable is misinterpretation or failure to take all available factors into proper account, for whatever reason, which leads to making a doubtful decision. In this respect it is very useful to have available a model. Models have a number of attractions:

1 In constructing a model, the builder needs to think very carefully about the way it is constructed, and what it is capable of doing. This thought-process can be of enormous help in understanding the way credit risks are analysed and decisions made.
2 Models require a fixed set of pieces in order to construct them. Information gathering can be geared towards collecting those pieces, and it thus imposes a routine which ensure the full range of information is available for inspection.
3 Model results are always consistent. They will provide a firm platform from which the credit grantor can decide how useful the result is in relation to the problem in hand (remember that models should never be the sole basis on which to make a decision).
4 Some models can be improved over time to suit the circumstances in which they are being used.

They have some less attractive features as well:

1 Their effectiveness depends on the amount and accuracy of the information which is fed in.
2 They may be complicated and time-consuming to calculate, although the increasing use of microcomputers can do much to reduce this disavantage.
3 There may be flaws in construction which can seriously impair their effectiveness.
4 Some models require stringent testing before they can be regarded as reliable.

In this chapter we will look at four models, examining their composition, purpose and effectiveness:

1 Z scores: measure how vulnerable a company is to failure.
2 Bathory's model: same as the Z score, using different ratios and formulae.
3 Working worth analysis: measures the general strength and size of a balance sheet.
4 Attribute analysis: assesses the general attractiveness of a customer, taking into account financial and non-financial information.

As can already be seen, models can be used for a range of purposes. Much effort has been concentrated on constructing a reliable model to predict company failure – a very worthwhile and specific pursuit. The Z score and Bathory's model fall into this category.

Working worth and attribute analysis are less specific in their intention. They aim more at helping the analyst to arrive at a balanced interpretation of the available information. These models are not predictive and therefore have a more general use in the analytical and decision-making process. They can also be adapted by the user to their own specifications. To distinguish between the two models in this book, they will be called 'predictive' and 'management' models.

In the consumer credit field, the use of models is now commonplace. The variables (age, occupation, salary, home ownership etc.) are easy to assess objectively. The volume of requests for personal credit is also higher. Models are therefore ideally suited in this environment.

Constructing models in the corporate credit field is much more difficult. Judgements tend to be more subjective, and information harder to obtain. The bulk of this chapter will be devoted to describing a corporate credit model – attribute analysis.

In examining the models, first the components will be described along with the computations required, followed by an evaluation of their purpose.

## 5.1 The Z score

The first work done on this model was in 1968 by Edward Altman. He used a technique called multiple discriminant analysis (MDA), along with statistical techniques, to arrive at a series of financial measurements which are a key to determining a propensity towards company failure.

### *5.1.1 Computation*

$$\frac{\text{Working capital}}{\text{Total assets}} \tag{5.1}$$

$$\frac{\text{Retained earnings}}{\text{Total assets}} \tag{5.2}$$

$$\frac{\text{Earnings before tax and interest}}{\text{Total assets}} \tag{5.3}$$

$$\frac{\text{Market value equity}}{\text{Book debt value}} \tag{5.4}$$

$$\frac{\text{Sales}}{\text{Total assets}} \tag{5.5}$$

The Z score was the sum of (5.1) to (5.5).

This work was taken up by Richard Taffler who further developed the model using similar ratios, but including a weighting factor to take account of the varying significance of the ratios:

$$\frac{\text{Earnings before tax and interest}}{\text{Opening total assets}} \times \text{Weighting factor} \tag{5.6}$$

$$\frac{\text{Total liabilities}}{\text{Net capital employed}} \times \text{Weighting factor} \tag{5.7}$$

$$\frac{\text{Current assets less stock}}{\text{Total assets}} \times \text{Weighting factor} \tag{5.8}$$

$$\frac{\text{Working capital}}{\text{Net worth}} \times \text{Weighting factor} \tag{5.9}$$

$$\text{Stock turn} \tag{5.10}$$

The Z score was the sum of (5.6) to (5.10).

The model was further developed by Howard Tisshaw who, in 1976, suggested some ratios well suited in particular to study non-quoted companies:

$$\frac{\text{Earnings before tax and interest}}{\text{Average total liabilities}} \tag{5.11}$$

$$\frac{\text{Pre-tax profit}}{\text{Sales}} \tag{5.12}$$

$$\frac{\text{Net capital employed}}{\text{Total liabilities less deferred tax}} \tag{5.13}$$

$$\frac{\text{Current assets less stock}}{\text{Net capital employed}} \tag{5.14}$$

$$\frac{\text{Current assets less stock}}{\text{Current liabilities}} \tag{5.15}$$

Further development by Richard Taffler in 1977, which included comparing a group of 46 failed companies with solvent companies of similar size and nature, caused the following revision of the Z score formula:

$$\frac{\text{Pre-tax profit}}{\text{Average current liabilities}} \times \text{Weighting factor} \tag{5.16}$$

$$\frac{\text{Current assets}}{\text{Total liabilities}} \times \text{Weighting factor} \tag{5.17}$$

$$\frac{\text{Current liabilities}}{\text{Total assets}} \times \text{Weighting factor} \tag{5.18}$$

$$\text{No-credit interval} \quad \times \text{Weighting factor} \tag{5.19}$$

Z score = sum of (5.16) to (5.19). A negative score suggests vulnerability.

It is immediately clear from this range of formulae that there are many variations on a theme. Some adjustments have been made to take account of continued research and testing. Their objective, which is central to predicting insolvency, is that they must cover all the main financial elements which contribute to a company's existence. Using the groups outlined in the previous chapter, liquidity, operations, gearing (capital structure) and performance, the ratios immediately above are well suited to the task:

1 Ratio (5.16) is a performance measure, suggesting the return in relation to the current debts used to generate income.
2 Ratio (5.17) is a combined operation and gearing measure, showing the value of quickly realisable assets in relation to the total capital used to produce them.
3 Ratio (5.18) is another operating/gearing ratio, which measures how well priority debt is covered by total assets available.
4 Ratio (5.19) is a composite ratio measuring how long a company could continue to trade without generating income.

### *5.1.2 Evaluation*

The final set of four ratios, with their appropriate weightings, have been shown to be capable of predicting insolvency in 97.6 per cent of cases, it was found that the event itself usually occurred within roughly three years of a company first displaying a negative score. A powerful weapon indeed in helping the credit grantor to avoid a bad debt.

However, there are three problems in adopting a Z score for everyday use:

1 The weightings have not been made publicly available. To construct a similar model, using, MDA, is a very complex task probably beyond the capabilities of most credit grantors, and is only accurate in a few industry groups.
2 They rely on a range of figures which are not always available on the smaller companies (the ones who have a greater tendency to fail).
3 The 46 samples used are, in statistical terms, too few on which to base a predictive model.

Z scoring information and computer software is commercially available, and is in use mainly in larger corporations. Z scores are not, however, a common feature in the everyday credit report.

Despite these weaknesses, the Z score has proved a useful model to its users, and has pioneered much thought and work in financial analysis.

The big question is – *when* will the company go bust? There is no model in existence which can predict both the event *and* the timing. Technically insolvent companies are trading in their thousands, lurching successfully through year after year of difficulties. Company survival is a very powerful motivator, for obvious reasons, and there are many managers well practised in the art. The 'magic' ingredient which can be used to forecast the moment when future survival has still not been discovered, though it will almost certainly be an item not contained in a balance sheet.

Nevertheless the Z score fulfils its responsibilities as a model, that of giving the analyst the ability of spotting early the potential failure, tracking from year to year, continuously monitoring deterioration or improvement in the score.

## 5.2 BATHORY'S MODEL

Alexander Bathory, another leading financial analyst, has developed a model capable of use across all sectors of business, and without requiring complex calculations.

### *5.2.1 Computation*

$$\frac{\text{Profit after tax, depreciation and deferred tax}}{\text{Current debt (bank debt, tax and leasing obligations)}} \qquad (5.20)$$

$$\frac{\text{Pre tax profit}}{\text{Capital employed}} \qquad (5.21)$$

$$\frac{\text{Equity}}{\text{Current liabilities}} \qquad (5.22)$$

$$\frac{\text{Tangible net worth}}{\text{Total liabilities}} \qquad (5.23)$$

$$\frac{\text{Working capital}}{\text{Total assets}} \tag{5.24}$$

The model score is the sum of 0.2 (sum of (5.20) to (5.24). A low or negative score suggests vulnerability. Compared with the four ratio measures:

1 Ratio (5.20) is a performance measure with a better defined calculation for both the profit generated, and the priority of the current debt.
2 Ratio (5.21) is another performance measure, showing the return on capital employed.
3 Ratio (5.22) is a gearing ratio which looks at the value of equity (here equity could be regarded as the same as net assets) in relation to short-term obligations.
4 Ratio (5.23) is similar to (5.22), but excludes intangible assets (if they exist), and includes all liabilities.
5 Ratio (5.24) is a liquidity measure showing the proportion of working capital, or net current assets, to total assets.

### *5.2.2 Evaluation*

Early tests of the model, on a sample group of 40 companies, produced a 95 per cent accuracy level.

Their calculation is straightforward except for (5.20), which introduces figures which may not be available in modified accounts (though the same might apply with the pre-tax profit figure required for (5.21)).

A look at the ratios reveals a similar picture to the Z score. They are variations on the more commonly recognised ones noted in the previous chapter, but no less valid for that. An operating ratio, like the stock turn in Taffler's early model, is not present in this group, though this is not a significant absence. In theory efficient operations (stock turn and cash collection) should result in good liquidity, and this is measured in ratio (5.24). The sum of the ratios, according to the formula, should be reduced to 20 per cent of the actual result – smaller figures are more manageable, one assumes.

A distinct benefit of this model is that it can be computed routinely without having to do a full-blown analysis of accounts. This means that microcomputer help (in the form of a spreadsheet) is not necessary. It is also capable of dealing with any normal set of accounts (abnormal sets being those of banks and financial institutions).

Bathory's model is sufficiently similar in nature and intent to the Z score that some of the reservations noted above also apply. No element of timing can be attached to the model.

Like the Z score, the clear purpose is to predict insolvency, However, emphasis of this ability detracts from another obvious but equally important credit consideration – predicting strength. There is no reason these models should not be used to monitor customers at the top end of the financial strength spectrum.

Analysts should use the results of these models to the best possible effect. Just because a score looks healthy does not mean that it should be filed as a waste of time. Profitable trading can best be achieved by concentrating effort on successful customers and a high model score is a good way of identifying those which fit into this important category.

This leads into the next model, which is a 'management' model, and is therefore not concerned with prediction, so much as identifying strong and weak customers so that the most appropriate form of credit monitoring can be applied.

## 5.3 Working worth analysis

This model was developed in 1981 by the author and published in *Credit Management* (June 1984). As with Bathory's model, it is a multipurpose measure which can be obtained from the most brief of financial accounts. There are two stages to its computation.

### *5.3.1 Working worth computation*

$$\frac{\text{Working capital} + \text{net worth}}{2} \tag{5.25}$$

This is a measure of the 'size' of a company, not in terms of its sales turnover, but in relation to the levels of working funds and its paper value. The figure is for use as a 'yardstick' of the possible level of acceptable credit.

It is a useful and commonly used way of attaining underwriting consistency and one or other of these measurements may figure high on the list of preferred yardsticks. However, there is a marked tendency among many companies for the financial figures to vary widely. Many have, according to their balance sheets, limited or even negative working capital, while still displaying an overall worth when taking into account the whole balance sheet picture. The use of a single figure may then be either overly restrictive or liberal.

Working worth, as its name suggests, combines working and equity capital, then averages them by dividing by two.

### *5.3.2. Balance sheet rating computation*

$$\frac{\text{Current assets}}{\text{Current liabilities}} \tag{5.26}$$

$$\frac{\text{Current assets} - \text{stock}}{\text{Current liabilities}} \tag{5.27}$$

*Table 5.1* Calculating the working worth

| Ratios/Measures | Examples | | | |
|---|---|---|---|---|
| | A | B | C | D |
| Current | 2(:1) | 1(:1) | 0.8(:1) | 1.5(:1) |
| Quick | 1(:1) | 0.5(:1) | 0.4(:1) | 1.0(:1) |
| ST debt–eqty | 0.75(:1) | 1.25(:1) | 2.9(:1) | 2.5(:1) |
| Tot debt–eqty | 1.25(:1) | 2.0(:1) | 2.9(:1) | 3.5(:1) |
| Rating | −1 | −1.75 | −4.6 | −3.5 |
| Working cap | 300,000 | 800,000 | (10,000) | 100,000 |
| Net worth | 800,000 | 300,000 | 100,000 | (10,000) |
| Working worth | 550,000 | 550,000 | 55,000 | 55,000 |

$$\frac{\text{Current liabilities}}{\text{Net worth}} \tag{5.28}$$

$$\frac{\text{Total liabilities}}{\text{Net worth}} \tag{5.29}$$

Rating = (5.26) + (5.27) − (5.28) − (5.29).

Ratios (5.26) and (5.27) are the common current and quick liquidity measures.

Ratios (5.28) and (5.29) are the common gearing ratios.

The rationale of this ratio is that the liquidity ratios should be as high as possible, and the gearing ratios as low as possible. Thus the rating relies on the inverse relationship between them. The higher the result the better.

### *5.3.3 Evaluation*

Working worth analysis is a very simple and surface level model. It concentrates on liquidity and gearing, though in the former case an element of operation efficiency is present. Since the net worth includes an element of retained earnings, the latter ratios reflect company performance. Since no actual performance measures are required, this model can be effectively applied to modified accounts.

There are two important differences between this and the two preceding models. They are concerned with the aggregation of a group of carefully chosen ratios, whereas the Working worth rating looks at a key relationship between four common ratios. This simple relationship goes straight to the heart of an instinctive concern of all credit grantors – their customer's dependence on others, and their perceived ability to pay. Though the result of the rating is insufficiently broad to be able to predict anything, it does give a good general impression of the state of health of a company, whether good or bad.

The second difference is that Working worth analysis can be used positively to calculate a credit line. To illustrate this, Table 5.1 gives some examples (as shown in the original publication):

*Table 5.2* Working worth rating scale

| Rating | Risk description | Level of confidence | Working worth % |
|---|---|---|---|
| −4.6 or less | High | Low | 0 |
| −3.9 to −4.59 | High | Low | 2.5 |
| −3.2 to −3.89 | High | Low | 5.0 |
| −2.5 to −3.19 | High | Low | 7.5 |
| −1.8 to −2.49 | High | Low | 10.0 |
| −1.1 to −1.79 | Limited | Medium | 12.5 |
| −0.4 to −1.09 | Limited | Medium | 15.0 |
| 0.3 to −0.39 | Limited | Medium | 17.5 |
| 0.9 to 0.29 | Limited | Medium | 20.0 |
| 1 and above | Low | High | 25.0 |

Taking first the relationship between the ratios, a trend is shown with Examples A–C, of worsening liquidity and increasing indebtedness. Example D paints quite a good picture on liquidity, but also a high gearing dependence, resulting in a lower rating than, for example B, which has a poorer set of liquidity ratios. By using the inverse relationship, Example D shows the balancing-out effect of the rating which should prevent an overly optimistic view to be taken of the liquidity measures.

This same balancing-out effect applies on the Working worth calculation, especially with Examples C and D, where negative figures are present. A constant dilemma facing credit grantors is the reconciliation of good and bad points of a risk. This model does so. For those who may be reluctant to give a credit limit to a company which could be described as technically insolvent (as with C and D), the realities of business often mean that some compromise is needed.

We can now link together the two components of the model. Having assessed the stability of the balance sheet, and determined a yardstick of its size, Table 5.2 is a rating scale which can be used for this purpose:

An alternative to this table is the graph in Figure 5.1 which shows a descending 'line of decision' according to the size of the balance sheet rating.

This linking device can be used to calculate a 'preferred credit limit', by applying a percentage of a yardstick according to the rating of the balance sheet. This is shown in Table 5.3 overleaf.

We can see how different credit levels can be applied to similar yardsticks, by taking into account the nature of the balance sheet.

The rating scale and yardstick percentages were developed in the early 1980s, for use in the electronics industry sector. However there is no reason whatever why they cannot be individually tailored to reflect conditions in different sectors, or even general economic conditions which have a bearing on the solvency and gearing of companies. The yardstick percentages can be regularly adjusted according to current credit and sales policy. Higher percentages could be given during expansionary periods, either in company or general

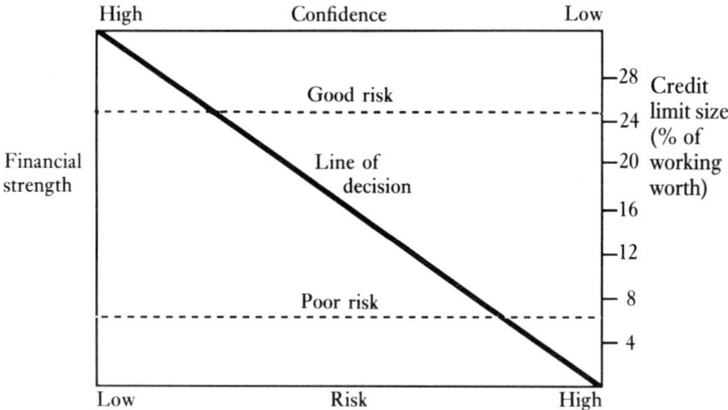


*Figure 5.1* Working worth analysis, 'line of decision'

economic terms. Both the scales can be adjusted according to experience. It helps to use a microcomputer to capture this experience and attention to this will be given in Chapter 11 on computers.

*The adaptable nature and simplicity of the working worth model is its greatest strength.*

*Table 5.3* 'Preferred level' calculations

| | Examples | | | |
|---|---|---|---|---|
| | A | B | C | D |
| Rating | −1 | −1.75 | −4.6 | −3.5 |
| Working worth | 550,000 | 550,000 | 55,000 | 55,000 |
| Preferred C/L | 82,500 | 68,750 | 0 | 2,750 |

However, one note of caution. The word 'preferred' should be emphasised when calculating credit levels using this technique. Its purpose is to consistently measure a reasonable credit figure, but there are many other considerations ('customer-speak' attributes, which have already been discussed) which influence the final credit judgement. In this case the 'management' part of the model comes to the fore. It can be used to highlight cases particularly where the actual credit line is above the preferred one. These are cases which merit a higher degree of supervision and monitoring. Working worth analysis can thus be used to ensure management resources are allocated in the most effective way.

## 5.4 Attribute analysis

This is a new model, developed by the author. It uses as one component a part of the Working worth model. However, the scope of attribute analysis is much broader, taking into account the full range of financial and non-financial considerations. It is a 'management' model which aims to build up a sort of 'identikit' picture of a customer. The benefits of doing this are many, and will be explained in detail later.

### 5.4.1 Computation

The eighteen attributes, in three major groups, are outlined below:

Customer attributes
- Outward impressions
- Product description
- Demand for product
- Strength of competition
- End-customer profile
- Management ability

Priority attributes
- Profit margin acceptability
- Ease of production
- Market attraction
- Market competition
- Security
- Replaceability

Credit attributes
- Trading experience
- Credit references
- Growth of equity and profit
- Balance sheet strength
- Gearing
- Capitalisation

The first scores to consider are the attribute weightings. In Section 5.4.2, item 3, this aspect is considered in greater depth. The weightings are a reflection of company policy and should not be the subject of constant change. The score range is from one to ten, a low score suggesting low importance. The rest of the model follows the three steps outlined below:

1 Step 1
The model involves giving a score, on a scale of one to ten, for each attribute (a scoring system which is familiar to all). The higher the score, the more attractive the attribute. A score of zero can be given if absolutely no information is available on any one attribute.

2 Step 2
The maximum possible score is calculated by multiplying each Importance Scale score by ten.

3 Step 3
The actual score is then multiplied by its Importance Score, to give a final Weighted Score. This can then be compared to the maximum score as a percentage.

The process is simple and fast. It is also ideal for operation on a microcomputer, and Figure 5.2 shows a sample spreadsheet of the model.

Note that besides the numbers, the spreadsheet has been designed to give a visual representation to the scores, shown by the asterisk markers. In most cases, the model requires a subjective approach to scoring each attribute. This does not imply lack of control over the way scores are given. Study Figures 5.3 A–C, which outline a three-part form for scoring each attribute.

Refer to Chapter 2 for a fuller discussion on the composition and meaning of each attribute. Though there are, as you can see, three suggestions on what individual score to give:

U – Upper scores (8–10) suggesting the circumstances which might merit a good score
M – Medium scores (4–7)
L – Lower scores (1–3)

Remember a score of 0 is given if nothing is known.

Embodied in the scoring system are three important features:

1 There is no 'middle' score. With average cases this is always the most tempting answer. In this model a score of 5 is just below average, 6 just above average.
2 By using a range of 1 to 10 , there is sufficient breadth for the analyst to exercise some judgement. Often the simple good/medium/bad trio does not adequately reflect the variety of situations that can arise. However for those who prefer this approach there is no reason the scores of 10, 6 and 1 should not be fixed early as the only scores available.
3 Space is devoted on the form for justifying comments. Every score must be backed up, and preferably recorded and signed. This way it is possible to do a *post mortem* to spot any areas where information had been misunderstood or misinterpreted. More important, given the threat of a *post mortem*, it should deter anyone from giving an unrealistically good score, in the hope it will swing the balance when making a credit level decision.

A final score, or percentage of the maximum, is the result of the model. In the case above it is 53 per cent. More attention will be paid to using the score later. For now, Table 5.4 gives some suggestions on general classifications:

### *5.4.2 Evaluation*

By now it should be clear that attribute analysis is a model which very cosely resembles the everyday routines which accompany credit decisions. All that is being done is to establish numerical values to describe each part of the jigsaw. For this reason, the following section will go into some depth on matters arising out of the model, and suggestions on how to make it work well.

Name: Coms (Northern) Ltd
Sect: Commercial vehicle spare part distribution
C/L scores

| | Customer | | | | | | Priority | | | | | | Credit | | | | | | Total |
|---|---|---|---|---|---|---|---|---|---|---|---|---|---|---|---|---|---|---|---|
| | 1 | 2 | 3 | 4 | 5 | 6 | 1 | 2 | 3 | 4 | 5 | 6 | 1 | 2 | 3 | 4 | 5 | 6 | |
| Score | 2 | 5 | 7 | 7 | 3 | 5 | 5 | 5 | 7 | 3 | 6 | 6 | 6 | 4 | 5 | 5 | 6 | 6 | |
| Weightings | 2 | 4 | 7 | 4 | 5 | 7 | 6 | 4 | 3 | 4 | 9 | 5 | 7 | 4 | 7 | 7 | 9 | 6 | |
| Maximum | 20 | 40 | 70 | 40 | 50 | 70 | 60 | 40 | 30 | 40 | 90 | 50 | 70 | 40 | 70 | 70 | 90 | 60 | 1000 |
| Final | 4 | 20 | 49 | 28 | 15 | 35 | 30 | 20 | 21 | 12 | 54 | 30 | 42 | 16 | 35 | 35 | 54 | 36 | 536 |
| Percentage | | | | 52 | | | | | | 54 | | | | | | 55 | | | 54 |

*Figure 5.2* Attribute analysis spreadsheet

CUSTOMER ATTRIBUTES

Date: A/c No:

Name: Credit limit:

Address: Time known (years):

---

Justifying comments

1 First impressions . . .

U Very professional, excellent appearances
M Workmanlike without being too special
L Dreadful in every way

---

2 Product description . . .

U Excellent product, high quality, impressive; innovative
M Basic but functional, medium quality
L Poor quality, shoddy, budget product

---

3 Product demand . . .

U Demand exceeds supply; huge potential
M Constant, well defined and predictable
L Supply exceeds demand; over-capacity; market as yet unestablished

---

4 Market competition . . .

U Little or none; customer dominant
M Normal competitive conditions
L Formidable competitors make life very difficult

---

5 End customer profile . . .

U Mainly blue chip, strong customers
M Mixed range of good and bad
L Selling to the bottom end of the market

---

6 Management team . . .

U Balanced with long experience; highly regarded/respected
M Competent
L Dictatorship; inexperienced; unbalanced

*Figure 5.3A* Scoresheet for use with attribute analysis – customer attributes

Priority attributes

Name:

Address:

---

| | | Comments |
|---|---|---|
| 7 | Products required . . . | |
| U | Strategically vital | |
| M | Standard line, bread-and-butter product | |
| L | Complex; unusual; special manufacture | |
| 8 | Profit margin . . . | |
| U | Well above average; highly profitable | |
| M | Acceptable | |
| L | Low; loss leader | |
| 9 | Competition . . . | |
| U | Token | |
| M | Tough but controllable | |
| L | Formidable, thankful for any order | |
| 10 | Market attraction . . . | |
| U | Strategic target; demand exceeds supply | |
| M | Normal conditions | |
| L | Supply outstrips demand; difficult market | |
| 11 | Terms and security . . . | |
| U | Highly secure, suitable guarantees; prepayment | |
| M | Standard terms, no special security | |
| L | Extended terms | |
| 12 | Replaceability . . . | |
| U | Major valuable customer; excellent potential | |
| M | Regular customer; valued business | |
| L | Easily replaceable; inconsequential | |

*Figure 5.3B* Scoresheet for use with attribute analysis – priority attributes

FINANCIAL ATTRIBUTES

Date:

Customer name:

Address:

| | | |
|---|---|---|
| A/c controller: | Major (y/n) | Time known |
| (years): | | |
| A/c No: | Credit limit: | D&B rating: |
| Credit terms: | Credit rating: | |

---

13 Trading experience . . .

U Always very prompt
M Generally acceptable record
L Almost always on stop

---

14 Credit references . . .

U Generally excellent
M Some reservations but generally OK
L Generally unsatisfactory

---

15 Growth/profitability . . .

U Healthy growth pattern in profit and worth
M Average growth pattern
L Profit/worth indicators in serious decline

---

16 Balance sheet rating . . .

U Rating > 1
M Rating < 1 and >–2.5
L Rating < –5

---

17 Bank/parent reliance . . .

U Gearing ratios in good shape
M Average gearing
L Heavy reliance on bank and/or parent

---

18 Capitalisation . . .

U Very well capitalised with good returns
M Average capitalisation and returns
L Very poor returns with minimal shareholding

*Figure 5.3 C* Scoresheet for use with attribute analysis

*Table 5.4* Attribute percentage score classification

| Score | Classification |
|---|---|
| 0–20 | Little to no merit in trading. Known attributes are adverse and several are probably missing, reflecting insufficient knowledge to justify trading. Severe weakness is possible. |
| 21–45 | Low attraction, higher risk, or recently formed customer. Possible strengths in some areas outweighed by weakness or lack of knowledge in others. Degree of latitude on exceeding a 'preferred' credit level restricted. Trading justified, but under close credit supervision. Lower sales priority suggested. |
| 46–65 | Valued customer. No major weakness or apparent vulnerability to failure. Long-term sales prospect. Wider degree of latitude on exceeding 'preferred' credit level. |
| 66+ | Highly attractive customer, in good shape. Very good long-term prospects. High sales priority recommended and a non-restrictive credit level. |

*Table 5.5* Calculating the 'trading level' based on attribute analysis

| Score | Latitude | Score | Preferred level | Adjst level |
|---|---|---|---|---|
| 0–20 | None | 18 | 10,000 | 10,000 |
| 21–45 | 'Preferred' level +21% to 45% of PL | 40 | 10,000 | 14,000 |
| 46–65 | 'Preferred' level × 1.5 +46% to 65% of PL | 50 | 10,000 | 20,000 |
| 66+ | 'Preferred' level × 2 +66% or more of PL | 70 | 10,000 | 27,000 |

1 Attribute scores and their significance:
The final score is a summation of all the pros and cons of dealing with a customer. It is not necessarily for use in determining a 'preferred' credit level – this is the function of working worth analysis, which can be operated in tandem with this model.

(a) Trading levels: the score is all-important at identifying just how much flexibility on the trading level is feasible. Table 5.5 is for guidance purposes only.

The adjusted level in Table 5.5 takes account of the 'preferred' level (calculated using working worth) and then loads it according to the score. As the score and general attractiveness of risk increases, the latitude formula suggested increases the adjusted level at an accelerated rate.

For the score of 50 the calculation is:

10,000 × 1.5 = 15,000 plus
10,000 × 50% = 5,000
20,000

*Table 5.6* Grading scale based on attribute analysis

| Score | Grade |
|---|---|
| 0–20 | D |
| 21–45 | C |
| 46–65 | B |
| 66+ | A |

For the score of 70 the calculation is:

$$
\begin{aligned}
10{,}000 \times 2.0 &= 20{,}000 \text{ plus} \\
10{,}000 \times 70\% &= \phantom{0}7{,}000 \\
&\phantom{=} 27{,}000
\end{aligned}
$$

The most important points to this part of the model are: first, that all the variables which affect the calculation of the adjusted credit limit – the working worth rating scale, and the loading factors above, can be tailored to suit individual needs and preferences; second, the adjusted level need not be the final level – this may be higher if need be, but the model has enabled a more realistic approach to be taken about what is a reasonable level taking into account all the circumstances.

(b) Customer grading and monitoring: many credit departments establish a grading system, used mainly to highlight cases requiring close supervision. The criteria often revolve around the nature and size of companies. Further discussion on grading systems appears in Chapter 8.

Here the grades can be linked to the attribute score, as in Table 5.6.

Sales targeting can also be based on the attribute score in a similar way.

(c) Underwriting authority: another function of the score could be to determine who should deal with a case. Underwriting authority levels have long been a concern, especially in larger companies and banks. Often, larger cases are much easier to underwrite than smaller ones. Incidence of company failure is also more common among the latter group, referral to a higher authority can be assigned according to the score and the number of levels of authority which exist.

(d) Score sub-groups and corroboration: a percentage (or score) has been calculated for the three attribute groups – customer, priority and credit. In Chapter 4 we talked about corroboration – non-financial features should be mirrored by financial ones. Looking at the example above, customer and credit attributes are close to each other, which is as it should be. Where full financial information is available, the customer and credit subscores should not differ widely – if they do one or other set of scores may be inaccurate. This is a good way of cross-checking a salesperson's scores for accuracy. Alternatively, if there

*Table 5.7* Attribute sub-totals

| | Examples | | |
|---|---|---|---|
| Attribute group | A | B | C |
| Customer | 51 | 51 | 38 |
| Priority | 72 | 25 | 59 |
| Credit | 28 | 28 | 39 |
| Total | 50 | 35 | 45 |

is a difference, the activities of the customer concerned may have changed for the better since publication of the last balance sheet. That should be taken into account when deciding the trading level. Attribute analysis is capable of allowing credit grantors to act on 'dynamic' information instead of solely relying on out-of-date financial figures.

2 Balanced decision-making:
In the sections above we examined some of the ways customer and credit attributes could be used together. They represent what could be termed the 'external' input to a credit decision. 'Internal' input refers to those priority trading attributes which influence how beneficial it is to trade with a company. Once again the components have been discussed in Chapter 3, but how do they fit into the model?

Taking into account priority attributes is an automatic, almost subconscious function of credit granting. To start with, it is assumed that trading will be profitable, and the production department will be ready and willing to supply the customer. However, the more experience you get at dealing with troublesome cases (or 'credit crunches'), the greater the attention which is paid to these attributes. When all avenues of investigation on 'external' information are spent, discussions quickly turn to priority matters. Here are some examples of situations which can arise:

(a) there is an exceptionally good profit margin;
(b) the customer is in a market in which your company is anxious to extend business;
(c) you need to sell to a customer to keep a production line running and staff employed;
(d) your company wants to get rid of some obsolete stock;
(e) entry into a new market means that goods are being supplied at a loss ('loss-leaders');
(f) some form of extra payment security is available;
(g) a customer will be very difficult to replace;
(h) an order has been obtained against the background of heavy competition;
(i) the customer order is for special items requiring extra production cost, and which cannot be resold elsewhere.

Each one of these situations can, on its own, seem to justify extending credit above the 'preferred' level. How can one cope with them?

Priority scoring is the 'balancing' feature of the model, designed to deal with this problem. It allows sales and marketing policy issues to be carefully considered. Take the following example of some attribute scores, in Table 5.7:

The overall attribute score on Example A falls into group B, the others into the higher risk 31–50 group (group C). In each case the priority score acts as the balancing factor.

In Example A, a reasonable customer score is counteracted by the low credit score. However, in priority terms, there is obvious benefit in doing business with the customer.

In Example B, whereas the customer and credit attributes are the same as for A, a much lower priority score has significantly reduced the attractiveness of the proposition.

In Example C, there is little to recommend the customer, except for a high priority score.

In all the examples, the credit grantor is faced with a difficult situation in view of the low credit score. The model has provided valuable guidance on what action to take.

3 Corporate policy and importance weightings.

Every credit decision has to be made within a framework of corporate policy. Perhaps sales policy demands very liberal credit underwriting. Alternatively, in times of general economic difficulties, credit considerations assume paramount importance. Larger companies especially can be known for their particular bias towards either sales or finance-oriented control.

Any management handbook on the subject will say that corporate policy should be well known and well defined. A manager's role is to ensure policy is carried out, and where necessary flexibly interpreted. The higher the level of authority, the more flexibility is permitted.

In the credit department, trading with most customers falls within policy limits. However, a small minority can provide a constant source of aggravation, because of either payment or trading level problems. It is with these cases that conflicts in priority can be encountered – the sales department is anxious to be flexible in its policy towards a customer, where the credit department is not. At worst this can result in an emotional trial of strength, leaving the loser feeling overlooked and overruled. Not the best of situations for improving the teamwork necessary for effective customer management.

Attribute analysis has a significant part to play in these circumstances. Setting importance weightings is a way of building corporate policy into the model. It should be done with great care, probably at a senior level, including joint discussions between sales, marketing and credit. Weightings could be set to cover more than one sector if appropriate, and can be occasionally adjusted to reflect changes in policy. But, most importantly, this process should involve

*Table 5.8* Four variations of Importance Weightings

| Attributes | Importance scores | | | |
|---|---|---|---|---|
| Orientation | Finance | Sales | Balanced | New company |
| **Customer** | | | | |
| Outward impressions | 2 | 4 | 3 | 3 |
| Product description | 4 | 6 | 5 | 5 |
| Demand for product | 7 | 5 | 6 | 6 |
| Strength of competition | 4 | 8 | 7 | 7 |
| End customer profile | 5 | 8 | 5 | 7 |
| Management ability | 7 | 10 | 8 | 8 |
| Sub-total | 29 | 41 | 34 | 36 |
| **Priority** | | | | |
| Profit margin acceptability | 6 | 6 | 6 | 6 |
| Goods/services required | 4 | 5 | 5 | 5 |
| Market attraction | 3 | 5 | 5 | 5 |
| Market competition | 4 | 4 | 4 | 4 |
| Security | 9 | 7 | 8 | 8 |
| Replaceability | 5 | 5 | 6 | 6 |
| Sub-total | 31 | 32 | 34 | 34 |
| **Credit & financial** | | | | |
| Trading experience | 8 | 8 | 7 | 7 |
| Credit references | 8 | 5 | 4 | 4 |
| Growth of equity and profit | 7 | 7 | 6 | 2 |
| Balance sheet strength | 7 | 5 | 5 | 2 |
| Gearing | 9 | 6 | 7 | 2 |
| Capitalisation | 6 | 4 | 6 | 2 |
| Sub-total | 45 | 35 | 35 | 19 |

discussion and agreement on the policy *in advance*, rather than let it become an issue of conflict as each troublesome case arises.

Individual cases should be treated on their individual merits, rather than policy issues. Discussions should centre on the justification for scoring, and it is here that flexibility and underwriting skill are so very important.

(a) Importance and weighting examples: Having discussed the significance and approach to setting weightings, it is worth looking in more detail at some examples of how this can be done. Table 5.8 shows how they can vary according to the orientation of a company:

Four types of weightings have been shown, though one of them, the new company column, appears for a different purpose which will be explained later.

Look at the subtotal figures: there is a wide variance between the customer and credit attributes in the finance and sales columns, reflecting policy bias. Not only will this have a numerical impact in the model, it also has psychological implications. Assuming the model is in regular use, and that the relevant sales and credit personnel are aware of the composition of the

*Table 5.9* Final attribute score taking into account different weightings

| Orientation | Customer | Priority | Credit | Final |
|---|---|---|---|---|
| Finance | 52 | 54 | 47 | 50 |
| Sales | 50 | 54 | 46 | 50 |
| Balanced | 52 | 55 | 48 | 51 |
| New company (A) | 52 | 55 | 17 | 41 |
| New company (B) | 52 | 55 | 31 | 48 |

weightings, policy bias is a way of letting each party know where they stand. Decisions made as a result of the model are easier to enforce because the differing priorities of the two departments have been considered.

There is an escape route for those who want to steer a middle course – balanced weightings can be used, and a suggestion of the importance scores is shown above. In terms of the relationship between sales and credit, a balanced approach can be perceived as being fair, and it also tends to produce slightly higher final scores.

However, the deliberate introduction of bias into the model does not mean that the power and authority of one department is being projected at the expense of the other. Nor, as you will see in the recommendations in Table 5.10, does it mean there will be wide variations in the suggested credit level. Table 5.9, using the example in Figure 5.4A–E illustrates this effect.

Note (A): Scores calculated on the assumption that no financial information is available, using the balanced weightings.

Note (B): As with (A), but using the new-company weightings.

Taking the final weighted score of the first three examples, 50, 50 and 51, there is no marked variance, even though the importance scores did differ widely. Interestingly, the subscore for customer attributes when sales bias is applied, is actually lower than it is with finance bias. This is because the better customer attributes have a low importance, whereas the lower scores have a higher importance.

Similarly, the credit subscores remain the same irrespective of whichever policy bias is applied. This is because they are mainly in the medium score range of 5 and 6.

In effect the model is acting in a very sophisticated way. The final weighted score treats the high scoring attributes of a case favourably, penalises the low scores and deals evenly with average scores. The way it does so can be finely tuned by the user.

Finally Table 5.10 shows credit recommendations it gives when applied to the actual figures given in the previous chapter to Coms (Northern) Ltd:

| | |
|---|---|
| Working worth (1987) | 324,577 |
| Rating | −1.18 |
| Rating scale percentage | 12.5 |
| 'Preferred' credit level | 40,572 |

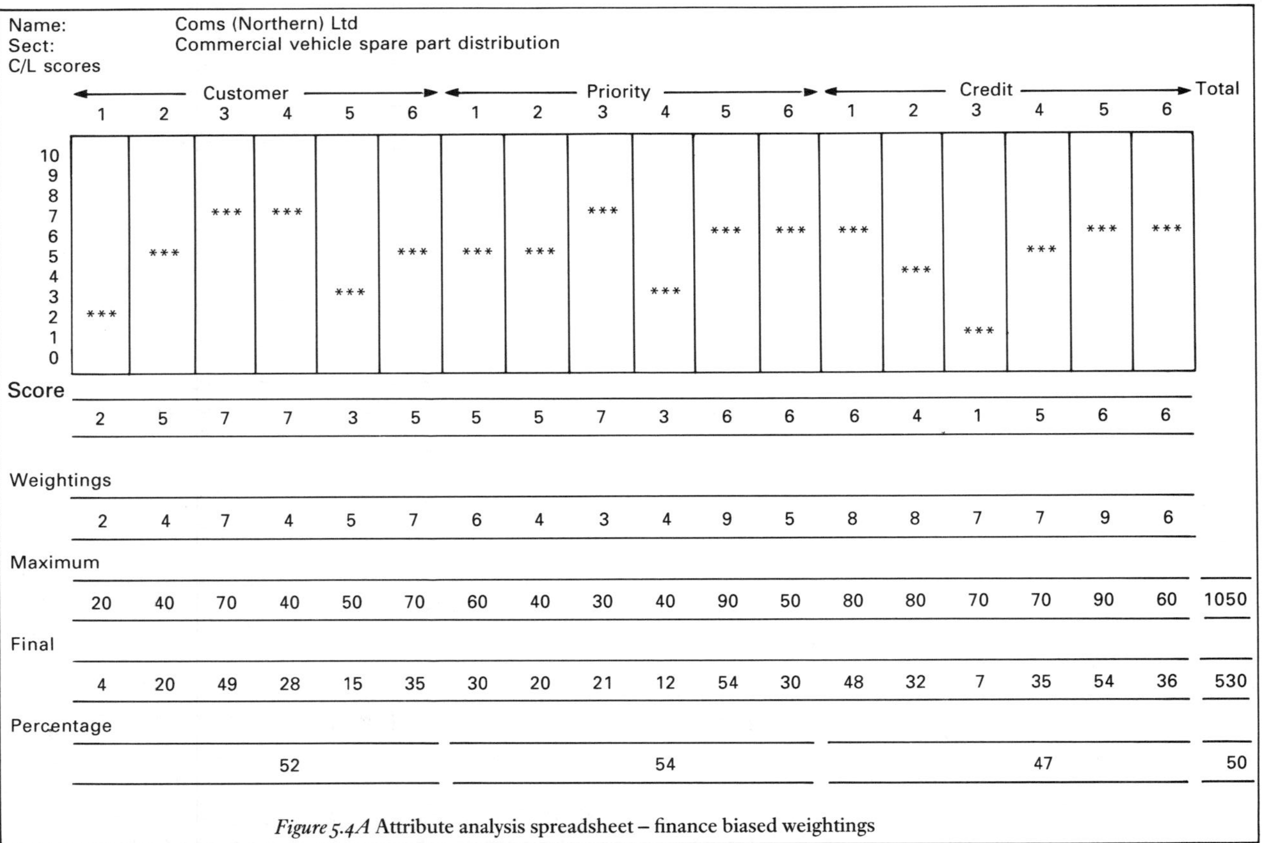

Name: Coms (Northern) Ltd
Sect: Commercial vehicle spare part distribution
C/L scores

| | Customer 1 | 2 | 3 | 4 | 5 | 6 | Priority 1 | 2 | 3 | 4 | 5 | 6 | Credit 1 | 2 | 3 | 4 | 5 | 6 | Total |
|---|---|---|---|---|---|---|---|---|---|---|---|---|---|---|---|---|---|---|---|
| Score | 2 | 5 | 7 | 7 | 3 | 5 | 5 | 5 | 7 | 3 | 6 | 6 | 6 | 4 | 1 | 5 | 6 | 6 | |
| Weightings | 2 | 4 | 7 | 4 | 5 | 7 | 6 | 4 | 3 | 4 | 9 | 5 | 8 | 8 | 7 | 7 | 9 | 6 | |
| Maximum | 20 | 40 | 70 | 40 | 50 | 70 | 60 | 40 | 30 | 40 | 90 | 50 | 80 | 80 | 70 | 70 | 90 | 60 | 1050 |
| Final | 4 | 20 | 49 | 28 | 15 | 35 | 30 | 20 | 21 | 12 | 54 | 30 | 48 | 32 | 7 | 35 | 54 | 36 | 530 |
| Percentage | | | | 52 | | | | | | 54 | | | | | | 47 | | | 50 |

*Figure 5.4A* Attribute analysis spreadsheet – finance biased weightings

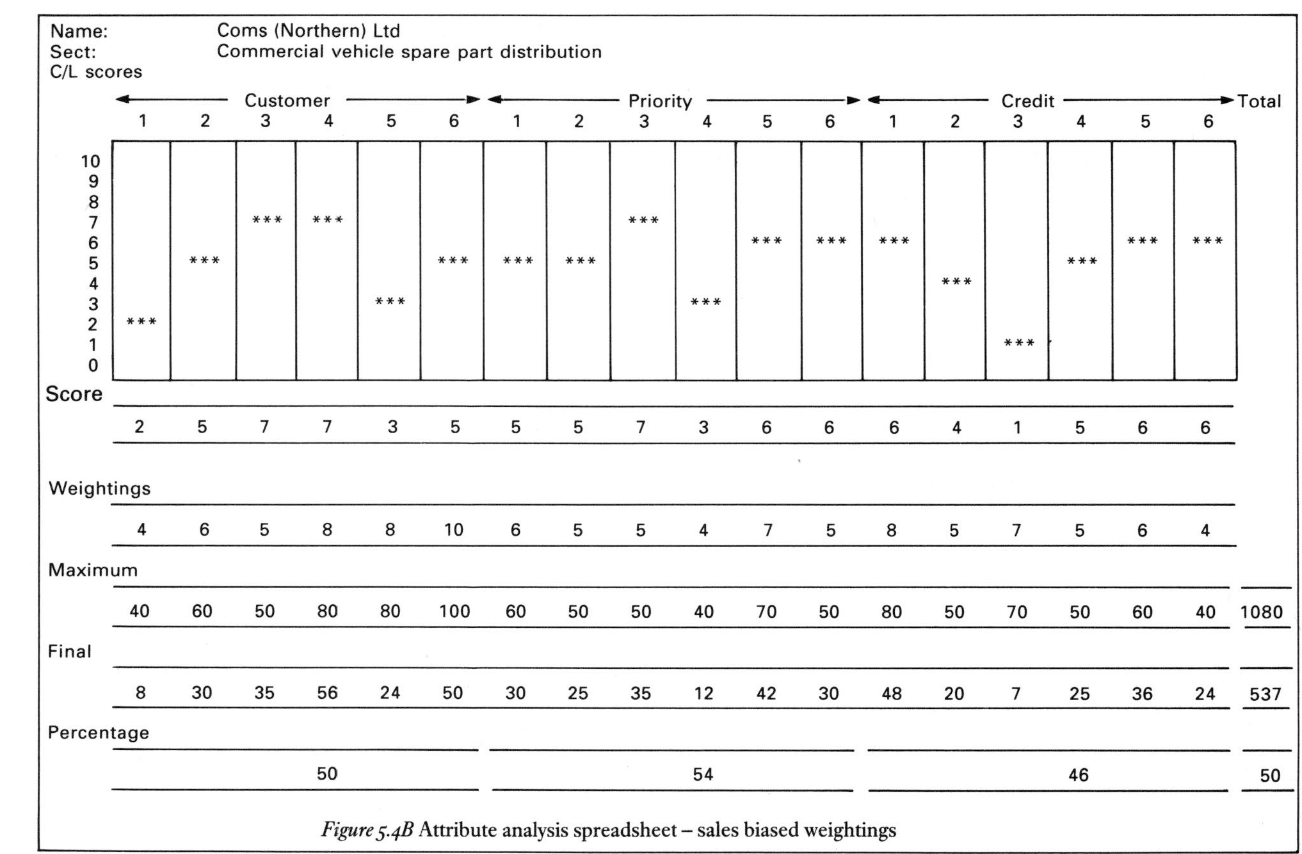

Name: Coms (Northern) Ltd
Sect: Commercial vehicle spare part distribution
C/L scores

| | Customer 1 | 2 | 3 | 4 | 5 | 6 | Priority 1 | 2 | 3 | 4 | 5 | 6 | Credit 1 | 2 | 3 | 4 | 5 | 6 | Total |
|---|---|---|---|---|---|---|---|---|---|---|---|---|---|---|---|---|---|---|---|
| Score | 2 | 5 | 7 | 7 | 3 | 5 | 5 | 5 | 7 | 3 | 6 | 6 | 6 | 4 | 1 | 5 | 6 | 6 | |
| Weightings | 4 | 6 | 5 | 8 | 8 | 10 | 6 | 5 | 5 | 4 | 7 | 5 | 8 | 5 | 7 | 5 | 6 | 4 | |
| Maximum | 40 | 60 | 50 | 80 | 80 | 100 | 60 | 50 | 50 | 40 | 70 | 50 | 80 | 50 | 70 | 50 | 60 | 40 | 1080 |
| Final | 8 | 30 | 35 | 56 | 24 | 50 | 30 | 25 | 35 | 12 | 42 | 30 | 48 | 20 | 7 | 25 | 36 | 24 | 537 |
| Percentage | | | | 50 | | | | | | 54 | | | | | | 46 | | | 50 |

*Figure 5.4B* Attribute analysis spreadsheet – sales biased weightings

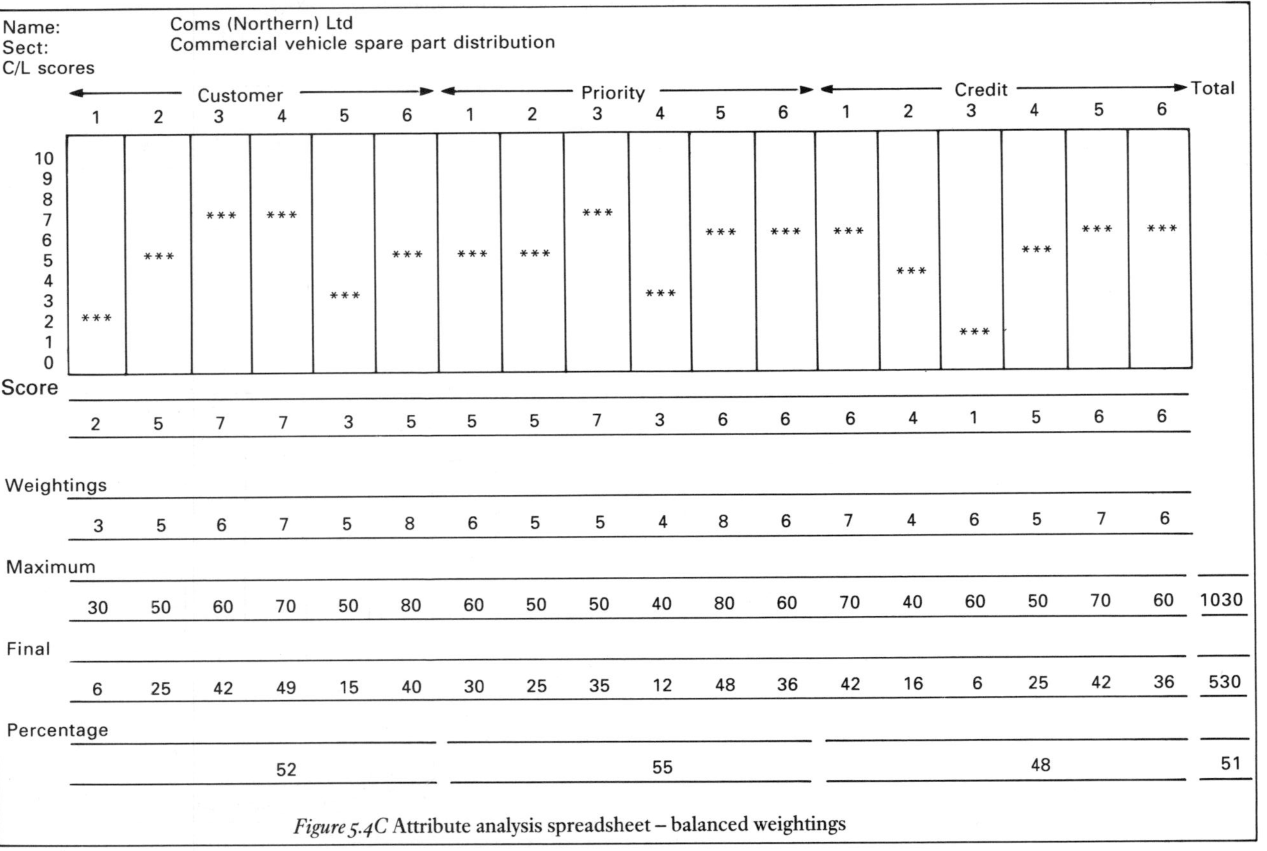

Name: Coms (Northern) Ltd
Sect: Commercial vehicle spare part distribution
C/L scores

| | Customer 1 | Customer 2 | Customer 3 | Customer 4 | Customer 5 | Customer 6 | Priority 1 | Priority 2 | Priority 3 | Priority 4 | Priority 5 | Priority 6 | Credit 1 | Credit 2 | Credit 3 | Credit 4 | Credit 5 | Credit 6 | Total |
|---|---|---|---|---|---|---|---|---|---|---|---|---|---|---|---|---|---|---|---|
| Score | 2 | 5 | 7 | 7 | 3 | 5 | 5 | 5 | 7 | 3 | 6 | 6 | 6 | 4 | 1 | 5 | 6 | 6 | |
| Weightings | 3 | 5 | 6 | 7 | 5 | 8 | 6 | 5 | 5 | 4 | 8 | 6 | 7 | 4 | 6 | 5 | 7 | 6 | |
| Maximum | 30 | 50 | 60 | 70 | 50 | 80 | 60 | 50 | 50 | 40 | 80 | 60 | 70 | 40 | 60 | 50 | 70 | 60 | 1030 |
| Final | 6 | 25 | 42 | 49 | 15 | 40 | 30 | 25 | 35 | 12 | 48 | 36 | 42 | 16 | 6 | 25 | 42 | 36 | 530 |
| Percentage | | | | 52 | | | | | | 55 | | | | | | 48 | | | 51 |

*Figure 5.4C* Attribute analysis spreadsheet – balanced weightings

Name: Coms (Northern) Ltd
Sect: Commercial vehicle spare part distribution
C/L scores

| | Customer | | | | | | Priority | | | | | | Credit | | | | | | Total |
|---|---|---|---|---|---|---|---|---|---|---|---|---|---|---|---|---|---|---|---|
| | 1 | 2 | 3 | 4 | 5 | 6 | 1 | 2 | 3 | 4 | 5 | 6 | 1 | 2 | 3 | 4 | 5 | 6 | |
| 10 | | | | | | | | | | | | | | | | | | | |
| 9 | | | | | | | | | | | | | | | | | | | |
| 8 | | | | | | | | | | | | | | | | | | | |
| 7 | | | *** | *** | | | | | *** | | | | | | | | | | |
| 6 | | | | | | | | | | | *** | *** | *** | | | | | | |
| 5 | | *** | | | | *** | *** | *** | | | | | | | | | | | |
| 4 | | | | | | | | | | | | | | *** | | | | | |
| 3 | | | | | *** | | | | | *** | | | | | | | | | |
| 2 | *** | | | | | | | | | | | | | | | | | | |
| 1 | | | | | | | | | | | | | | | | | | | |
| 0 | | | | | | | | | | | | | | | *** | *** | *** | *** | |
| Score | 2 | 5 | 7 | 7 | 3 | 5 | 5 | 5 | 7 | 3 | 6 | 6 | 6 | 4 | 0 | 0 | 0 | 0 | |
| Weightings | 3 | 5 | 6 | 7 | 5 | 8 | 6 | 5 | 5 | 4 | 8 | 6 | 7 | 4 | 6 | 5 | 7 | 6 | |
| Maximum | 30 | 50 | 60 | 70 | 50 | 80 | 60 | 50 | 50 | 40 | 80 | 60 | 70 | 40 | 60 | 50 | 70 | 60 | 1030 |
| Final | 6 | 25 | 42 | 49 | 15 | 40 | 30 | 25 | 35 | 12 | 48 | 36 | 42 | 16 | 0 | 0 | 0 | 0 | 421 |
| Percentage | 52 | | | | | | 55 | | | | | | 17 | | | | | | 41 |

*Figure 5.4D* Attribute analysis spreadsheet – balanced weightings/new company

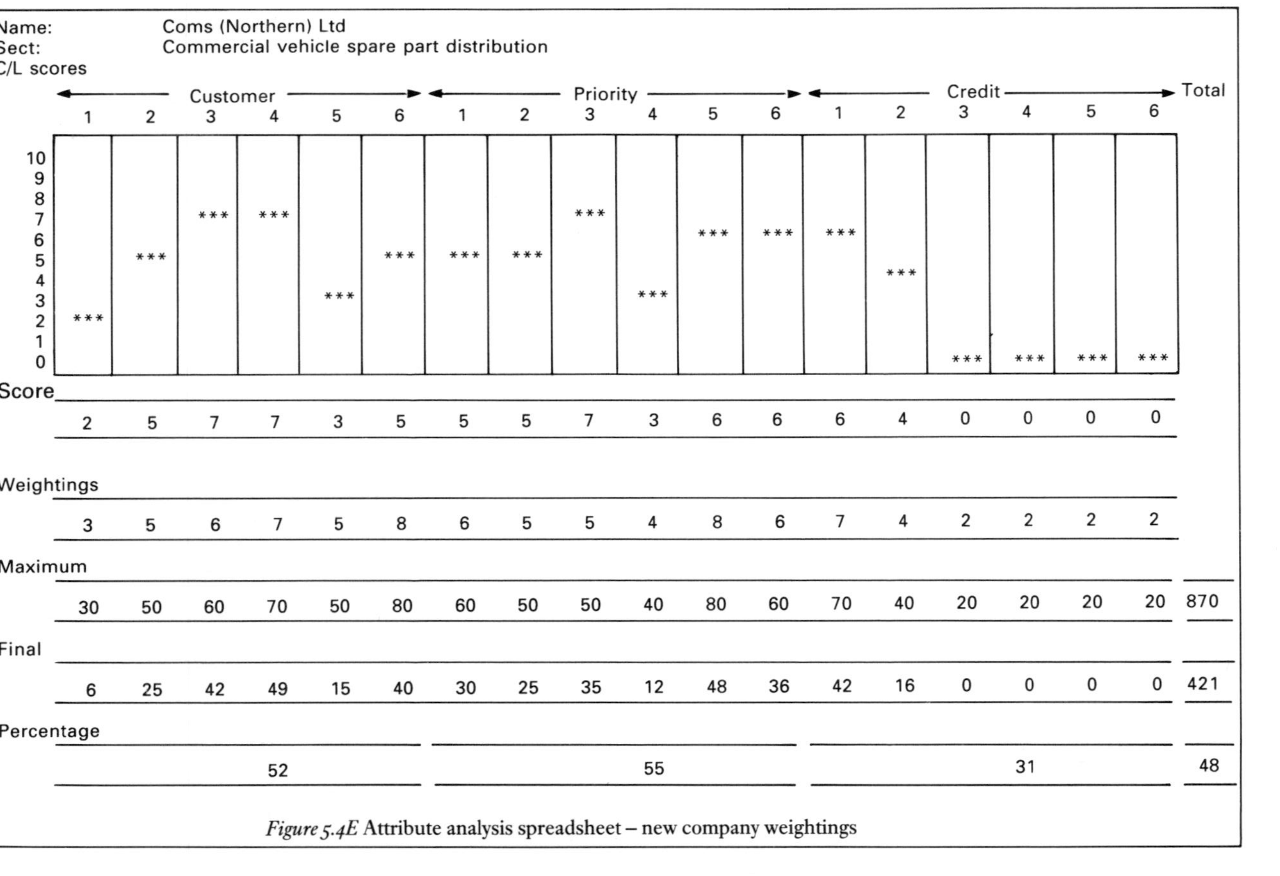

Name: Coms (Northern) Ltd
Sect: Commercial vehicle spare part distribution
C/L scores

| | Customer 1 | Customer 2 | Customer 3 | Customer 4 | Customer 5 | Customer 6 | Priority 1 | Priority 2 | Priority 3 | Priority 4 | Priority 5 | Priority 6 | Credit 1 | Credit 2 | Credit 3 | Credit 4 | Credit 5 | Credit 6 | Total |
|---|---|---|---|---|---|---|---|---|---|---|---|---|---|---|---|---|---|---|---|
| Score | 2 | 5 | 7 | 7 | 3 | 5 | 5 | 5 | 7 | 3 | 6 | 6 | 6 | 4 | 0 | 0 | 0 | 0 | |
| Weightings | 3 | 5 | 6 | 7 | 5 | 8 | 6 | 5 | 5 | 4 | 8 | 6 | 7 | 4 | 2 | 2 | 2 | 2 | |
| Maximum | 30 | 50 | 60 | 70 | 50 | 80 | 60 | 50 | 50 | 40 | 80 | 60 | 70 | 40 | 20 | 20 | 20 | 20 | 870 |
| Final | 6 | 25 | 42 | 49 | 15 | 40 | 30 | 25 | 35 | 12 | 48 | 36 | 42 | 16 | 0 | 0 | 0 | 0 | 421 |
| Percentage | | | 52 | | | | | | 55 | | | | | | 31 | | | | 48 |

*Figure 5.4E* Attribute analysis spreadsheet – new company weightings

*Table 5.10* Attribute score taking into account different weightings

| Policy bias | Adjusted credit level |
|---|---|
| Finance | 81,144 |
| Sales | 81,144 |
| Balanced | 81,549 |

It is up to the reader to decide how valid these levels are. Based on the information we know on the company, they have a poor collection record which has adversely affected profits and worth. On the plus side management is experienced and market factors are favourable, as is gearing, which offsets the adverse profit/equity growth. Certainly the balancing factor – the priority attributes, points very much to Coms (Northern) being a worthwhile and valuable customer.

The important point to note with these recommendations is that a very comprehensive range of financial, non-financial and policy features have been combined using this model in a totally consistent way.

(b) Dealing with recently formed customers: this idea has appeared several times above, so it is appropriate to deal with this aspect before looking at the rationale to setting importance scores.

Financial information is sparse to non-existent on newly formed companies. How then can we apply the working worth rating to gauge a 'preferred' credit level, and what is the effect on the scoring system? The answer to the first part is, of course, we cannot 'calculate' any credit level. The second question can also be well catered for in the model.

Here, the new company importance weightings come to the fore. Notice how customer weightings have been given a slightly higher importance, but the finance weightings have been marked down to a score of 2 for all the financial attributes. Figure 5.4E compares the final score outcome using both balanced and new company biased importance scores. Despite the absence of any financial information, a score of 48 has been justified when new company bias is applied. The model has evened out the gap in customer information.

In the real world, where credit grantors have to work with minimal financial information, no-one can afford the luxury of outright credit refusal if no figures are available. Some attempt must be made to judge the position sensibly. Once again the model can come to the rescue. Assuming over a period of time, the model is applied to a reasonable number of customers, both recently formed and well established. Having condensed a large amount of customer information into numbers, it is possible to compare any one case with similar model scores of others, to find out the credit levels given to them. Using this technique a high degree of underwriting consistency can be achieved.

For this purpose, a simple microcomputer database can be constructed to store, retrieve and compare attribute information. This is a good example of how modern technology can play an important role in sophisticated credit management.

(c) Weighting score rationale (priority): in order to get an attribute analysis model in operation quickly, the first step is to set some importance scores which are generally applicable across a broad range of customers. For those trading in just one market, this is all that is needed.

It is best to start with the priority weightings, since they will reflect the company policy which governs trading. Next, identify any attribute which stands out as crucial to the trading decision.

In the examples in Figure 5.4E, payment security has been chosen. This is because if, by some stroke of luck, a cast-iron guarantee is available, or maybe the payment terms are cash with order, then this almost alone could mean the difference between go or no-go.

Market attraction can be very important if company policy has been set to increase penetration in a particular market. A high priority would be appropriate. In the model, the score is lower on the assumption that no specific policy applies.

Profitability ought to be considered next. The higher the variance in profitability, the more important the weighting should be.

Replaceability is an ever-present consideration. Most companies constantly search for new customers, either to expand sales or to compensate for the loss of existing customers. However, this attribute is very market sensitive. In static or contracting markets, companies can find themselves with a static customer base, where replacement would be very difficult. In this situation, a high importance score is justified.

Market competition is another ever-present feature. There are few markets where orders can be obtained with ease, there being no other competitors. The importance score here depends on how busy the salesforce are. If they are spread thinly, then it becomes preferable to concentrate in areas where the likelihood of being beaten by the competition is high. A high importance score would be justified in this case. If competitive conditions are of the more typical 'nip-and-tuck' nature, then a lower score is more suited.

The importance of goods or services required, to making a decision, depends on the nature of the business. Distributors dealing mainly with ex-stock items need to attach lower importance to this aspect. Manufacturers supplying custom-built products need to set a higher importance weight.

(d) Weighting score rationale (credit and financial): as we have already discussed, the importance of financial attributes depends on the availability of information. The suggestions below assume there is such information available.

Gearing is arguably the most important. Many failures that are caused by a bank calling in a receiver. It follows that highly geared companies are at greatest risk and, with a high importance score, such companies would be rightly penalised by the model.

Payment experience is almost in the same league. Serious deteriorations in payment patterns are a good signpost of impending failure. As this attribute is the most readily available, and easiest to judge objectively, a high importance is suggested.

Growth of equity and profit follows next in the pecking order. If a company appears to be progressing well, then this may well be sufficient to offset any current weakness in the balance sheet. However, this attribute is market sensitive if the general trend is one of stagnation then a lower importance is more suitable.

On a par with the above, capitalisation plays an important role in the longevity of a company. Undercapitalisation is a common feature on insolvency, but usually accomplished by an even worse gearing position.

The importance score for balance sheet strength is the one most prone to individual preference. It plays its part in the solvency of a customer, but how precisely can it be expressed? Any one of the three preceding models could be used to decide the actual (rather than importance) score – if working worth analysis is used then the scores could even be linked to the rating scale. An average score of 5 has been given in the example, implying that neither too much nor too little is attached to the importance of this attribute.

Finally credit references, obtained from a third party has been included. This is an integral part of the information gathering process, but can be unreliable. A higher importance is justified if no financial information is available, otherwise a lower weight is recommended.

(e) Weighting score rationale (customer): customer attributes are the most subjective in nature of the entire group. Different interpretations of the circumstances are quite possible. Getting the relevant information relies on having a closer relationship with the customer, or using credit reports which specialise in giving full background information. There is a good argument for setting generally low priorities to this attribute group to take account of the above. Nevertheless, they do address some important issues.

Management ability is top of this list, and should carry one of the highest importance weightings in the model. So much of a company's success depends on the ability, balance and experience of its management.

Strength of competition is also very important. Take the Laker Airways collapse in the early 1980s. A well-financed and managed company was forced into liquidation as a result of competition (later judged to be unfair).

The nature of the Product and, separately, the demand or market for it, will be a strong influence on company success.

End-customers are an integral part of the trading chain. This is especially so if a customer has only a small number of them. The 'domino effect', as amply illustrated when DeLorean collapsed, has a destructive effect on the smaller suppliers who existed solely to service its needs. Smaller, or more recently formed customers, often have less power to manage their customers, and can run into cashflow problems. This attribute is difficult to judge accurately and, though important, is suited to a lower importance score.

Finally, outward impressions. These can be the easiest to misinterpret, but also the most readily scored. Every piece of contact with a customer goes towards building up an outward impression, however a consistently low importance has been established to this attribute.

4 Information gathering (and information scarcity).
The model requires basic and readily obtainable information to be assessed.

Credit attributes cover four major financial and two track record measurements which can be assessed as part of a standard credit investigation. Priority attributes are based on major elements of marketing, sales and credit policy fundamental to any credit risk. Customer attributes describe essential information on the customer which will determine its long-term attractiveness. They can be obtained from some credit reports, or from people with close contact with the customer – the salesforce.

The model imposes a desirable regime on the balance and quantity of information whch should be obtained. It can even compensate for lack of information on new companies. Its most obvious and important use is for dealing with those customers:

(a) who are key accounts, representing a large volume of business;
(b) on whom there is a conflict of priorities between the credit and sales departments;
(c) who are perceived as being high risk;
(d) where insufficient financial data is available to support the desired level of trading;
(e) where full information is needed to support important or difficult sales or credit negotiations.

In all the above it is essential to be fully equipped with customer information. Absence of information, especially on attributes with a high importance score, will seriously reduce the final score. It is thus in everyone's interest to find out as much as possible on a customer. In many instances the burden will fall on the sales department to contribute as much as possible. If they require a difficult credit decision to be made in their favour, then this is entirely fair.

5 Implications on underwriting
The attribute analysis model, used properly, imposes a methodical and consistent approach to credit granting (though any credit level recommendations are for guidance purposes only). It can be adapted to meet any situation, and requires a high degree of cooperation between all parties involved with customers for it to work properly. Company policy and underwriting preferences can be built in. Its components are basic and easily understandable. It produces results which predict nothing, but can be used for management purposes to identify risk and allocate resources accordingly.

The model follows all the instinctive elements in credit underwriting. However, what about 'gut-feel' underwriting? The answer is that the model does not remove the right to make the final judgement, using any of these methods. Underwriters need to think carefully about the 'gut-feel' for the following reasons:

(a) It is never wrong: when a high risk is assumed on this basis, if it does go wrong then the underwriter will look back and say 'my feelings were right'. Alternatively if the risk was declined, you may never find out if you were wrong.
(b) Emotional underwriting is a way of making a credit decision without getting a sufficient depth of information to make an informed decision.
(c) 'Gut-feelings' may not be understood by other parties, especially if the decision goes against them, or the case subsequently goes wrong.
(d) A 'gut-feeling' used to decline a risk can be regarded by some as a misuse of authority, rather than an exercise in judgement.

The word 'imposed' has been used on several occasions. The attribute analysis model does represent an imposition when compared to some methods of underwriting. Other forms of models, and here I refer to the extensive use of credit ratings, are popular because the work in compiling them is done by a credit agency.

Underwriters need to consider this aspect carefully. In the author's experience of underwriting, one maxim has so often proved correct: the quality of underwriting, and the level of respect earned by the underwriter, is determined by the amount of work done in order to make the decision and monitor the risk. Set in this context, attribute analysis is a way of streamlining the underwriting process by concentrating effort in the most important directions.

## 5.5 The role of credit models

A credit model is a way of combining customer information in a rational and logical way. 'Predictive' models like the Z score and Bathory's model have a very specific objective in mind. The working worth and attribute analysis models are more general in nature – and are thus best suited as guides to the quality of the risk, and the monitoring required.

*The results of a model are much more useful if viewed over a period of time to establish a trend, rather than used in isolation.*

The weight which is attached to models will depend on how well understood they are. This is a drawback to the Z score because of its dependence on proprietary ratio weightings. A model over which the user has a high degree of control, such as attribute analysis, can be continually tested and refined to increase the reliability of the result. The same applies to a lesser extent with working worth analysis. Bathory's model can also be continually tested for accuracy, though there is no direct provision for adjustment.

Models are ideal candidates for computerisation. In the long term, computers save calculation time and they can more efficiently store the results for future recall. Now that credit information can be both obtained and manipulated (using models) at speed, the way is paved for the microcomputer to take the place of the calculator on the credit grantor's desk. Software is becoming easier to use, so that the time and effort needed to acclimatise to computers is steadily reducing, as is their cost.

Models should not be used as replacements for the human decision, except perhaps when the credit requested is low. A notable example of over-reliance on models can be found in the Stock Market's crash in October 1987, which was compounded by the automatic selling of shares by one computer to another. In the consumer credit field, with a large volume of application asking for comparatively small amounts of credit, automated underwriting using models can be justified. Not so in corporate credit, where subjective measurement and experience plays such an important role.

## Chapter summary

Four models have been described.

1 The Z score, used to predict insolvency. Tested as 97.6 per cent accurate, but no prediction of timing given. Model requires the use of proprietary weightings and applies in a limited number of industry sectors.
2 Bathory's model, used to predict insolvency. Tested as 95 per cent accurate, but again timing not predicted. Can be used in all sectors except financial.
3 Working worth analysis used to access balance sheet stability and calculate a 'preferred' credit limit. Useful for classifying risk. Applies across all sectors. Can be adjusted to suit the circumstances of the user. Based on readily available financial information. It can be calculated in three stages:
   (a) Balance sheet ratings: calculates balance sheet strength.
   (b) Working worth: a yardstick on which to base a credit level.
   (c) Rating scale: for use in applying a percentage of the yardstick based in the financial rating. This scale can be tailored by the user. The result could be described as a 'preferred' credit level.
4 Attribute analysis: a comprehensive numerical model for taking into account 18 major elements of a credit decision, financial and non-financial. Can be tailored by the user to suit almost all corporate credit granting applications, results in a weighted final score, used to classify risk, and calculate an 'adjusted' credit level.
   (a) Importance score weighting. Before starting general use of the model, a weighting score of 1 to 10 (bad to good) is given for each attribute, which can be occasionally refined thereafter.
   (b) Attribute scores. Awarded for each attribute on the same scale as the weightings. Where no information is available, a score of zero is given.

(c) Maximum score. This is calculated by multiplying the highest possible score for each attribute (10) by its importance score.
(d) Weighted score. The actual attribute scores are multiplied by their importance score.
(e) Attributable final score. The weighted score as a percentage of the maximum score which can if required be subdivided into three main groups.
(f) Adjusted credit level calculation. Based on the 'preferred' credit level calculated by working worth analysis, if available.

CHAPTER 6

# CASE STUDIES

We know what to look for when assessing risk, and where to get it. Balance sheets have been explained, along with techniques for analysing them using ratios. Suggestions have been made on various models, which can be used to ensure a consistent approach to credit underwriting. Now is the time to put all this into practice.

This chapter contains details of three fictional companies. The main information on these companies is based on some real-life cases, but names and other details have been altered to ensure anonymity. The basic information is presented in the form of a Dun & Bradstreet standard business information report. Industry norm ratios, as compiled by ICC Business Publications Ltd, have also been included. I must thank both companies for their cooperation in supplying these data.

The analyses will be made in four separate phases – a thorough picture being built up as we go along, leading to a final credit-granting conclusion:

1 A general description of the customer information available.
2 Balance sheet analysis, including ratios, common-size analysis and two model calculations – Bathory's model and working worth analysis. Itemised financial figures for the most recent year have been given, along with general figures for the previous two years (see the format of the business information report).
3 Comparison of the ratios for the latest year, against the industry norm.
4 A review of non-financial features, using the attribute analysis model. This is done using edited extracts from a Sales Report. For the sake of example, it is assumed that marketing information is also contained in this report. Where possible, the scores have been chosen by the salesperson completing the report, not the credit grantor.
5 A final credit-granting conclusion.

The greatest problems faced by credit analysis tend to be with smaller companies, who commonly require credit above their perceived creditworthiness, and where information is incomplete. Hence the choice of these examples.

A requested credit level for each case has been given. It should be assumed this is open account or revolving credit with no security available. Our task is to see whether it can be granted, giving reasons for our decision.

It should be stressed that any conclusions and recommendations made during the course of this chapter are individual to the author. Credit granting is very much subject to individual preference and attitudes, and including current credit policy. No two analysts will share identical views, perhaps the most important facet is to be able to justify a credit decision, and I hope this will be satisfactorily done in each case.

All the case studies apply primarily to corporate credit granting so that the Attribute Analysis model can be described for each. Bankers will however find Case Study Two of interest. Credit is required to fund an expansion of the business and it could well be that the fictional company may also borrow from the bank for this purpose.

At the conclusion of this chapter, instead of the normal summary, there will be a brief review of the case studies, to see just how useful are some of the techniques described in this book.

---

## 6.1 CASE STUDY 1 (refer to Figure 6.1)

*Name*: High Quality Homes Ltd

*Industry sector*: House building

*Credit required*: £30,000

*Previous experience*: This customer has been known for the last six years, and has a current credit limit of £5,000. During this time payments have been slow, and the account has been frequently stopped, though full payment has always eventually been made.

*Sales report extracts*: 'The premises are a bit untidy, with materials lying all over the place. Not much better in the offices, provisions for keeping wooden components do not seem very effective, considering its importance to timber-framed construction. Demand for such houses in this tourist area is good, and competition from other builders is heavy. Management appear to know their business but, judging from appearance, do not seem to have good control over operations. However, their current orders are with a blue chip construction company, and all the goods they want from us will be going to meet these orders.

They have asked for goods which are in stock, for supply over the next seven months. I have negotiated a good price with above average profit, despite heavy competition from four other potential suppliers.

Because of the above, and the fact that their end buyers are first class, I would like the credit limit raised to £30,000 to cover this order. Even though we have had problems with the customer in the past, they have assured me there will be no problems with this one.'

---

BUSINESS INFORMATION REPORT
STANDARD REPORT
DATE PRINTED 15 APR 19Y9

DUNS: 00-100-1000

HIGH QUALITY HOMES LTD RATING --

SOMMERFIELD INDUSTRIAL ESTATE,
TAUNTON
SOMERSET

TEL. XXXX-XXXXX

TIMBER FRAMED HOUSING MFRS & BLDRS
SIC(S): 2452

ANY AMOUNTS HEREAFTER ARE IN POUNDS STERLING UNLESS OTHERWISE STATED

SUMMARY

| | | | |
|---|---|---|---|
| STARTED | 19X8 | SALES | (EST) 1,500,000 |
| DATE INC | 19X8 | NET WORTH | 9,000 |
| LEGAL FORM | PRIV LTD CO | EMPLOYS | 30 |
| REG NO | XXXXXXX | NOM CAP | 300,000 |
| CONDITION | FAIR | ISS CAP | 251,000 |
| TREND | DOWN | | |
| FINANCING | SECURED | | |

PRINCIPALS
Geoffrey H Holmes, chairman.
Adrian P Drake, managing director.
David G Soames, technical director.
Simon Evans, director and secretary.

PAYMENT SUMMARY

DATE RANGE: 04.Y8 - 03.Y9 HI CREDIT: 20000 AVG HI CREDIT: 6800

| | ANTIC/DISC | PROMPT | SLOW TO 30 | SLOW 31 TO 60 | SLOW 61+ | TOTAL |
|---|---|---|---|---|---|---|
| ALL SOURCES: | 0 | 13 | 3 | 7 | 0 | 15 |
| HIGHEST CR: | 0 | 20000 | 2000 | 9000 | 0 | |
| PLACED FOR COLLECTION: | 0 | | | | | |

In some instances, payments beyond terms can be the result of overlooked invoices or disputed accounts.

PUBLIC RECORD
INFORMATION

XXXXXX COUNTY COURT JUDGEMENTS (CORPORATE)

CO NAME: HIGH QUALITY HOMES LTD
CO ADDR: SOMMERFIELD INDUSTRIAL ESTATE,
TAUNTON
SOMERSET

(Cont'd)

*Figure 6.1A* Sample DunsPrint report

HIGH QUALITY HOMES LTD 15 APR 19Y9
TAUNTON UK

PUBLIC RECORD INFORMATION
(Cont'd)
DATE: DDMMY8
CASE NO: XXXXXXX AMOUNT: 289.87
CT NAME: TAUNTON OF SOMERSET

BANKERS
National Westminster Bank PLC, Taunton, Somerset

FINANCES

| | Fiscal 31.12.Y5 '000s | Fiscal 31.12.Y6 '000s | Fiscal 31.12.Y7 '000s |
|---|---|---|---|
| Net Worth | (26) | 36 | 9 |
| Fixed Assets | 196 | 201 | 249 |
| Total Assets | 546 | 494 | 448 |
| Current Assets | 350 | 293 | 199 |
| Current Liabs. | 487 | 393 | 437 |
| Working Capital(Deficit) | (137) | (100) | (238) |
| Long Term Debt | 85 | 65 | 2 |

Abstract from fiscal balance sheet as at 31.12.Y7:
The undermentioned accounts have been audited and approved in accordance with Sections 247-249 of the Companies' Act 19Y5, which changed disclosure requirements for companies classified as "small".

| | '000s | | '000s |
|---|---|---|---|
| Capital | 251 | Total tangible assets | 249 |
| Reserves | 29 | | |
| Retained Earnings | (271) | | |
| Other Def. Liabs. | 2 | | |
| Current Liabilities: | | Current Assets | |
| Other Current Liabs. | 437 | Stock & Work in Prog | 109 |
| | | Debtors | 90 |
| Total Current Liabs. | 437 | Total Current Assets | 199 |
| Total Liabilities | 448 | Total Assets | 448 |

Statement obtained from Companies' Registry on 30.11.Y8.
Other current liabilities include Accruals: 10, Payment received on account: 1, Bills of exchange payable: 59, Other Creditors: 7, Social Security: 8, Other taxes: 11. The above accounts have been audited and approved in accordance with section 247-9 of the companies act 1985 which has changed disclosure requirements for companies classified as small or medium.

(Cont'd)

*Figure 6.1B* Sample DunsPrint report (cont.)

FINANCES
(Cont'd)

Charges have been registered including: Registered in 19Y2 a debenture to National Westminster Bank PLC.
Registered in 19Y2 a mortgage to National Westminster Bank PLC.
Registered indebtedness at annual return date was shown as 189676.
On 4.1.Y8 Simon Evans submitted the following partial estimates.

Turnover for 31.12.Y8: 1,500,000
Projected annual turnover: 1,500,000

Subject has no current expansion plans.
An overdraft facility of 150000 is stated to be available but is not utilised.
Informants consider that suitable guarantees should be obtained. The balance sheet figures will be noted.

HISTORY

Geoffrey H Holmes - No other recorded directorships as at 30.11.Y8

Adrian P Drake - work history: Also responsible as production director. Date appointed 26.01.Y7 - also associated with Central Somerset Developments Ltd as at 30.11.Y8

David G Soames - work history: Also responsible as finance director. Date appointed 26.01.Y7. - also associated with Central Somerset Developments Ltd as at 30.11.Y8

Simon Evans - No other recorded directorships as at 30.11.Y8 - work history: Chartered Accountant. Date appointed 31.07.Y7.
Business started 19Y8.
99% of capital is owned by G H Holmes
The balance is owned by P Holmes
Private limited company registered 02.10.19X8.
Name changed from Frogsham-Eves Ltd on 16.3.Y3.
Nominal Capital 300,000. Issued Capital 251,000.
Search at Companies registry 30.11.Y8 showed annual return made up to 06.09.Y8

Auditors: Keep-Your-Books Ltd, High St, Taunton

OPERATIONS

Manufacturers and builders of timber framed housing (100%).
Territory: South England. Imports 1% from Sweden.
EMPLOYEES: 30.
Sells to: larger builders such as Wimpey & individuals. Terms are: Net 30 days. Number of accounts: 25. Territory: 100% National.
Product Names: none
Non seasonal business.
Owns offices, factory. The property covers 2 acres
Registered office: at heading address.

*Figure 6.1 C* Sample DunsPrint report (cont.)

| NAME | High Quality Homes Ltd | | | COMMON-SIZE ANALYSIS | | |
|---|---|---|---|---|---|---|
| C/L | | | | | | |
| SECT | BLD | | | | | |
| YEAR | 31/12/85 | 31/12/86 | 31/12/87 | | | |
| MONTHS | 12 | 12 | 12 | | | |
| DENOM | '000s | '000s | '000s | | | |
| SALES | NA | NA | NA | | | |
| PTPROF | NA | NA | NA | | | |
| FA_FIXED | 0 | 0 | 249 | 36 | 41 | 56 |
| FA_OTHRS | 0 | 0 | 0 | 0 | 0 | 0 |
| TOTAL | 196 | 201 | 249 | 36 | 41 | 56 |
| CA_STOCK | 0 | 0 | 109 | 0 | 0 | 24 |
| CA_DETRS | 0 | 0 | 90 | 0 | 0 | 20 |
| CA_OTHRS | 0 | 0 | 0 | 64 | 59 | 0 |
| TOTAL | 350 | 293 | 199 | 64 | 59 | 44 |
| FL_LOANS | 0 | 0 | 0 | 0 | 0 | 0 |
| FL_OTHRS | 0 | 0 | 2 | 15 | 14 | 0 |
| TOTAL | 85 | 65 | 2 | 15 | 14 | 0 |
| CL_CREDS | 0 | 0 | 437 | 0 | 0 | 100 |
| CL_BANK | 0 | 0 | 0 | 0 | 0 | 0 |
| CL_OTHRS | 0 | 0 | 0 | 85 | 86 | 0 |
| TOTAL | 487 | 393 | 437 | 85 | 86 | 100 |
| EQ_SHRS | 0 | 0 | 251 | | | |
| EQ_OTHRS | 0 | 0 | -242 | | | |
| TOTAL | -26 | 36 | 9 | | | |
| WCAP | -137 | -100 | -238 | | | |
| NASSTS | -26 | 36 | 9 | | | |
| WWORTH | -82 | -32 | -115 | | | |
| TOTASSTS | 546 | 494 | 448 | | | |
| TOTLIABS | 572 | 458 | 439 | | | |

| RATIOS | | | |
|---|---|---|---|
| CURRENT | .7 | .7 | .5 |
| QUICK | .7 | .7 | .2 |
| GEARING1 | -18.7 | 10.9 | 48.6 |
| GEARING2 | -22.0 | 12.7 | 48.8 |
| DSO | *VALUE! | *VALUE! | *VALUE! |
| ROS | *VALUE! | *VALUE! | *VALUE! |
| STOCK T/O | *VALUE! | *VALUE! | *VALUE! |
| CSH/CDEBT | *VALUE! | *VALUE! | *VALUE! |
| ROCE | *VALUE! | *VALUE! | *VALUE! |
| EQ/CL | -.05 | .09 | .02 |
| TNW/TL | -.05 | .08 | .02 |
| WC/TA | -.25 | -.20 | -.53 |
| BATMODSCR | NA | NA | NA |

| LOOKUP TABLE | | | |
|---|---|---|---|
| SCORE | 42.17 | -22.15 | -96.67 |
| C/L REC | 0 | 0 | 0 |

| RATING | PERCENT |
|---|---|
| -4.60 | 2.50 |
| -3.90 | 5.00 |
| -3.20 | 7.50 |
| -2.50 | 10.00 |
| -1.80 | 12.50 |
| -1.10 | 15.00 |
| -.40 | 17.50 |
| .30 | 20.00 |
| 1.00 | 25.00 |

*Figure 6.1D* Sample spreadsheet showing balance sheet, ratio and common-size analysis, working worth analysis

High Quality Homes Ltd

| RATIOS | 31/12/87 Company | 86/87 Sector |
|---|---|---|
| CURRENT | .5 | 1.6 |
| QUICK | .2 | .3 |
| GEARING1 | 48.6 | 1.6 |
| GEARING2 | 48.8 | 1.9 |
| DSO | NA | |
| ROS | NA | |
| STOCK T/O | NA | |
| ROCE | NA | |

*Figure 6.1E* Ratio comparison with industry norm
*Source:* ICC industrial performance analysis

### *6.1.1 General information*

The company is a well-established builder of timber-framed houses. The credit agency suggestion of seven thousand five hundred pounds falls well short of the amount we are looking for. Full financial information is not available, and that which is looks none too promising. Track record looks suspect, with slow payments and county court judgments. Coupled with our own trading experience, the prospect does not look good from a general point of view.

### *6.1.2 Balance sheet analysis*

The major balance sheet measures are unfavourable. Liquidity, now at 0.5 (current ratio) and 0.2 (quick ratio) is very limited with a negative working capital of £238,000. Indebtedness is split evenly between bank and creditors, and gearing ratios are very high. All debts are short term, increasing this company's vulnerability to action by creditors if bills are not met on time. The main weakness of the company is its profitability, or lack of it. Though no figures are given, the negative retained earnings figures suggest that severe losses have been made in the past, and current performance is failing to reduce this figure. Quite the opposite, the figure is increasing, and has resulted in the total equity, or shareholders' funds, reducing to £9,000.

On a more positive note, the shareholder/directors hold a good level of share capital £250,000, and other motivation to continue in business may be higher as a result. Also the split between fixed and current assets (56% to 44%) means there is some substance to the company, doubtless a comfort to the bank. Interestingly an overdraft of £150,000 is stated to be available but not utilised.

Name: High Quality Homes Ltd
Sect: House Builders
C/L scores

| | Customer | | | | | | Priority | | | | | | Credit | | | | | | Total |
|---|---|---|---|---|---|---|---|---|---|---|---|---|---|---|---|---|---|---|---|
| | 1 | 2 | 3 | 4 | 5 | 6 | 1 | 2 | 3 | 4 | 5 | 6 | 1 | 2 | 3 | 4 | 5 | 6 | |
| Score | 3 | 4 | 6 | 2 | 8 | 4 | 7 | 5 | 5 | 3 | 5 | 5 | 4 | 3 | 2 | 1 | 1 | 2 | |
| Weightings | 3 | 5 | 6 | 7 | 5 | 8 | 6 | 5 | 5 | 4 | 8 | 6 | 8 | 5 | 7 | 5 | 7 | 7 | |
| Maximum | 30 | 50 | 60 | 70 | 50 | 80 | 60 | 50 | 50 | 40 | 80 | 60 | 80 | 50 | 70 | 50 | 70 | 70 | 1070 |
| Final | 9 | 20 | 36 | 14 | 40 | 32 | 42 | 25 | 25 | 12 | 40 | 30 | 32 | 15 | 14 | 5 | 7 | 14 | 412 |
| Percentage | | | | 44 | | | | | | 51 | | | | | | 22 | | | 39 |

*Figure 6.1F* Attribute analysis spreadsheet

A reasonable though speculative view is that, given the decline in net worth, this overdraft level may not be available for much longer.

Using the two models, the figures have been echoed with the scores, Bathory's model has not been calculated due to lack of profit figures, and the working worth rating of −96.67 reflects the low liquidity and high gearing. The figure has also been getting rapidly worse.

The balance sheet trend is declining. Liquidity is getting worse and gearing getting higher.

### *6.1.3 Industry comparison*

Only ratios for liquidity and gearing are available. Gearing can be quickly dispensed with, since the subject's figures are very high. There is some slight consolation in that the quick ratio comparison shows a position only slightly worse than average, though the current ratio is much lower than average. This might suggest that, given an industry known for its illiquidity, there may be a higher degree of patience exercised by creditors.

### *6.1.4 Attribute analysis*

Since some important items fo financial information are lacking, it is especially useful to have available a fair report from an experienced salesman who knows the company well. The attribute scores have been carefully justified, and the main benefits of doing business succinctly described. In short we have a long established but unorganised customer, in a good area for housing, who has obtained a contract from a first class contractor. To cap it all, the margin on the goods is attractive, and obtained in the face of heavy competition.

The weighted scores of the analysis (Figure 6.1F), reflect this position well. The customer attribute percentage, at 44 per cent, is a little below average. The priority score of 51 per cent is better, but not spectacularly so. In achievement terms the salesperson has reason to feel pleased but there is nothing else special about the market, goods, credit terms or replaceability of the customer.

A score of 22 per cent for the credit attributes is the biggest problem. It has reduced what could have been a reasonable prospect into a very marginal case. Using working worth analysis, no credit level has been recommended, because of the low net worth and very high gearing. Even if one took the agency recommendation of £7,500 and adjusted it using the system suggested in Chapter 5, Section 4.2.1(a), a level just under £10,500 is the most that could be considered (£7,500 plus 39 per cent of that figure).

### *6.1.5 Credit decision*

This is an occasion where the reasonable non-financial information used to justify trading is not good enough to counterbalance the poor credit information. Even though the profit margin is good, the slow payment record of the customer may well erode the benefit. In addition the sales, profit and equity trends point towards this company being in severe trouble. True there may be a substantial unused overdraft facility to bale the company out but, with such poor figures, there is no guarantee that this will be permanently available. The credit decision is therefore no credit increase, and is a recommendation to wind down business with the customer. Close payment monitoring will be required, and the account stopped the moment overdues occur.

---

## 6.2 CASE STUDY 2 (refer to Figure 6.2)

*Name*: Sumptuous Furs Ltd

*Industry sector*: Fur and luxury clothing manufacturer.

*Credit required*: £200,000

*Previous experience*: None – new customer

*Sales report extract*: 'I was contacted by this old-established fur trader, because they have embarked on a major expansion of their production into high-quality woollen garments. This is because of the unpredictable demand for fashion furs.

These are very experienced people who know the clothing business well, and who have identified an area of expansion with excellent potential.

They have placed an order for wool and cotton materials, over twelve months, all ex-stock items at standard price and profit.'

---

### *6.2.1 General information*

This is an old-established company under family ownership. The payment record is favourable, though experience shown in the report has been extracted from only three sources. Nothing is known of the sales trend, but profitability swings widely from one extreme to another. A credit suggestion of fifteen thousand pounds falls well below the figure we have to consider.

### *6.2.2 Balance sheet analysis*

Sumptuous Furs is a merchanting and converting organisation, with virtually no fixed assets, and very little borrowing. Gearing ratios of just 0.6 suggest there is ample capacity for the subject to borrow more without relying too much on outside help. The liquidity ratios conflict in their nature. At first sight a current ratio of 2.7 may give some comfort, but a low quick ratio of 0.4 suggests that stock is slow moving. Since the market in furs is influenced by fashion, this trend can be expected. Profit margins on fashion goods are often very high.

BUSINESS INFORMATION REPORT
STANDARD REPORT
DATE PRINTED 15 APR 19Y9

DUNS: 00-100-1000

SUMPTUOUS FURS LTD

RATING U
(FMLY: DD)

1-5 THE STREET,
LONDON E2
UK

TEL. XXXX-XXXXX

FUR & SKIN EXPTRS & CONTRS
SIC(S): 3999

ANY AMOUNTS HEREAFTER ARE IN POUNDS STERLING UNLESS OTHERWISE STATED

SUMMARY

| | | | |
|---|---|---|---|
| STARTED | 18Y7 | NET WORTH | 1,802,831 |
| DATE INC | 19A0 | EMPLOYS | 11 |
| LEGAL FORM | PRIV LTD CO | NOM CAP | 25,000 |
| REG NO | XXXXXXX | ISS CAP | ALL |
| CONDITION | FAIR | | |
| TREND | DOWN | | |

PRINCIPALS

Joseph Zorb, managing director.
Frank Zorb, director.
David Zorb, director and company secretary.

PAYMENT SUMMARY

DATE RANGE: 10.X8 - 01.Y9 HI CREDIT: 90 AVG HI CREDIT: 77

| | ANTIC/DISC | PROMPT | SLOW TO 30 | SLOW 31 TO 60 | SLOW 61+ | TOTAL |
|---|---|---|---|---|---|---|
| ALL SOURCES: | 0 | 3 | 3 | 0 | 0 | 3 |
| HIGHEST CR: | 0 | 90 | 0 | 0 | 0 | |

PLACED FOR COLLECTION: 0

In some instances, payments beyond terms can be the result of overlooked invoices or disputed accounts.

BANKERS

Barclays Bank PLC, Branch X, London

FINANCES

| | Fiscal 31.03.Y5 | Fiscal 31.03.Y6 | Fiscal 31.03.Y7 |
|---|---|---|---|
| Pre-tax profit(Loss) | (10,296) | 72,629 | (133,728) |
| Net Worth | 1,877,918 | 1,936,034 | 1,802,831 |
| Fixed Assets | 19,458 | 47,356 | 47,438 |
| Total Assets | 2,627,738 | 2,803,573 | 2,819,223 |
| Current Assets | 2,608,280 | 2,756,217 | 2,771,785 |
| Current Liabs. | 749,820 | 867,539 | 1,016,392 |
| Working Capital(Deficit) | 1,858,460 | 1,888,678 | 1,755,393 |
| Long Term Debt | 0 | | |
| Employees | 10 | 11 | 11 |

(Cont'd)

*Figure 6.2A* Sample DunsPrint report

SUMPTUOUS FURS LTD
LONDON UK

FINANCES
(Cont'd)

Abstract from fiscal balance sheet as at 31.03.Y7:
The undermentioned accounts have been audited and approved in accordance with Sections 247-249 of the Companies' Act 19Y5, which changed disclosure requirements for companies classified as "medium".

| | | | |
|---|---|---|---|
| Capital | 25,000 | Fixtures & Equipment | 47,438 |
| Retained Earnings | 1,777,831 | | |
| Current Liabilities: | | Current Assets | |
| Trade Creditors | 957,700 | Stock & Work in Prog | 2,349,436 |
| Accruals | 1,628 | Debtors | 387,076 |
| Other Loans Payable | 5,000 | Prepaid Expenses | 659 |
| Directors Accounts | 28,159 | Cash | 34,614 |
| Taxation | 23,905 | | |
| Total Current Liabs. | 1,016,392 | Total Current Assets | 2,771,785 |
| Total Liabilities | 2,819,223 | Total Assets | 2,819,223 |

Profit and Loss Account: Annual from 1.4.Y6 to 31.3.Y7

| | |
|---|---|
| Gross Profit | 131,803 |
| Admin expenses | 263,933 |
| Payroll | 68,822 |
| Deprec./Amortisation | 10,710 |
| Net operating Income (Loss) | (132,130) |
| Interest payable | 1,598 |
| Profit before Taxes | (133,728) |
| Other Tax | (4,375) |
| Profit After Tax | (129,353) |
| Net Loss | 129,353 |
| Retained earning at start | 1,907,184 |
| Net Loss | 129,353 |
| Dividends | 0 |
| Retained earnings at end | 1,777,831 |

The notes to the accounts give the number of employess as 11, and Directors remuneration as 82,182.
Statement obtained from Companies' Registry on 4.1.Y9.
On 9.1.Y9 David Zorb confirmed general details in this report.

An overdraft facility is stated to be available.
Informants consider subject trustworthy for normal credit requirements, twentyfive thousand pounds or so mentioned as a guide.
The trading figures will be noted.

(Cont'd)

*Figure 6.2 B* Sample DunsPrint report (cont.)

```
SUMPTUOUS FURS LTD
LONDON  UK

(Cont'd)
HISTORY
        Joseph Zorb - also associated with Zorb Enterprises Ltd as at 04.01.Y9

        Frank Zorb - also associated with Zorb Enterprises Ltd as at 04.01.Y9

        David Zorb - also associated with Zorb Enterprises Ltd as at 04.01.Y9
        Business started 18Y7.
        50% of capital is owned by Frank Zorb
        The balance is owned by David Zorb
        Private limited company registered 26.12.19T0.
        The nominal share capital is divided into 500 "A" shares 500 "B"
        shares and 24,000 "Non voting Ordinary" shares, all shares are of one
        pound
        Nominal Capital 25,000. All issued.
        Search at Companies registry 04.01.Y8 showed annual return made up to
        31.12.Y7

        Auditors: Audit-expert Ltd, London

OPERATIONS
        Fur and skin merchants and converters.
        EMPLOYEES: 11.
        Sells to: Fur & Skin merchants (& some retailers). Terms are: Variable
        including net 30 days & letters of credit. Territory: 20% National.
        Exports 80% of sales to France, West Germany & ither EEC countries.
        Imports 80% of sales from Finland, Denmark.
        Owns offices, wharehouse covering 4000 sq.ft.
        Registered office: at heading address.
```

*Figure 6.2 C* Sample DunsPrint report (cont.)

| NAME | Sumptuous Furs Ltd | | | COMMON-SIZE ANALYSIS | | |
|---|---|---|---|---|---|---|
| C/L | | | | | | |
| SECT | FUR | | | | | |
| YEAR | 31/03/85 | 31/03/86 | 31/03/87 | | | |
| MONTHS | 12 | 11 | 12 | | | |
| DENOM | | | | | | |
| SALES | NA | NA | NA | | | |
| PTPROF | -10296 | 72629 | -133728 | | | |
| | | | | | | |
| FA_FIXED | 0 | 0 | 47438 | 1 | 2 | 2 |
| FA_OTHRS | 0 | 0 | 0 | 0 | 0 | 0 |
| TOTAL | 19458 | 47356 | 47438 | 1 | 2 | 2 |
| | | | | | | |
| CA_STOCK | 0 | 0 | 2349436 | 0 | 0 | 83 |
| CA_DETRS | 0 | 0 | 387076 | 0 | 0 | 14 |
| CA_OTHRS | 0 | 0 | 35273 | 99 | 98 | 1 |
| TOTAL | 2608280 | 2756217 | 2771785 | 99 | 98 | 98 |
| | | | | | | |
| FL_LOANS | 0 | 0 | 0 | 0 | 0 | 0 |
| FL_OTHRS | 0 | 0 | 0 | 0 | 0 | 0 |
| TOTAL | 0 | 0 | 0 | 0 | 0 | 0 |
| | | | | | | |
| CL_CREDS | 0 | 0 | 957700 | 0 | 0 | 94 |
| CL_BANK | 0 | 0 | 0 | 0 | 0 | 0 |
| CL_OTHRS | 0 | 0 | 58692 | 100 | 100 | 6 |
| TOTAL | 749820 | 867539 | 1016392 | 100 | 100 | 100 |
| | | | | | | |
| EQ_SHRS | 0 | 0 | 25000 | | | |
| EQ_OTHRS | 0 | 0 | 1777831 | | | |
| TOTAL | 1877918 | 1936034 | 1802831 | | | |
| | | | | | | |
| WCAP | 1858460 | 1888678 | 1755393 | | | |
| NASSTS | 1877918 | 1936034 | 1802831 | | | |
| WWORTH | 1868189 | 1912356 | 1779112 | | | |
| TOTASSTS | 2627738 | 2803573 | 2819223 | | | |
| TOTLIABS | 749820 | 867539 | 1016392 | | | |

| RATIOS | | | |
|---|---|---|---|
| CURRENT | 3.5 | 3.2 | 2.7 |
| QUICK | 3.5 | 3.2 | .4 |
| GEARING1 | .4 | .4 | .6 |
| GEARING2 | .4 | .4 | .6 |
| DSO | *VALUE! | *VALUE! | *VALUE! |
| ROS | *VALUE! | *VALUE! | *VALUE! |
| STOCK T/O | *VALUE! | *VALUE! | *VALUE! |
| CSH/CDEBT | *DIV/0! | *DIV/0! | -.14 |
| ROCE | -.01 | .04 | -.07 |
| EQ/CL | 2.50 | 2.23 | 1.77 |
| TNW/TL | 2.50 | 2.23 | 1.77 |
| WC/TA | .71 | .67 | .62 |
| BATMODSCR | NA | NA | .79 |

| LOOKUP TABLE | | | |
|---|---|---|---|
| SCORE | 6.16 | 5.46 | 2.02 |
| C/L REC | 467047 | 478089 | 444778 |

| RATING | PERCENT |
|---|---|
| -4.60 | 2.50 |
| -3.90 | 5.00 |
| -3.20 | 7.50 |
| -2.50 | 10.00 |
| -1.80 | 12.50 |
| -1.10 | 15.00 |
| -.40 | 17.50 |
| .30 | 20.00 |
| 1.00 | 25.00 |

*Figure 6.2 D* Sample spreadsheet showing balance sheet, ratio and common-size analysis, working worth analysis

A shareholding of £25,000 suggests a reasonable level of commitment by the directors, despite the losses made in the current year, the directors still withdrew just over £82,000 – a figure which could be regarded as a little high in the circumstances. However, when put in longer context, it is not unreasonable.

Using the models, Bathory's score 0.79 is somewhat above the critical danger level. The working worth rating of 2.02 is also good, though the trend over three years is on the decline, based on the working worth yardstick, a figure of £444,778 is suggested, which is well above that which we are concerned with.

A declining trend in the ratios is evident, especially with the quick ratio. Movement in the other ratios is less marked.

### *6.2.3 Industry comparison*

Again several of the ratios are missing due to lack of sales information. As could be expected, gearing ratios compare very favourably, as does the current ratio. The quick ratio and return on capital are lower than average.

### *6.2.4 Attribute analysis*

Sumptuous Furs has been around for a long time. The sales figure is unknown (in the region of £2–8m), so their market is limited in potential, leaving them vulnerable to pressures they cannot control. Expansion seems a very good idea in the circumstances. Assuming the market demand has been assessed correctly, their plans should have a good chance of success, hence a 60 per cent score for customer attributes. There are sufficient reserves, working capital and borrowing power for them to undertake the prophecy. Scores for balance sheet

Sumptuous Furs Ltd

| | 31/03/87 | 86/87 |
|---|---|---|
| RATIOS | Company | Sector |
| CURRENT | 2.7 | 1.4 |
| QUICK | .4 | 1.0 |
| GEARING1 | .6 | .9 |
| GEARING2 | .6 | 1.2 |
| DSO | NA | |
| ROS | NA | |
| STOCK T/O | NA | |
| ROCE | -7.0 | 19.0 |

*Figure 6.2 E* Ratio comparison with industry norm
*Source:* ICC industrial performance analysis

Name: Sumptuous Furs Ltd
Sect: Fur Traders
C/L scores

| | Customer | | | | | | Priority | | | | | | Credit | | | | | | Total |
|---|---|---|---|---|---|---|---|---|---|---|---|---|---|---|---|---|---|---|---|
| | 1 | 2 | 3 | 4 | 5 | 6 | 1 | 2 | 3 | 4 | 5 | 6 | 1 | 2 | 3 | 4 | 5 | 6 | |
| 10 | | | | | | | | | | | | | | | | | | | |
| 9 | | | *** | | | | | | | | | | | | | *** | *** | | |
| 8 | | | | | | | | | | | | | | *** | | | | | |
| 7 | *** | | | | | | | | | | | | | | | | | *** | |
| 6 | | *** | | | | | | | | | | | | | | | | | |
| 5 | | | | *** | *** | *** | *** | *** | | | *** | *** | | | | | | | |
| 4 | | | | | | | | | *** | | | | | | *** | | | | |
| 3 | | | | | | | | | | *** | | | | | | | | | |
| 2 | | | | | | | | | | | | | | | | | | | |
| 1 | | | | | | | | | | | | | | | | | | | |
| 0 | | | | | | | | | | | | | *** | | | | | | |
| Score | 7 | 6 | 9 | 5 | 5 | 5 | 5 | 5 | 4 | 3 | 5 | 5 | 0 | 8 | 4 | 9 | 9 | 7 | |
| Weightings | 3 | 5 | 6 | 7 | 5 | 8 | 6 | 5 | 5 | 4 | 8 | 6 | 8 | 5 | 7 | 5 | 7 | 7 | |
| Maximum | 30 | 50 | 60 | 70 | 50 | 80 | 60 | 50 | 50 | 40 | 80 | 60 | 80 | 50 | 70 | 50 | 70 | 70 | 1070 |
| Final | 21 | 30 | 54 | 35 | 25 | 40 | 30 | 25 | 20 | 12 | 40 | 30 | 0 | 40 | 28 | 45 | 63 | 49 | 587 |
| Percentage | 60 | | | | | | 46 | | | | | | 58 | | | | | | 55 |

*Figure 6.2 F* Attribute analysis spreadsheet

stability, gearing and capitalisation are all excellent, and amply make up for the lack of track record and downward profit trend. On the priority side, there is nothing exceptional to the business, except for a slight marking down of market attraction, and it appears competition for business is fierce.

Application of the attribute analysis scoring sytsem on the preferred level (£444,778 × 1.5 plus 55 per cent of £444,778) gives a suggested maximum level of £911,794.

### *6.2.5 Credit decision*

The credit level requested seems to be well above previously reported values. The losses recorded in the last balance sheet year cast a small shadow over the figures. However, taking all the other features into account, this is attractive business, for which a credit level of £200,000 can be quickly given. However, since the model results point to an even higher figure it may be worth granting a level of £400,000, just to emphasise that further orders are to be positively encouraged.

---

## 6.3 CASE STUDY 3 (refer to Figure 6.3)

*Name*: Excelsior Precision Ltd

*Industry sector*: Precision Engineers

*Credit required*: £50,000

*Previous experience*: Known fifteen years. Current credit limit £25,000. Trading record good.

*Sales report extract*: Customer specialises in hand tools and small items of precision machine tools. Occupy factory in good order on the trading estate. They pride themselves in the quality of goods produced, though from what I hear from other customers in this sector, many others produce tools just as good. They are in a very competitive market, selling to all sorts. I know the management well, and they have always impressed me as good managers.

Their order is for pressed steel sheets of a non-standard size. Lots of competition, so I exceptionally agreed a price below our norm thus profit not quite so attractive. However there was little choice since, if we do not take this contract, we may lose all the business to Joe Bloggs down the road – it would be difficult to find another customer with such a good track record in my area.'

---

### *6.3.1 General information*

Excelsior Precision is a well established engineering company. The shares are all family owned. Evidence of mortgage charges now fully paid off, creating an

```
BUSINESS INFORMATION REPORT
STANDARD REPORT
DATE PRINTED  15 APR 19Y9

DUNS: 00-100-1000

EXCELSIOR PRECISION LTD
                                                          RATING E
                                                          (FMLY: EE)

RIVERSIDE INDUSTRIAL ESTATE
WEDNESBURY
WEST MIDLANDS
UK

TEL.  XXXX-XXXXX                                PRECISN ENGRS
                                                SIC(S):  3429

   ANY AMOUNTS HEREAFTER ARE IN POUNDS STERLING UNLESS OTHERWISE STATED

SUMMARY

STARTED          19W6               SALES              1,656,058
DATE INC         19W6               NET WORTH          224,022
LEGAL FORM       PRIV LTD CO        EMPLOYS            50
REG NO           XXXXXXX            NOM CAP            100
CONDITION        FAIR               ISS CAP            ALL
TREND            EVEN

PRINCIPALS
          Wilfred Jig, director.
          Thomas Banks, director.
          Mavis Banks, director and secretary.

PAYMENT SUMMARY

DATE RANGE:  04.X8 - 03.Y9    HI CREDIT:    6000  AVG HI CREDIT:  2096

          ANTIC/DISC   PROMPT   SLOW TO 30  SLOW 31 TO 60  SLOW 61+  TOTAL
ALL SOURCES:      0         6          5             6           1      16
HIGHEST CR:       0      6000        900           900        1500
PLACED FOR COLLECTION:   0

In some instances, payments beyond terms can be the result of overlooked
invoices or disputed accounts.

PUBLIC RECORD
INFORMATION

XXXXXX          MORTGAGES & CHARGES LODGED
                SATISFACTIONS

CO NAME: EXCELSIOR PRECISION LTD

   DATE: 0601Y8

Satisfaction for charge created 19.01.W8

CO NAME: EXCELSIOR PRECISION LTD

   DATE: 0601Y8

Satisfaction for charge created 21.11.W7

                                                                  (Cont'd)
```

*Figure 6.3A* Sample DunsPrint report

EXCELSIOR PRECISION LTD
WEDNESBURY UK

PUBLIC RECORD
INFORMATION
(Cont'd)

CO NAME: EXCELSIOR PRECISION LTD

DATE: 0601Y8

Satisfaction for charge created 20.11.W7

CO NAME: EXCELSIOR PRECISION LTD

DATE: 0601Y8

Satisfaction for charge created 06.05.X7

BANKERS
LLoyds Bank PLC, Birmingham

FINANCES

| | Fiscal 31.11.Y5 | Fiscal 31.11.Y6 | Fiscal 31.11.Y7 |
|---|---|---|---|
| Turnover | 1,606,088 | 1,831,668 | 1,656,058 |
| Pre-tax profit(Loss) | 41,495 | 87,279 | 165,180 |
| Net Worth | 201,197 | 221,083 | 224,022 |
| Fixed Assets | 321,373 | 459,118 | 424,064 |
| Total Assets | 878,446 | 1,119,906 | 952,071 |
| Current Assets | 557,073 | 660,788 | 528,007 |
| Current Liabs. | 546,380 | 660,323 | 505,327 |
| Working Capital(Deficit) | 10,693 | 465 | 22,680 |
| Long Term Debt | 130,869 | 238,400 | 222,722 |

Abstract from fiscal balance sheet as at 31.10.Y7:

| | | | |
|---|---|---|---|
| Capital | 100 | Land & Bldgs | 163,242 |
| Reserves | 1,611 | Fixtures & Equipment | 260,822 |
| Retained Earnings | 222,311 | | |
| Deferred Taxation | 51,718 | | |
| Mortgages/Loans | 139,120 | | |
| Hire Purchase | 31,884 | | |
| Current Liabilities: | | Current Assets | |
| Bank Overdraft/Loans | 111,421 | Stock & Work in Prog | 97,937 |
| Taxation | 66,621 | Debtors | 414,950 |
| Other Current Liabs. | 327,285 | Tax recoverable | 15,120 |
| Total Current Liabs. | 505,327 | Total Current Assets | 528,007 |
| Total Liabilities | 952,071 | Total Assets | 952,071 |

(Cont'd)

*Figure 6.3B* Sample DunsPrint report (cont.)

```
EXCELSIOR PRECISION LTD
WEDNESBURY  UK

FINANCES
(Cont'd)

          Profit and Loss Account: Annual from 1.11.Y6 to 31.10.Y7

Net sales                                1,656,058

Deprec./Amortisation                        71,042
Net operating Income (Loss)                165,180
Profit before Taxes                        165,180
Other Tax                                   51,718
Profit After Tax                            43,709
Net Profit                                  43,709

Retained earning at start                  219,482
Net Income                                  43,709
Dividends                                   40,880
Retained earnings at end                   222,311

The notes to the accounts give the Directors remuneration as 53,878.
Statement obtained from Companies' Registry on 5.12.Y8.
Other current liabilities consist of: Other creditors
Registered in 19Y4 a mortgage to Lloyds Bank PLC.
Registered in 19Y6 a charge to Lloyds Bank PLC.
Registered indebtedness at annual return date was shown as 405137

Informants consider subject trustworthy for normal credit
requirements, ten thousand pounds or so mentioned as a guide.

HISTORY
Wifred Jig - No other recorded directorships as at 05.12.Y8

Thomas Banks - No other recorded directorships as at 05.12.Y8

Mavis Banks - No other recorded directorships as at 05.12.Y8
Business started 19W6.
99% of capital is owned by Thomas Banks
1% of capital is owned by M Banks
Private limited company registered 11.11.19W6
Nominal Capital 100. All issued.
Search at Companies registry 04.12.Y8 showed annual return made up to
09.08.Y8

OPERATIONS
Precision engineerants and converters.
EMPLOYEES: 50.
Sells to: Engineering industry. Terms are: net 30 days. Territory:
100% National.
Occupies factory
Registered office: at heading address.
```

*Figure 6.3 C* Sample DunsPrint report (cont.)

| NAME | Excelsior Precision Ltd | | | COMMON-SIZE ANALYSIS | | |
|---|---|---|---|---|---|---|
| C/L | | | | | | |
| SECT | ENG | | | | | |
| YEAR | 30/11/85 | 31/10/86 | 31/10/87 | | | |
| MONTHS | 12 | 11 | 12 | | | |
| DENOM | | | | | | |
| SALES | 1606088 | 1831668 | 1656058 | | | |
| PTPROF | 41495 | 87279 | 165180 | | | |
| FA_FIXED | 0 | 0 | 424064 | 37 | 41 | 45 |
| FA_OTHRS | 0 | 0 | 0 | 0 | 0 | 0 |
| TOTAL | 321373 | 459118 | 424064 | 37 | 41 | 45 |
| CA_STOCK | 0 | 0 | 97937 | 0 | 0 | 10 |
| CA_DETRS | 0 | 0 | 414950 | 0 | 0 | 44 |
| CA_OTHRS | 0 | 0 | 15120 | 63 | 59 | 2 |
| TOTAL | 557073 | 660788 | 528007 | 63 | 59 | 55 |
| FL_LOANS | 0 | 0 | 139120 | 0 | 0 | 19 |
| FL_OTHRS | 0 | 0 | 83602 | 19 | 27 | 11 |
| TOTAL | 130869 | 238400 | 222722 | 19 | 27 | 31 |
| CL_CREDS | 0 | 0 | 327285 | 0 | 0 | 45 |
| CL_BANK | 0 | 0 | 111421 | 0 | 0 | 15 |
| CL_OTHRS | 0 | 0 | 66621 | 81 | 73 | 9 |
| TOTAL | 546380 | 660323 | 505327 | 81 | 73 | 69 |
| EQ_SHRS | 0 | 0 | 100 | | | |
| EQ_OTHRS | 0 | 0 | 223922 | | | |
| TOTAL | 201197 | 221183 | 224022 | | | |
| WCAP | 10693 | 465 | 22680 | | | |
| NASSTS | 201197 | 221183 | 224022 | | | |
| WWORTH | 105945 | 110824 | 123351 | | | |
| TOTASSTS | 878446 | 1119906 | 952071 | | | |
| TOTLIABS | 677249 | 898723 | 728049 | | | |

| RATIOS | | | |
|---|---|---|---|
| CURRENT | 1.0 | 1.0 | 1.0 |
| QUICK | 1.0 | 1.0 | .9 |
| GEARING1 | 2.7 | 3.0 | 2.3 |
| GEARING2 | 3.4 | 4.1 | 3.2 |
| DSO | 0 | 0 | 93 |
| ROS | 2.6 | 4.8 | 10.0 |
| STOCK T/O | 0 | 0 | 22 |
| CSH/CDEBT | .32 | .37 | .25 |
| ROCE | .12 | .19 | .37 |
| EQ/CL | .37 | .33 | .44 |
| TNW/TL | .30 | .25 | .31 |
| WC/TA | .01 | .00 | .02 |
| BATMODSCR | .22 | .23 | .28 |

| LOOKUP TABLE | | | |
|---|---|---|---|
| SCORE | -4.04 | -5.05 | -3.61 |
| C/L REC | 2649 | 0 | 6168 |
| RATING | PERCENT | | |
| -4.60 | 2.50 | | |
| -3.90 | 5.00 | | |
| -3.20 | 7.50 | | |
| -2.50 | 10.00 | | |
| -1.80 | 12.50 | | |
| -1.10 | 15.00 | | |
| -.40 | 17.50 | | |
| .30 | 20.00 | | |
| 1.00 | 25.00 | | |

*Figure 6.3D* Sample spreadsheet showing balance sheet, ratio and common-size analysis, working worth analysis

impression of sensible and responsible borrowing. However, a look at the trading experience available shows that Excelsior may not be the best of payers. A credit suggestion of ten thousand pounds falls well short of requirements. Full financial information has been disclosed, perhaps showing the owner's willingness to display evidence of their good management. Whether this is the case we shall see.

### *6.3.2 Balance sheet analysis*

There is a very well balanced and stable 'feel' to the accounts. Looking at the common-size analysis, assets are evenly split between fixed and current, and the proportion of fixed and current liabilities is reasonable. Note the decrease in long-term liability which, when reduced to common size, is an increase from 25 to 31 per cent.

A deeper examination of the figures shows that this stable feeling is more an illusion than reality. Liquidity is a weak point. There is only just sufficient current assets to meet current liabilities, though the position changes little if the stock figure is removed.

Amounts borrowed/owed compared to equity (the gearing ratios of 2.3 and 3.2) are high. Very little share capital has been placed in the busness by its management.

The current sales figure is down on the previous year, but pre-tax profit has nearly doubled. It is a little difficult to decide how to regard these figures. A reduction in sales to a figure attained two years ago may be a disappointment. But to double profits every year is a spectacular success.

Excelsior Precision Ltd

| | 31/10/87 | 86/87 |
|---|---|---|
| RATIOS | Company | Sector |
| CURRENT | 1.0 | 1.7 |
| QUICK | .9 | .9 |
| GEARING1 | 2.3 | .9 |
| GEARING2 | 3.2 | 1.3 |
| DSO | 93 | 74 |
| ROS | 10.0 | 6.0 |
| STOCK T/O | 22 | 94 |
| ROCE | 37 | 13.3 |

*Figure 6.3E* Ratio comparison with industry norm
*Source:* ICC industrial performance analysis

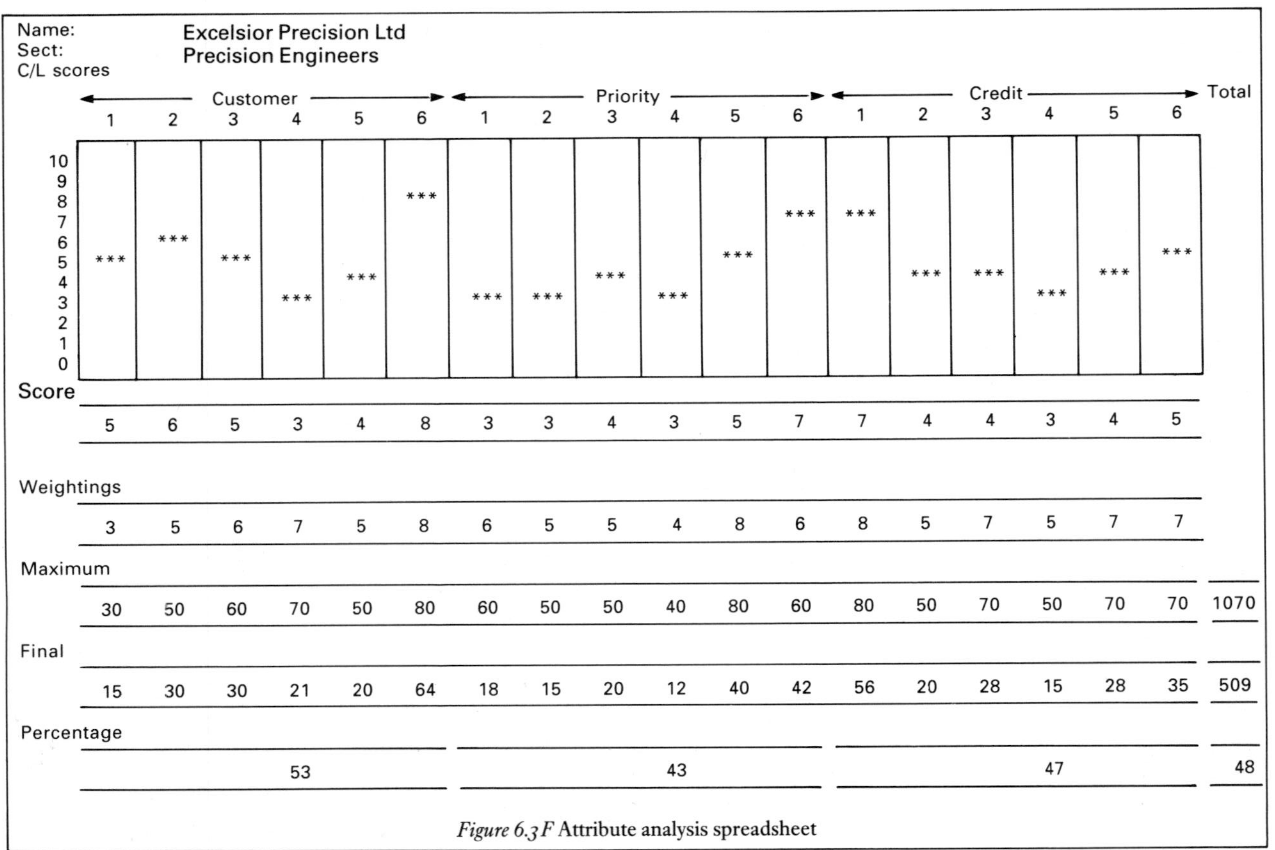

Name: Excelsior Precision Ltd
Sect: Precision Engineers
C/L scores

| | Customer | | | | | | Priority | | | | | | Credit | | | | | | Total |
|---|---|---|---|---|---|---|---|---|---|---|---|---|---|---|---|---|---|---|---|
| | 1 | 2 | 3 | 4 | 5 | 6 | 1 | 2 | 3 | 4 | 5 | 6 | 1 | 2 | 3 | 4 | 5 | 6 | |
| Score | 5 | 6 | 5 | 3 | 4 | 8 | 3 | 3 | 4 | 3 | 5 | 7 | 7 | 4 | 4 | 3 | 4 | 5 | |
| Weightings | 3 | 5 | 6 | 7 | 5 | 8 | 6 | 5 | 5 | 4 | 8 | 6 | 8 | 5 | 7 | 5 | 7 | 7 | |
| Maximum | 30 | 50 | 60 | 70 | 50 | 80 | 60 | 50 | 50 | 40 | 80 | 60 | 80 | 50 | 70 | 50 | 70 | 70 | 1070 |
| Final | 15 | 30 | 30 | 21 | 20 | 64 | 18 | 15 | 20 | 12 | 40 | 42 | 56 | 20 | 28 | 15 | 28 | 35 | 509 |
| Percentage | 53 | | | | | | 43 | | | | | | 47 | | | | | | 48 |

*Figure 6.3 F* Attribute analysis spreadsheet

Moving to the operating ratios, collection and stock turnover periods, figures of 93 and 22 days respectively shows a mixture of fortunes. A 22 days stock turnover suggests the company is good at getting its goods out of the door quickly. Its collection record of 93 days is unimpressive when compared with their standard credit terms of 30 days.

The trend in the ratios is stable, with an improvement in gearing ratios. Bathory's model and the working worth rating are improving, though they are both lurking rather close to danger level.

### *6.3.3 Industry comparison*

Excelsior Precision is average or below on all the ratios except profitability and stock turnover. This emphasises that the company has an attractive product which is easy to sell – shame about their sales performance.

### *6.3.4 Attribute analysis*

Taking first the customer attributes, reasonable scores have been given in the circumstances, all except the score of 8 for management ability. Has the sales person been influenced by his personal knowledge of those concerned? Possibly management on the production side is good, but we have seen from the figures and general credit information that financial management leaves something to be desired. Cash collection is below average and their payment record with others could be better. A drop in sales, despite the attractiveness of their goods, is a sign that sales are not being managed effectively. The attribute score in this instance is not justified, 3 being suggested in its place.

A score of 43 per cent on the priority attributes is unimpressive. They contain a slight contradiction – the margin on goods (which are non-standard) is low, but the customer is regarded as being worth keeping. Surely the ones worth keeping are those who yield a high profit?

An average score of 47 per cent is given for the credit attributes. The weakest link is the balance sheet rating which, as mentioned above, is low but improving. There is scope for improvement on the financial management side.

If we leave the scores as shown in Figure 6, then an adjusted credit level is £12,212 (£6,168 × 1.5 plus 48 per cent of £6,168). This is a figure very close to that recommended by the credit agency. However, if we change the management ability score to 3 as suggested above, it has the effect of reducing the customer attribute score to 41 per cent, and the overall score to 44 per cent. Again using the adjusted credit level calculation as explained in Chapter 5, the level is reduced to £8,881 (£6,168 plus 44 per cent of £6,168).

### *6.3.5 Credit decision*

Despite having researched the case as much as possible, and weighed up the pros and cons in an even way, the suggestion of a suitable level is below the existing credit limit! Therefore in the circumstances it is not possible to increase the existing level of £25,000. For those readers who feel this decision is too restrictive, we will come back to it at the beginning of the next section.

## 6.4 Making credit decisions

I hope that the above credit levels are reasonable in the circumstances but, just in case of disagreement, I will make a few more observations on my own decisions.

Case Study 3 is the one which I feel least comfortable about. The customer is long established, with a good track record. All that is required is a doubling of the level of £50,000. Maybe it is justified when set against a working capital level of £22,680, net worth of £224,022 and creditors' figure of £327,285? I would not want to be accused of handing on a plate all the business to a competitor. What other 'saving graces' might there be to justify the higher level?

Thankfully there is one – it does not appear Excelsior Precision are in imminent danger of collapsing. That being the case, it is a very convenient but perfectly valid justification for 'taking a flier' and agreeing the limit. Some underwriters would take the same decision, using 'gut feel' as justification. Either way, under extreme pressure I would give a £50,000 credit level, but mark the customer for a three-monthly review to monitor progress.

As you will have realised, Case Study 3 is carefully designed to broach some of the most difficult problems facing the credit grantor. For instance it shows how difficult it is to rely on a model-based formularised approach to underwriting. Credit scoring is fine for high-volume, low-value credit decisions. For larger cases scoring can be used to gauge the degree of difficulty or risk in giving a credit level. But it cannot and should not be used to make the decision.

Another point with Case Study 3 is the use of the ultimate salesman's ploy – the threat that good business will go elsewhere if credit is limited. Often it is a perfectly genuine statement. The customer may be using this ploy himself to force the best deal. A weak salesman is particularly prone to this tack, or a company which has no strong 'unique selling point' (to use the marketing jargon) to their products. There are two ways of dealing with these circumstances:

1 Call the salesman's bluff.
2 Avoid it, by giving the salesman a list of companies doing well. With any luck he will not have time to get round to less creditworthy cases like this one.

Case Study 2 is an example of positive credit underwriting. Quite without prompting, a level has been given well above that required. Setting a target for the salesman to aim at is to be encouraged as much as possible. It saves time, and creates a good impression on the sales department. Also it shows how adverse points, such as recent losses suffered by that company, are put in proper perspective when set against seventeen other items of information.

Case Study 1 is the most straightforward of the three. The company in question is in serious financial decline, and the positive elements to the case were not powerful enough to have any influence.

To conclude this chapter it is worth repeating – there is no such thing as a 'right' decision. Consistent decisions, taken after full and balanced considerations, are closest to being 'right' – though even they can go wrong. The key to greater consistency is:

1 thorough investigation;
2 balanced analysis;
3 accurate interpretation.

# CHAPTER 7

# THE SALES/CREDIT RELATIONSHIP

The credit department is one of four having close contact with customers, the others being marketing, sales and production. Each has what can be described as its specific 'area of effectiveness', although there are also areas of overlap. The credit department should be most effective when converting happy customers into cash. The others play their part in making sure there are as many happy customers as possible, by assuming different areas of effectiveness. Figure 7.1 shows this relationship.

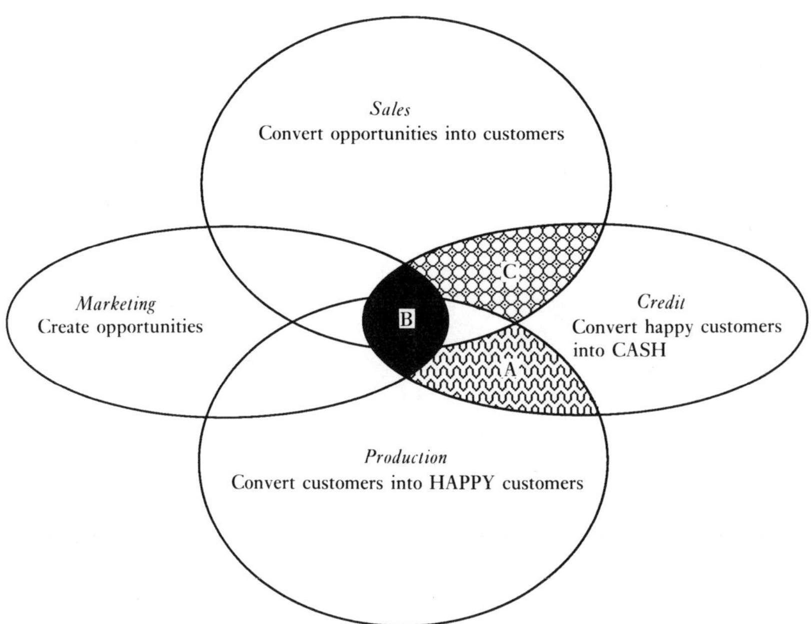


*Figure 7.1* Areas of effectiveness

The ellipses represent 'areas of effectiveness' and the overlaps are marked A, B and C.

'A' is the link between production and credit. This takes the form of correct delivery of goods to the customer. Any errors in this area, such as late or early delivery; incorrect pricing; end of month delivery; delayed issuing of credit notes; result in unhappy customers and unwanted disputes, which are coordinated by the credit department. This is a constant source of problems and can adversely influence company profitability.

'B' is the link with marketing. Given the expertise and ability to provide first-class company information, the credit department is well placed as a prime intelligence source. Many credit managers regard this relationship as very important, especially if it gives them a chance to influence the sort of customers and markets traded with.

'C' is the relationship between sales and credit. The two work hand in hand to make sure a realistic trading level is maintained after taking into account the creditworthiness of customers. The success of the relationship is measured in terms of profit.

From time to time, the credit department can be asked to take a course of action with a customer which, in their eyes, appears risky and undesirable. This is the point where commercial expediency takes over from credit considerations. Put another way, credit department priorities are pushed into a secondary role to sales department priorities.

This chapter examines the nature of the credit department and highlights issues which affect their relationship with the sales credit department, how they arise and how they can be handled. No examination of the credit function would be complete without mention of this phenomenon, mainly because it can have a significant effect on the way credit decisions are taken. Bearing in mind some of the previously described techniques for analysing risk, which are more 'scientific' in nature, applying them with success is a definite 'art'. Good communications between credit and sales is essential.

Before going any further it should be stressed that no implication is intended, either in this or other chapters, that the sales and credit departments are like cat and dog, always at each other's throats. Quite the opposite, I hope. However, a source of frequent discussion in the corporate credit world is the occasional friction which occurs between the two. Usually it is a minor matter, but sometimes it can develop into something much more serious.

## 7.1 The sales and and credit departments put into perspective

The sales and credit departments differ both in role and nature. An evaluation of these differences can be described as follows:

| | Sales | Credit |
|---|---|---|
| 1 | Aggressive | Methodical |
| 2 | Dynamic | Governed by routine |
| 3 | Forward-looking | Clear up after the event |
| 4 | Trusting | Mistrusting |

1 Aggressive/Methodical
The sales department is continually battling against the competition. They have to persuade customers that the products they sell are the best in every way for the job, and having done so, convince them to continue to buy them.
The credit department is methodical in the way they collect money. Care is taken not to be too aggressive lest it should put off the company from doing further business. The competitive elements underlying the salesperson role are of little significance to the job of getting the money in.
2 Dynamic/Routine
The sales department have to dance to the customer's tune in order to keep the business or to get new customers. Urgent calls, weekend or evening meetings, all have to be accommodated.
The credit department use strict routines, or cycles, to collect money. Certain periods of the day may be set aside for phone calles, cash matching, handling disputes, etc., and collection activity peaks at the end of a trading month.
3 Forward-looking/Clear-up after the event
A salesperson's mind will primarily be focused on where the next order is coming from. Orders obtained yesterday are history – in the hands of the production and distribution departments.
The credit department spends its time collecting invoices which were actual orders three months or more ago. At worst, time has to be spent sweeping up the mess created when the order was taken or goods delivered.
4 Trusting/Mistrusting
Having spent much time and energy in persuading a customer to buy, it is convenient for the salesperson to assume the goods are needed and the order can be afforded.
The implication of the phrase 'credit limit' is that a customer cannot be trusted with the unlimited benefit of credit. This has to be so, of course – many companies would much prefer to use a supplier as a free source of finance instead of a bank, especially if they are small and undercapitalised.

This perspective – which could easily be interpreted as portraying the credit department as a plodding, mistrusting, back-room organisation which sweeps up other people's mess – could perhaps be regarded as a little melodramatic or unfair. In fact great skill is needed to coax money out of a customer who would rather not pay just now if he could help it. Also a saleperson's skill and dynamism is completely wasted if a customer does not pay for his goods. 'A sale is not a sale until it's paid for' is the phrase which appears in every manual on selling.

Whether or not you go along completely with this perspective, the difference between departments cannot be ignored. The 'areas of effectiveness' are clearly defined and the personalities different. This can be summed up by the 'dentist' analogy which is held by some salespeople:

'The credit manager is like a dentist. He's a nice bloke, and I know he's very skilled. I know I ought to consult him when necessary. However I still prefer to put it off until the last moment.'

Here the world of business and our own dental health care converge, because often the 'last moment' is too late.

## 7.2 The 'no-win' situation

Continuing for the moment on the theme of putting into perspective the credit role, we are burdened with an impossible task – the 'no-win' situation. Here are three reasons which illustrate this point.

1 The credit grantor is charged with the task of deciding how much a customer can afford. This is almost impossible. If a customer definitely wants the goods, he will find a way of paying for them. How can a precise figure be put on this willingness? If a trading level of £10,000 is set, does this mean that an £11,000 level is out of the question? There is no real way of knowing except by taking the chance. Even if a customer has a track record, which shows that payments get slower when the amount exceeds a certain amount, as long as the money is eventually collected then there is at least some justification for a continuing credit account.

When a restrictive credit limit is given, it is important to remember that a common sales response, though rarely given within earshot of the credit manager, is 'what does he know?'

2 No-one has yet found a way of reliably predicting insolvency. No matter how weak a customer looks, the majority still find a way of keeping going. This is a phenomenon we have already examined – there is a very strong survival instinct which plays a major role in business. Statistically speaking the incidence of insolvency in most companies is still very low – so low that some feel able to conduct their credit function with little or no credit checking.

3 It is quite common for insolvency to occur with no warning. A post-mortem may even reveal that nothing untoward appeared to be happening on the balance sheet, and payments were being received satisfactorily right up to shortly before the event. This can be termed an 'unavoidable' bad debt – it happens to everyone, through no fault of their own. Thus it is regarded a fact of life for which bad debt reserves have been allocated.

In combination these three aspects have played a major role in shaping the attitude towards credit assessment. If you are in a 'no-win' situation, why try to combat it – surely it is better to concentrate resources on collecting money? This at least keeps the money coming in, and in the process can be used as a signpost of insolvency.

Of course this attitude is highly dangerous, and many have had their 'fingers burned' as a result. Such companies can be easily spotted. They react after the event by advertising for an experienced credit manager, with customer assessment expertise, needed to reorganise the credit function.

Credit insurance companies also see the after-effects. This is a time when interest in insuring against bad debts is at its highest. A major attraction of a credit insurer is the support it gives the credit department when difficult credit decisions are necessary. An unbiased, expert third-party opinion is very useful in persuading others of the validity of a credit decision. But credit insurers are also in the 'no-win' situation. Despite a large budget for credit information, they regularly fall prey to the unpredictability of business. This is exactly why they are in business.

## 7.3 The impact of company policy on the sales/credit relationship

The two departments have different 'areas of effectiveness', and company policy must reflect this. Is the area of overlap properly addressed?

Many companies like to distinguish clearly between the two. 'A salesman is a salesman, not a credit person.' 'We don't want a salesman to spend his time on matters which should be dealt with by someone else. He has enough to do as it is.'

An analogy which is often used is the 'football team principle'. A salesman is a forward, continually foraging into other people's territory with the specific task of scoring goals (getting sales). The credit person is in the defence, making sure no goals (bad debts) are incurred.

This is a very good analogy, not only for its succinct description of the position, but also it can be used to prove another point about the relationship. In the modern game, a forward is expected to lend a hand when his team is under attack, and to 'stay in the game' as much as possible. Similarly, good defenders are distinguished by their ability to attack and score goals, as well as being solid in defence. Irrespective of their roles (areas of effectiveness), all the players on the field have one objective – to win.

Those companies which adopt the attitudes above may be taking too narrow a view on the overall objectives of the sales and credit departments. There is a common objective for them both – to maximise sales and minimise profit erosion through slow collection and bad debts.

This objective is usually given to the credit department. Certainly they are responsible for collecting quickly, which is a function of good judgement and efficient organisation. How can they be held solely responsible for maximising sales? Surely this is also the responsibility of sales to sell as much as possible at the most attractive profit margin. Marketing contribute by identifying the areas where profitable sales can be made. Production help by providing attractive goods with the greatest efficiency. Maximising sales is a 'lofty' goal which is by no means the sole province of the credit department.

The sales department has a responsibility to help minimise profit erosion. This aspect cannot be stressed too highly. It means concentrating effort on customers who have proved, or appear on paper, to be attractive long term customers and reasonable payers. If they hear through the 'grape-vine' that one of their customers is in trouble, they have a responsibility to let the credit department know. More than once I have heard a salesman say, after his customer went bust 'Oh! I knew about that customer being in trouble weeks ago, but I thought you would have heard it for yourself through your own channels'.

The companies most at risk for failing to impress this common objective on the salesforce, are the ones who pay a commission, and base it solely on invoiced sales. There is little incentive for the salesperson to take the proper care when selling to customers. There are many ways of encouraging the salesforce, and one of the best is to pay a normal salary with bonuses based on sales *and* profit targets.

## 7.4 Interpersonal relationships and negotiations

The success of the sales/credit relationship is closely linked to the people involved, their attitudes, and ability to compromise. This is summed up in the following:

1 It revolves as much around personalities within the sales and credit functions, as it does around the customer case in question.
2 They involve negotiations, not just with the customer, but also between internal departments.
3 Linked to the negotiating element, there should never be a clear winner and loser – the 'win/win' factor (a negotiating tactic based on this principle) should always be adopted.

Now for two examples which illustrate the range of sales/credit relationships.

Example 1 – credit dominance:
Some while ago I spent a few hours chatting to an experienced credit manager. He explained that he had been given the authority to have the final word on every trading decision. He had never been overruled. What is more, if he ever was (and it would have to come in the form of a directive from the board), he would seriously consider resignation.

Example 2 – sales dominance:
The building and construction sector is well known for its sales-consciousness. While speaking to several credit managers in this sector, a common source of discontentment emerged. Company policy had no firm guidelines on when an

account should be suspended because of late payments. Attempts to place customers on stop were often overruled. In addition, tenders for work were issued without consulting the credit department beforehand and, if accepted, were presented as a 'fait accompli'. No attention was being paid to initial credit vetting, and bad debts had thus become a serious problem.

Let's examine some of the implications to these examples:

1 In both cases, there must be a sufficient profit in the business for the situations outlined to be allowed to continue. If the bottom line is satisfactory why 'rock the boat'?
2 There are losers in both examples – the sales department in example one, and the credit department in example two.
3 The influence of personalities is in evidence. The autocratic manager of example one could be viewed as having an emotional view of his role, possibly created by pride in his ability to resolve skilfully every decision to his advantage (if this is the case). In example two, the morale of the credit department is seriously eroded.
4 Both examples are 'tinderbox' in nature. In example one the 'loss of face' caused by a decision of his being overruled seemed to him to be so significant, that resignation became a real possibility. In example two the danger is that morale will get so low, the only option is to seek other more satisfying employment. Another danger is that they will be hit by a very large insolvency which could have been avoided.
5 The respective boards of directors have a lot to answer for. In example one there is a high degree of bias towards the financial side of the business. In example two the opposite is the case.

Although these are perhaps extreme examples, some elements, maybe in a milder form, can exist in many companies.

## 7.5 THE 'CREDIT CRUNCH'

This is a term which can be used to describe a situation credit grantors dread. It takes two forms:

1 The new customer who wants to place a big order, but on whom the best available information is adverse. An 'all or nothing' situation.
2 The existing customer, who may be a source of constant payment problems, has placed orders which will take his account well over the credit limit. An 'over-limit' situation.

### *7.5.1 The 'all-or-nothing situation'*

Here, the credit grantor is being put on the spot and is being given the total responsibility of making the decision (the 'hot potato'). From the salesman's point of view, this is the best way to go about getting an order cleared. The later he leaves it before notifying the credit department, the better his chances of getting a favourable result.

There are three ways of dealing with the circumstances:

1 Try to ensure that credit policy stipulates that the credit department has to be involved at an early stage in any order, and that all salespeople know of this rule. The best time is at enquiry stage, where an idea of the order size is available, but no firm offers or contracts have been discussed. The earlier a salesman is compelled to inform the credit department of such an event, the better. If he fails to give early enough warning then the whole case can be turned around – any difficulties are as a result of not being informed at the proper time. If subsequently it proves impossible to do the order, the responsibility for the outcome is shifted onto the salesman.
2 Involve him in the decision as much as possible. Here is a case where attribute analysis can be so handy. It forces the salesman to justify the merits of trading with the customer, while allowing the credit difficulties to be presented in an understandable and rational way. Again some of the burden of the decision must be shifted onto the salesman. He does not want a reputation of getting the company bad deals. It helps if the credit grantor is a member of a credit club. Other companies can be contacted at credit manager level, to see if they have been approached with the same deal, and if so whether they turned it down. If this does turn out to be the case, then it is clear you are being 'suckered' into doing business that no-one else wants to touch.
3 Make sure there is an escape route or higher authority who, as a very last resort, can be used to mediate in the issue. The finance director is the obvious person, though even better may be a credit committee formed by senior sales and finance managers. In some organisations the committee style is often used in decision-making, especially for very large potential credit exposures.

### *7.5.2 The 'over-limit' situation*

This is possibly more difficult to deal with. The customer already has a credit account, and the onus is very much on keeping the customer satisfied. The way of dealing with it depends on what sort of experience is available.

1 'Over-limit' with poor experience situations, provide a golden opportunity for trade-offs with the customer:

> Dear buyer,
>
> We understand you have placed orders, the value of which will take your credit account over its present limit. We are delighted that you should want to do so, and are happy to increase your limit accordingly.

However, on past experience, we have found that your payments have been late, which has on occasions forced us reluctantly to suspend trading. A number of invoices are outstanding well beyond their due date (give details).

Therefore this increase in your limit is conditional upon outstanding invoices being paid, and your agreement that the new credit level applies only in the event that future invoices are settled in accordance with our credit terms.

We are sure you will regard these conditions as being fair in the circumstances, and that this agreement will lead to better continuity of supply.

Yours sincerely etc.

This letter could be sent by the credit department, or amended slightly so that it could be sent by the salesman. It is addressed to the buyer because he is more interested in getting the goods rather than paying for them. He is therefore in a good position to influence his purchase ledger department to agree to the conditions.

If the terms are accepted, the increased credit limit given, and they still refuse to pay on time, then the limit can be reduced and no-one can complain.

If there is doubt about the actual ability of the customer to meet an increased credit level, then the letter can be adjusted so that further financial information must be provided before the increase can be agreed. If it is not forthcoming then no increase. If it is supplied, and it looks bad, then there is equal justification for not increasing the limit.

2 'Over-limit' with good experience should be less of a problem. This is the moment to obtain fresh credit information on which to base the credit limit. Using on-line services, this can be done very quickly. Alternatively the customer could be asked for the information, on the understanding that it will help you be more flexible in adjusting the limit in the future, should business continue to increase.

There is a constant theme to the methods above. Make sure it is possible to find out, as early as possible, of an impending 'crunch'. Forewarned is forearmed. There are several ways of doing this:

(a) Establish an understanding, backed up by policy guidelines if necessary, that sales should contact credit before not after the crunch. It helps to ensure they have the means of finding out what the credit limit and current account balance are.
(b) If possible, credit should be made aware of outstanding orders, call-offs, contract deliveries, etc., so that there is a means of identifying the 'crunch' before it happens. Computerised systems can be set up to provide this.

One last observation. 'All-or-nothing' attitudes by the customer should be treated with care. They could be (and in my experience very often are) part of a negotiating tactic to get the best price and terms knowing full well they are a bad credit risk. The salesman can unwittingly become involved in these tactics by appearing to be in sympathy with the customer in trying to get the best credit deal for them, when he should be in sympathy with his own colleague (credit manager) who is also doing his best to protect the interests of the company.

The key point here is that the 'credit crunch' can only be handled properly if full customer information is available, and full cooperation exists between the sales and credit departments.

## 7.6 How and when to compromise

Given a conflict of priorities between departments, it is important to have some good compromise solutions. This section looks at the main ones, and some of the pitfalls in using them.

### *7.6.1 Temporary credit limits*

This is the first and perhaps most often used means of compromise.

The temporary credit limit is a way for the credit manager to admit modestly that he cannot infallibly judge what is a correct limit, show that he has his doubts on the risk, and that the limit is given for a limited period only. All these are laudable sentiments, and by giving what amounts to the benefit of the doubt, it is the best way to solve the problem.

In some industries temporary limits are routine, being given during seasonal peaks in the trading (e.g. summer stocking and crop credit).

However, the term 'temporary' is open to abuse. It can be taken as an open invitation to bend the rules. The next time a 'crunch' occurs the salesman will be fully expecting another 'temporary' solution to the extent that he may not even bother to consult the credit department until it is a 'fait accompli'.

A customer who is told he is being given a temporary increase may also have mixed feelings about it. 'Either I am worthy of a £15,000 credit limit, or I'm not. Who do they think they are?' The converse also applies – they may be very relieved to get a temporary increase, though this is possibly a sign they are in desperate need of extra support.

So the temporary solution should be used with care. If a customer appears to be worth the risk, give him the benefit of the doubt with a permanent credit limit if possible. If a temporary increase is the only resort, make sure it is given as a one-off, and as reluctantly as possible so that the sales department are fully aware of how flexible and commercially aware you are.

### *7.6.2 Extending terms*

This is a form of compromise which is rarely used, and if so as a very last resort. News travels fast: the moment one customer is given them, others will follow.

### *7.6.3 Giving favours*

If a credit manager has a particularly good relationship with his sales colleagues, then this is a very effective form of compromise. It should be given as a trade-off for favours in return, perhaps in the form of helping in a difficult credit problem, or just simply to store up for the next 'crunch' situation if you are not prepared to be flexible.

There are some tactics which can be employed here. Be more prepared to do a favour when the amount involved is small. Smaller bad debts tend to be unavoidable, and a concession here and there may not have too serious impact on the bad debt result. Not so with bigger cases. Any decision on these must be treated with the utmost care for obvious reasons.

### *7.6.4 One-off cases*

This has already been mentioned in a different context above. There are occasions where something exceptional has created a credit problem. Maybe it is an increase in prices, or deliveries have to be made over a shorter period. Or just simply that the circumstances which created the problem will not recur. A flexible decision is probably clear cut, but make sure it is made with suitable 'reluctance'.

### *7.6.5 Relaxing the trade suspension period*

This is a slightly more acceptable way of extending terms – most suitable for use with medium to large customers. It is used where there is no limit problems, but the customer refuses to abide by the standard terms of credit. Like the temporary credit limit, however, it can be open to abuse.

## 7.7 Improving the image of the credit department

Credit assessment is still an up-and-coming corporate discipline which, as we have seen above, has to be handled very carefully. Its place in the pecking order depends as much on its results, as the way those results are achieved. Strong negotiating techniques and a flexible approach are both very necessary skills. There are some things which can be done which help (and hinder) the regard placed on the credit department by others.

### *7.7.1 'Negative vibes'*

I have named this subsection after a phrase from *Kelly's Heroes*, a well known and lighter-hearted war film. The hero Kelly, a somewhat weird tank commander, manages to pull off some spectacular feats. While planning each battle compaign, all of them seemingly impossible, any suggestion to this effect was met by the response 'No man, not those negative vibes again. Think positive.'

The 'negative vibes' trap is easy to fall into. For every advantage to doing business that a salesman can see, the credit manager can answer it with a disadvantage. After a few such cases, the salesman knows that the next time there is debate on a customer's credit account, the first thing he will hear is 'negative vibes'.

Of course 'every silver lining has a cloud', but there are ways of dealing with them. This goes back to the art of negotiating, always start by sympathising with the other person. Then gradually build up your own case for justifying whichever course of action you feel most suitable.

### *7.7.2 Speed of reaction*

There never seems enough time to make a proper, measured decision. Credit problems always have to be dealt with quickly, otherwise either money or opportunities are lost. As we have already examined, sometimes a case has been deliberately left to the last moment, again as a negotiating ploy by sales.

The only thing which can be done here is to make sure customer information can be gathered rapidly from the file, or if necessary from another source such as an on-line credit agency.

### *7.7.3 Frequent contact with the sales department*

Never turn down an opportunity to meet salespeople, and actively work to increase this contact.

The sales meeting is an ideal place for discussing credit matters, especially if it is being held in an exclusive luxury hotel. It is a good opportunity to talk about current credit problems, with emphasis on the lessons which can be learned from them. Salespeople respect a person who feels it is important enough to talk with them on their own ground. Be prepared for a rough time, but it is worth it.

Sales visits are another opportunity to build up personal relationships and also learn as much about each other's work and attitude towards it, as possible.

## Chapter summary

1 The relationship between the credit and sales departments depends on good interpersonal contact, and an ability to negotiate. The styles and roles are different:

| Sales | Credit |
|---|---|
| AGGRESSIVE<br>There are tough competitors out there, so get in quick | METHODICAL<br>Careful planning is required to collect the largest amount of cash |

| | |
|---|---|
| DYNAMIC<br>Keep the daily call rate high, extending into evening and weekends if the customer wants | ROUTINE<br>Work to fixed deadlines. Confined to the hours when people can be contacted. Often highly computerised |
| FORWARD-LOOKING<br>Today's small customer may be tomorrow's 'major' | CLEANING-UP AFTER THE EVENT<br>Today's late invoice was a sale three months ago |
| TRUSTING<br>If an order is received, it implies the goods are both wanted, and can be paid for | MISTRUSTING<br>The simple phrase 'credit limit' implies disbelief and restriction |

2 Company policy should recognise that the sales department have as much responsibility for maximising sales and minimising credit as the credit department.

3 The 'credit crunch' occurs when the desired trading level is above the 'preferred' one, or where the customer is threatening to take his business elsewhere if he is not given a suitable credit limit. The onus and responsibility for the decision is placed on the credit manager. Methods of overcoming them include:
   (a) ensuring the position is highlighted before it becomes a problem;
   (b) getting the customer to concede on prompt payment in return for a higher credit limit (if he was paying slowly before);
   (c) involving the salesman in the decision as much as possible.

4 Ways of compromising over difficult credit situations are:
   (a) temporary credit limits;
   (b) extending terms, though recommended as a last resort;
   (c) doing favours in return for other favours;
   (d) one-off cases, where truly exceptional circumstances are taken into account;
   (e) relaxing the trade suspension period, for use when medium to large customer insists on longer credit terms.

5 The respect and credibility of the credit department can be improved by:
   (a) not appearing too negative;
   (b) attending meetings of and joint visit with the salesforce;
   (c) reacting quickly.

CHAPTER 8

•

# CREDIT RISK MANAGEMENT

Credit risk management is a term which describes the methods and systems used to minimise credit losses. These could arise either from credit trading, or some form of borrowing.

However, management differs between banks and corporations. In banking, risk management is always a central activity – essential given the billions of pounds risked by each major lender. With standard forms of loans/overdrafts, banks do not have to invoice clients. Charges, fees, interest and commissions are all deducted from an account. Risk management therefore requires them to keep a close eye on each account, and take suitable action.

In the corporate field less emphasis tends to be placed on credit risk management. The figures at risk per company are smaller. They have far fewer customers than banks do. A close eye is automatically kept on their customers as part of the collection cycle. As a result other methods of credit risk management can sometimes be neglected. The extent to which this happens depends on variables such as:

1 Level of credit expertise and resources allocated.
2 Past record of bad debts.
3 The size of the company.
4 The nature of their market(s).

There are many similarities of approach between bank and corporate credit management, even though there may be some differences of emphasis. This chapter will deal with corporate and bank credit risk management respectively.

## 8.1 Corporate credit risk management

At the heart of this subject is the role of the credit department. The onus is on this function to minimise bad debts, but they are by no means the only party involved. We have already discussed the role of the sales department. The fundamental nature of their contribution cannot be stressed too highly, to the extent that it should be included in the policy guidelines under which they operate. A serious credit problem requiring drastic action should never be regarded as a hindrance to sales, but rather a concerted campaign to protect the profit of the company.

There is one major obstacle to achieving this objective. There is probably not a single person in a sales department who would not be prepared to cooperate fully in minimising a credit problem, as long as it definitely was a problem. The trouble is there can be a tendency amongst credit departments to be too cautious in their attitude.

At first sight, the last sentence may seem to contradict the whole purpose of credit risk management. Surely the wider the scope of monitoring, the better the chance of 'nipping in the bud' a potential bad debt? The trouble with this method is that it can suffer from 'overkill'. It is possible to end up with a sufficiently large number of cases under review, that the real effectiveness of the operation comes into question. A balanced approach to the issue is very important, and ways to achieve this will be suggested throughout the chapter.

A bad debt means a lost customer, and a loss of profit and future sales. Equally, the seriousness of a loss can be quickly measured in monetary terms. However there is more to it than that. What happened? Could it have been reduced or avoided? Can systems be changed to prevent it happening again? All these questions are asked in the traditional bad debt post mortem. My point is that the circumstances surrounding the event are as significant as the actual amount lost. So before going any further, I would like to introduce three categories of bad debts which take account of circumstances:

1 'The inevitable bad debt.' This is a fact of life. Despite all reasonable effort being made to prevent these from happening, they will occur. Usually they will be small or minor in nature. Though on infrequent occasions they could be a major bad debt (sometimes called a catastrophe bad debt) where there was no prior warning or danger signals.
2 'The unavoidable bad debt.' Again this is a fact of life, but the difference being that warning signs were picked up before the event, and all measures were taken to minimise the resultant loss.
3 'The avoidable bad debt' is one where the warning signs were there, but not heeded resulting in a loss that, with hindsight, could have been prevented.

The success of a credit risk management system can be judged by examining each bad debt suffered to see into which category a bad debt falls. A good reason for making this classification is that credit policy and procedures can be geared with it in mind. The idea is to concentrate effort in minimising unavoidable bad debts, and to make absolutely sure that no avoidable bad debts occur. If that means pulling resources away from trying to control inevitable bad debts, then so be it. These terms will be amplified as the chapter progresses.

## 8.2 Controlling shipments

During my time as an 'excess of loss' credit insurance underwriter, there was one question of paramount importance when assessing a company's ability to control credit risk – does the credit department have the power to prevent shipments to a customer effectively? I found on many occasions where no such power existed, that bad debts had been higher than necessary due to 'seepage' of invoices dated after the recommendation to suspend trade.

This element of company organisation is a continuous source of debate and conflict. Some companies, particularly if they have a deliberate sales bias, keep control of the dispatch and invoice cycle. The credit department is thus reliant on the alertness and cooperation of sales to suspend shipments when instructed. Other companies are so diverse in organisation that it becomes a major logistical problem to inform all the right people that supplies should be stopped.

On the other side of the coin are companies, usually with an integrated computerised system, who give the credit department the ability to suppress the issuing of paperwork which precedes the shipment. At the same time, the computer is used to inform the sales department of the current account status.

The broadcasting of information is absolutely crucial to controlling a credit account, and where possible it should be done via computer on a range of interfaces with sales, rather than by producing paper-based lists for weekly circulation to a limited number of people.

In the writer's opinion, the credit department should always have direct control over the production of shipping documents and dispatch of goods. Also every effort should be made to ensure this potent weapon is used as little as possible. The one valid criticism by opponents of this measure is that it gets used too often, which can disrupt customer relations and leave sales staff feeling frustrated that they cannot fully perform their role in making sure sales contracts are fulfilled. There are two reasons for stopping supplies:

### *8.2.1 Slow payments:*

A typical chasing cycle will begin with gentle reminders by letter, or phone calls to the larger customers. However there comes a point where, if the customer still does not pay, a less gentle method is used – the suspension of trade. In this case the customer is in breach of his contract (all sales contracts should have a credit period, and the results of exceeding it, clearly stated). In addition he may be in some financial trouble which prevents honouring of the contract, and trade suspension halts any further exposure.

The trade suspension period (TSP) should be properly defined in company policy. This is very important, because it is often misunderstood by sales that trade suspension is at the discretion of a 'trigger-happy' credit department. In fact it should be the other way round, where a customer is reluctantly put 'on stop' as a matter of company policy, which the credit department has been given the responsibility to carry out.

What is the best length of time for a TSP? This is a very difficult question to answer because there are so many variables which affect it. It could be said as a general rule that the longer the credit terms, the shorter the TSP. An average length would be sixty days after due date, if the standard net monthly or thirty-day terms were used. Many larger companies are able to set a TSP of thirty to forty-five days, on the basis that they are a major supplier whom the customer cannot afford to do without. Also, with a larger level of receivables, it is important in cashflow terms to be stringent in controlling customer payment delinquency. One exception that proves the rule is the perishable food sector, who deal on seven- to fifteen-day credit periods, and have a correspondingly short TSP, for obvious reasons.

### *8.2.2 Credit limit excesses:*

This is a very much more controversial use of the trade suspension weapon. Unlike slow payments which are defined by company policy, its use is at the discretion of the credit department.

The motive behind limiting trade is the belief that a customer's financial capability is also limited, and by exceeding it the company is exposed to higher credit risk. As we have already examined in previous chapters, there are grave difficulties in deciding what this level is. If the credit limit excess has been caused by slow payments then there is clear evidence that the customer has reached the 'limit' of his credit. To limit trade in the absence of a tardy payment record is a subject we shall discuss in the next section.

## 8.3 The credit limit as a means of controlling risk

This is an often used, and abused technique. Throughout this book, its use as a term has been avoided as much as possible, 'credit level' or 'trading level' or 'preferred level' being used in its place. In the author's opinion the word 'limit' is inappropriate, especially when there are no less than three perfectly adequate alternative phrases. It has negative connotations which can be misconstrued as an attempt to restrict trading to a precise figure set by someone who in all probability has no insight whatsoever into the cashflow of the customer.

Setting semantics aside, whether called a 'limit' or 'level', it is set in recognition of certain circumstances or used as a trigger to some sort of action. They are:

### *8.3.1 'Whichever is the lower' credit level*

A natural formula for deciding the necessary credit level is the perceived creditworthiness or 'expected level of monthly trading times two', whichever is the lower. The formula assumes a thirty-day credit period, and is sufficient to allow two months to be outstanding at any one time. It can be adjusted according to the standard credit terms, and also the trade suspension period.

Its use can lead to problems. If ICI placed an initial order for £10,000, the range of possible credit levels stretches from £20,000 (using the formula) to a six- or maybe even seven-figure number, the lower figure being chosen under these circumstances. However what happens if the order level increases? Would shipments be withheld until the credit level had been increased?

Though an extreme example, it does highlight a flaw in this approach. If an initial credit limit is set, and then subsequently increased with no difficulty when trading increases, it:

1 negates the reason for setting it in the first place;
2 creates extra work for the credit department;
3 possibly delays shipments while the credit level is being sorted out;
4 leaves the sales department with a bad impression of the original decision, even if it was based on policy guidelines.

### *8.3.2 'Whichever is the higher' credit level*

This is another basis for setting a credit level – as high as possible, even if it falls above what appears to be adequate at the time.

Sometimes the response I get when talking to credit managers about this issue is . . .

*'we don't set credit limits higher than necessary because it might be used as a target by the sales department.'*

There is some merit in being conservative, certainly in setting an initial level, because it gives time to judge from trading experience how creditworthy the customer is. However when, using all the techniques of analysis, it appears that a higher than necessary limit is feasible, then why not set a target for the sales department? This a valuable and positive role the credit department can play in helping to identify areas where sales expansion is possible. Setting the highest possible level also avoids having to do further work to increase it, if trading gradually increases.

### *8.3.3 Credit levels to control risk*

There can come a point where, taking into account a possibly unsatisfactory track record, and also that the credit level is around or above a 'preferred' level, it is useful to monitor individual shipments to the customer. If the organisation is such that the credit manager can prevent shipments being made if the outstanding belance exceeds the credit level, then this is a valid control technique.

Again it is not without its problems. The biggest danger is that it gets used too often. If the track record is satisfactory, and the level is being controlled merely because the trading level falls above the 'preferred' level, then the comments in 8.2.1 apply. Over-cautiousness can be counter-productive, creating customer dissatisfaction and internal friction rather than less bad debts.

### *8.3.4 'Quick-start' credit levels*

As its name implies, this is a level given to a new customer, just to start off his trading account.

There can come a point where to do a reasonably thorough credit vetting job on every customer can become time-consuming and expensive. It may even delay the initial shipment of goods to the detriment of customer relations. The solution is to set a fixed level which will normally be above that which is required for the first order.

This is a common procedure in larger companies. A level which can range from £500 to £10,000 can be given after minimal credit investigation (rating books are ideal for this purpose), provided nothing adverse is known, or even if nothing is known at all. Some companies subsequently get more information if they have time; others are prepared to leave it at that unless the trading experience is poor or level of business goes above the quick start level, in which case a full investigation is done.

The disadvantage to this method is that some customers go bust after just one or two shipments and nothing was done to find out which ones were most vulnerable. On the other hand, the quick start level is usually at a low enough level for such a bad debt to fall into the 'inevitable bad debt' category – an unavoidable and therefore acceptable feature of business.

### *8.3.5 No credit level at all*

There are some strong arguments in favour of having no credit limit system at all. This can be justified by looking at the make-up of a typical customer base, which comprises:

1 Major accounts, who are of such importance that restrictions on the level might jeopardise future business. About 10 per cent of the customer-base will fall into this category.
2 Small accounts, representing approximately 50 per cent of customers. They may be regular customers, though some will only place the occasional order. As such they are an important trading asset, but individually have less impact on sales, and should failure occur, would be an inevitable bad debt.
3 Medium accounts: about 35 per cent of customers will provide regular and attractive business. Some may even rise into the major category, while others will graduate from the small category.
4 Risky accounts: around 5 per cent of customers create 75 per cent of the difficulties of the credit department, either in collecting money, solving disputes or finding the right credit level. They will range in size from small to major accounts and, if they fail, would be unavoidable bad debts.

Viewed in this light, only 5 per cent of the customer-base requires any

*Table 8.1* Grading system based on company type

| Grade | Comments |
|---|---|
| A | Blue chip company, or government backed agency |
| B | Large company, with no apparent credit weakness |
| C | Medium company, reasonable information held |
| D | Small company, nothing seriously adverse known |
| E | High-risk customer, with weak finances and poor record |

additional credit risk management, so why try to put some sort of limit on the others? In its place could be put some 'referral criteria' which could be used to trigger further credit action.

The message here is that the absence of credit limits does not imply absence of control, if something is used in its place or in combination with limits. This leads on to the next section, which covers *grading* or *rating* systems.

## 8.4 Grading systems for controlling risk

A customer grading or rating, established according to pre-defined criteria, is in common use as a risk control trigger (here the word rating should not be confused with the credit rating which is part of the services of some credit agencies). In this section we shall look at ways to set customer grades, and how they can be combined with credit levels.

The credit limit is an imperfect measure of creditworthiness. At worst it can be used as a excuse for unnecessary disruption to an otherwise satisfactory account. In isolation it is inappropriate as a description of risk. A customer grade is a much better indicator of risk. Table 8.1 outlines one type of grading system.

This grading system concentrates on customer size and the nature of the information available, the lowest grading, 'E' being reserved for difficult cases. In doing so it conveys two different messages, and makes it useful if the 'no credit limit system' is adopted. With only one grade reserved for difficult cases, it is easy to spot on computer tabulations (which are a common form of internal customer information). The one slight weakness of this system is that the choice is too wide. What is the difference between a large and blue-chip company, or between a small and medium one? These are the sort of questions which can be resolved by setting the criteria as part of credit policy. Note also there is no grade for 'unacceptable risk', on the assumption that such a customer would only be traded with on cash terms.

Another type of grading system, shown in Table 8.2, is based on the perceived risks of trading.

This system is ideally suited for use in combination with credit limits. No element of size is included in the above, just a suggestion of the regard in which a credit account is held. This is a significant point, because small customers on

*Table 8.2* Grading system based on perceived risk

| Grade | Comments |
|---|---|
| A | No risk, highly creditworthy company |
| B | Acceptable risk; satisfactory experience |
| C | High risk; unsatisfactory experience |
| D | Unacceptable credit risk, cash terms only |

whom little or no information is available can be just as good as their larger counterparts, and thus merit a 'B' grade. With just four possible grades, there is a more limited choice and the most difficult decision to make is when to move an account from acceptable to high risk. Credit policy should be designed to precisely define the distinction between the two. A good way of doing this is to adopt the working worth or attribute analysis models, to calculate a 'preferred' trading level, and then measure the difference between that and the actual level allowed. If the difference is more than *x* per cent (percentage up to individual preference) then the case can be classified a 'C' risk.

Both of these systems share one very important feature – only one grade is reserved for high-risk customers. The reason for this is very clear cut. A high risk customer should be instantly identifiable on computer tabulations, subject to close monitoring, and credit information renewed on a regular basis.

Grading systems are very much up to the individual company to construct. If this is the case, two golden rules should be observed:

1. always make sure there is a properly defined distinction between each grade; and
2. try not to leave a 'compromise' or 'average' grade for use when undecided about which grade is most appropriate.

## 8.5 Monitoring and reviewing the customer base

There is a distinction between monitoring and reviewing. The former relates to monitoring on-going trading experience, the latter involves the regular update and review of credit information.

All currently-trading customers are the subject of constant monitoring, simply because their payment experience comes under scrutiny during collection routines. High-risk customers, or ones who are particularly important, should in addition be subject to a review which includes the renewal of information from appropriate sources. The best sources are:

1. The salesforce, who should constantly have their 'ears to the ground' for any hint of problems suffered by their customers. This is a no-cost form of information.
2. Credit reports can be renewed once a year, and should be obtained to coincide with the availability of financial accounts. An even better, though

more expensive way, is to use continuous service reports. These will be sent every time there is a noteworthy event such as the lodging of accounts.

3 Credit clubs are another low cost avenue of information which can be used for review purposes.

The scope and use of review systems varies considerably. A common and rather miserly attitude is to forgo the expense of renewing credit information and rely solely on monitoring action. Such companies lose the opportunity to distinguish between the habitually tardy payers, and those in genuine financial difficulties. The earlier such cases can be identified, the sooner damage limitation measures can be instigated. 'Avoidable bad debts' normally results from failure to carry out a proper review system.

Another variant of the review system is to renew information on just 'C' or 'D' (depending on which grading system is used) customers. This at least means that signs of failure are likely to be picked up earlier.

However, there is a strong case for including those few 'A' grade customers (using Table 8.2 grades) who form the greater part of the sales ledger. The volume of invoices with such companies, and the accompanying level of disputes, can sometimes mask a deterioration in payment. There is a high probability that there will be an incidence of major customer failure in one year out of every five. The purpose of reviewing here is to spot the danger signals before payment experience deteriorates into the unacceptable category. However, if none are apparent, the exercise has not been a waste of time, because the information can be used to highlight those doing well, so that the sales department can target them properly.

Renewal and review of carefully selected customers is so important, that it may be worth setting up a supplementary 'R' (for review) rating. This could be reserved for those customers judged to be in danger of failure in the near future, and those who are so big, that it makes sense to know all about them all the time.

## 8.6 Who has responsibility for credit risk management?

We have already discussed the role the salesforce can play in being alert to customer difficulty and letting the credit department know. Who in this department should be responsible for keeping customers under review?

There are two schools of thought on this matter. In many companies, customer monitoring and review are both done by the cash collector. They have first-hand experience of the payment record and are thus best placed to notice any serious deterioration. In addition, the range of their duties is more varied if risk management is added to their job description. For companies with a small customer base, or a high level of staffing, then this approach can work well.

However, there comes a point where the pressures of collecting money to fiscal targets involves so much collection work, that the finer points of customer review can be neglected. It becomes too difficult to set aside these duties so that credit reports can be ordered and analysed, and changes to the credit level or grading made. Another difficulty is one of training. Some analytical expertise backed up by a knowledge of company accounts is needed, qualities that not all cash collectors have. In these circumstances it is better to have a specialist credit controller whose sole responsibility is to set, monitor and review credit levels. Often these duties fall on the shoulders of the credit manager.

One further alternative is to operate a rotation system, though this is only feasible in larger organisations. In order to improve the variety of the job, and expertise in doing it, a rotation system means that each collector spends, say, six months as a credit analyst. The advantages are that job satisfaction many be increased. The disadvantage is that continuity both in collecting and risk management may suffer, and also that some people may find themselves more suited to one job or the other – not both.

## 8.7 Computers and credit risk management

Computers have a prime role to play in the task of monitoring customers. With a customer-base numbered in the thousands, the job of spotting the potential bad debts can be difficult. This is where exception reports have an important role. Some examples of these are:

1 The aged receivable report: shows the ageing of all outstanding invoices. It is used by collectors to identify customers who are late payers.

2 The over-limit report: this can be a separate report or combined with the aged receivable report, and shows those instances where the balance is above the credit level. A judgement on what action to take can be made after taking into account the invoice ageing.

3 The stop list: showing all customers where trade has been suspended. Account balance and credit level details can help immediately identify cases requiring close attention.

4 The DSO Report: showing the collection record in terms of the number of days it is taking for invoices to be paid. This report is more complex to set up, and requires more computing power, but is nevertheless very useful at condensing a customer's track record into an easily assessable form.

5 The cost of credit report: follows on from (d). If a single DSO figure can be calculated and compared to the actual credit terms, payment received after this period can be said to represent extra cost to the company, since the overdue portion will have to be temporarily replaced out of the company's own funds or

*Table 8.3* Cost of credit calculations

| | |
|---|---|
| Amount outstanding | £10,000 |
| DSO | 100 days |
| Average daily invoice value | £100 |
| Credit terms | 60 days |
| Average late payment value (40 days × £100) | £4,000 |
| Annual interest cost (13% overdraft rate) | £520 |
| Monthly cost (£520/12) | £43.33 |

overdraft. This results in profit erosion. There are several ways this can be calculated, Table 8.3 showing one suggestion.

This is a very simple example calculation, using averages. There is no reason that, using a computer, the actual value of overdue invoices cannot be identified for the purpose calculating the interest cost.

Information of this type is absolutely vital to the credit department, by giving them the ammunition with which to emphasis how important it is to keep within credit levels and payment terms. It can be circulated to top management and the sales department to keep them informed of profit erosion due to late payment.

6 The orders on hand report: This can be used to identify, in advance, instances where the credit level may be exceeded in the future because of orders on hand. It gives the credit department time to increase this level, or increase collection pressure, so that the balance falls within the credit level.

In all these examples it is possible for specific cases to be easily identified as requiring action by the credit department.

## 8.8 The crisis visit

We have already seen how a customer visit is an excellent way to gather valuable information. It is also necessary under less favourable circumstances, when there has been a serious breakdown in trading relationships. Probably payments have been unacceptably slow, with a high incidence of disputes, and the background information is unfavourable. The objectives of a crisis visit is usually to:

1 assess the viability of the customer;
2 reach agreement on payment schedules;
3 decide what future trading is feasible.

Every credit manager should be alert to the signs of a possible crisis, and enlist the salesperson's help to arrange a meeting. The earlier such a meeting can be arranged the better – prevention is better than cure. Specific people closely involved with the case should be available both from your own company and the customer's.

### *8.1 Looking for signs of failure during a visit*

Many of the standard features discussed before come into play. Particularly important are the outward impressions since these are more difficult to disguise. An overstocked warehouse, or the refusal to be allowed to look at it, is one common feature. Board resignations another, and so too is an unwillingness to discuss certain aspects of the customer's finances. However most difficult to interpret are any plausible explanations given by the customer to the circumstances leading to the crisis and the way they are going to cope with them.

This is a time when 'smokescreens' can be erected. If a customer has had half a dozen creditors visit him in the last few weeks then it is natural to assume that any smokescreen will, by then, have been carefully rehearsed (a quick call to a few members of your credit club may confirm whether they too have made a visit). The only way to combat the smokescreen is to ensure a report of what was said at the meeting is sent afterwards to the customer. The moment any promises made are broken, then this serves as a reference document, and strengthens your position in asking for the matter to be put right. Inability to meet promises made at a crisis meeting are the surest possible signs of an impending failure.

### *8.8.2 General points on customer visits*

It takes practice to develop a good technique at handling customer visits. Great care must be taken not to offend the customer while also getting all the information you need. Always prepare beforehand a checklist of the main points you want answered. These will be different for every case, and the main questions have been covered above.

Spend as much time listening as possible, and try to gently steer the meeting around those questions, rather than methodically move from one prearranged point to another. The meeting should flow with ease rather than be a series of staccato questions and answers. Always remember that with every meeting, you will forget or not get the opportunity to ask one or two interesting questions, so make sure the most important ones are firmly fixed in your mind and are covered as early in the meeting as possible. Appear sympathetic and understanding about a customer's less good points. This will encourage him to be a little more open about his business in the knowledge it is not going to be overly criticised by an outsider.

## 8.9 Crisis management

Despite taking all reasonable measure to minimise credit risk, there comes a time where a crisis has to be dealt with. This is the point where the customer is in imminent danger of collapse and steps have to be taken immediately to protect the interests of your company. Judging when this becomes a real possibility is difficult, some of the circumstances being:

1 Notification that a receiver/administrator has been appointed.
2 Information that a winding-up petition has been issued.
3 Contact from the customer requesting an increase in payment terms and a rescheduling of payments.
4 Information received through the 'grape-vine', either from the sales department or credit club.
5 Evidence of multiple writs issued against the customer is received.
6 Attempts to recover overdues through the courts have failed, and it is apparent that the only remaining method is to issue a winding-up order yourself.

One useful feature to these circumstances is that there can be no doubt about their gravity, and cooperation between all involved is absolutely imperative. The credit manager in effect assumes the role of chief coordinator. Each case will have its own individual characteristics, but the action which is required falls into the following broad categories:

### *8.9.1 Notification*

Everyone concerned with the company, from the sales desk to the finance director, should be informed immediately, first by phone, then in writing. It helps if such a situation can be broadcast on the various computer screens which may be available.

### *8.9.2 Suspend trading*

Stop all shipments, and if necessary and possible, recall all deliveries that have just been made. It is better to 'shoot first and answer questions later' if the customer becomes aggrieved at this action.

### *8.9.3 Compile a neat record of all outstanding orders and invoices*

It helps to know exactly where you stand with a customer, and be able to talk in precise terms to him. These details may subsequently be required by a receiver in establishment of a claim against the estate.

### *8.9.4 Get an urgent bank report*

It is worthwhile asking the opinion of banks even though some have occasionally been known to give a reasonable report one week, then appoint a liquidator the next. This is a time when a specific query should be made as to whether a cheque which is presented in the next few days will be honoured.

### *8.9.5 Speak to the customer*

Both the sales and credit departments should speak to their respective contacts. By doing this a range of responses can be subsequently analysed for their implications. First contact of this nature is often met by confident responses that any current difficulties are only temporary and that no-one should worry too much. This sort of reply is often the precursor to insolvency.

If possible make a joint sales/credit visit to the customer. It can be done on the pretext of being concerned with the position, and expressing anxiety to sort matters out so that the relationship can be restored to a more even keel. Beware of the 'smokescreen'.

### *8.9.6 Put everything into writing*

Any promises or rescheduling agreements should be put in writing. A copy of a meeting report should not only be circulated throughout the company, but it could also be given to the customer just so that their comments are on the record.

### *8.9.7 Exercise retention of title*

This applies if a receiver has been appointed, or is just about to be. A quick strike has the best chance of success, but for it to be effective, goods must be marked to be clearly identifiable.

### *8.9.8 Obtain extra security*

If insolvency is not immediately imminent, there appears to be some chance of the company surviving, and if the customer requests further goods to put his stock in saleable condition, this is a good opportunity to insist on secured terms. At the very least, a bill of exchange is a way of formally recording a customer's liability to pay. If subsequently it is not honoured then no further trading should be considered. At best ask for cash before delivery, making sure the cheque is cleared before shipment. There are some legal measures which, if successful, can provide added confidence to trading. By this I refer to the garnishee order, which legally assigns any money received by the customer, through the sale of his goods or other assets, to your company.

### *8.9.9 Consult other suppliers*

Often the continued survival of a company requires continuity of supply from several different sources. Sometimes the actions of one major creditor can mean the difference between survival and failure. This type of information may well be volunteered by the customer, or if not can be obtained on request. Get in touch with the other companies – it is in everybody's interest if a coordinated policy towards the customer is formed.

## 8.10 Bank credit risk management

A quick review of the section headings will show how many of the principles above apply also to banks. Of course there are differences:

1 In banks the distinction between sales and credit activity is not as clear as it is in a company. The bank manager often does both roles. Once a corporate customer opens an account, the manager must ensure services and charges are tailored to suit the customer, while keeping the interests of the bank secure.
2 The competitive element is different. A credit manager will always be careful to not over-manage credit risk. Excessive zeal can result in a lost customer, where a tolerable position may otherwise have been possible. Banks face the greatest competition in getting new accounts, and keeping them. However, when it comes to risky situations, bank managers have more authority to impose restrictions and tightly manage the account. Companies often rely on their banks in times of hardship – it is unlikely that another lender would happily take over the account of a company in severe difficulties.
3 Although (a) and (b) may imply that it is easier for a bank manager to effectively manage credit risk, he is faced on occasions, with a much more delicate task – the closure of a business who are unable to meet their obligations.

## 8.11 Controlling accounts

A customer's bank account status is always available, either on computer screen or printout. While debits and credits will be marked in chronological order, the significance of time is much less relevant than in a statement of outstanding invoices. The bank statement calculates the account balance, which can then be compared to the overdraft or lending limit. Comparisons and variances can be calculated from month to month or year to year. Slow payments have no relevance in this event.

If a borrowing limit is exceeded, or the account balance appears to be getting close to that limit, it is necessary to contact the customer and find out why. That is assuming the customer does not contact the bank first. Mostly the position is caused by temporary cash flow problems which will clear themselves after a short time.

An alternative course of action when an account exceeds its balance, is to refuse to honour any further cheques. This not only inconveniences the customer, it can have very damaging consequences. If bills are not paid, and suppliers find out that the support of the bank has been lost, a company is placed in very grave danger of being liquidated. The decision by the bank to take this action is not made lightly. A preferable course of action, if the circumstances merit, is to place the account in the hands of a department which specialises in nursing customers through periods of severe trading difficulty. In banks this is often known as an 'intensive care unit'.

## 8.12 The borrowing limit as a means of controlling risk

In corporate credit management, the credit limit can be manipulated in different ways according to the perceived credit risk of the customer. Following on from above, the bank overdraft or borrowing limit is just as important, but is not manipulated in the same way. It is set after carefuly analysis of, and discussions with, a customer.

## 8.13 Grading systems

Customer grading is a good way to code, in an easily recognisable way, credit risk or customer size. However, it is an optional facility, often adopted as a result of personal preference of the credit grantor. This is also the case in banking.

## 8.14 Monitoring and reviewing the bank customer case

While a statement of outstanding invoices gives information on products amounts and dates, the bank account is a positive mine of useful and interesting information. Some of the main features which can be examined to assess the current state of a client, are:

### *8.14.1 Turnover*

The amounts of money earned by a company can be approximated by calculating the credits to the account. This figure can be totalled for a year, and compared to previous periods. An instant picture is thus formed of current performance. Action can be taken to discuss the account with the customer, if figures appear to be inexplicably declining. Similarly, the frequency of credits can also be used to measure sales success.

### *8.14.2 Average balance and trends*

A series of monthly balances can be averaged, for comparison to the current balance. An analysis of the balance trend will quickly reveal if anything untoward is happening.

### *8.14.3 Rounded amounts*

A customer suffering from cash flow problems may not want to tell his bank. However this does not mean the event can be disguised. Rounded amount cheques are a sign of this event These are usually 'on-account' payments made to silence a supplier's protest at not being paid.

### *8.14.4 Standing orders and direct debits*

Standing orders, or direct debits, are convenient ways to make sure regular bills are not overlooked. Conversely when cash is tight they can be an unwanted drain on scarce resources. One way to eliminate this difficulty is to cancel the standing order, or reject the debit. In so doing, the bank is immediately alerted to a possible cause for concern.

## 8.15 Who has responsibility for credit risk management in banks?

The bank manager and his assistants assume the prime responsibility for credit risk management. There is no dilemma about whether collection clerks should be given this task. Great emphasis is placed on training bank staff to do this function, and there is a formal hierarchy of authority levels.

As a rule the bank manager will be given a level of underwriting authority sufficient to allow him almost total discretion over the activities of his branch. For larger loan levels, or in cases where a bank customer is in severe difficulty, reference to a higher authority may be needed. In the first instance this will be to a regional centre, who act as a buffer between the branches and headquarters. Here the largest credit decisions are taken, usually by a credit committee.

## 8.16 Computers and credit risk management in banks

The computer-produced account balance statement can be requested in order that the features noted in Section 8.14, can be picked up.

## 8.17 The crisis meeting

The relationship between a bank and its client, is more intimate than between corporate supplier and customer. In the early days of a business account, three- or six-monthly meetings are often held. This arrangement may relax as business gets established on an even keel. If not then regular meetings will be maintained. Therefore a crisis visit is not so relevant to a banking situation. More likely the frequency of visits will increase during a crisis.

Much information which will be requested in these situations. The bank will need audited and unaudited accounts, cash flow statements, budgets, details of orders-on-hand, and any other supporting information, like management accounts.

## 8.18 Crisis management

The last thing a bank would wish to do is to force his customer out of business – it does nothing for their reputation. Strenuous efforts are made to project a positive, caring and understanding image. Nevertheless companies that are less well managed, or who are victims of the swirls and eddies of economic trends, get into severe difficulties.

All banks have some form of intensive care unit, whose specific task is to care for such companies, and hopefully help them overcome their difficulties. While the existence of such departments is well known, banks understandably prefer to keep private their 'nursing methods'. Therefore a general review of the steps taken by a bank to manage a customer crisis are:

### *8.18.1 Early warning*

The early warning signs have already been noted in 8.4.4 above.

### *8.18.2 Ask questions*

It is often the case that a company in the early stages of trouble, will be reluctant to admit it. However, if the signs are there the bank will start to ask questions, and ask for further information – a process often resented by a customer whose pride has been hurt. However if the questions are not answered, or the answers appear ominous, and the amounts involved of sufficient size, the bank will move to the next stage – an independent analysis of the position.

### *8.18.3 Call in an outside adviser*

Accountancy firms are often asked by banks to look at the books of a company and make recommendations. The results of this investigation will be used to formulate a survival plan.

### *8.18.4 Set conditions and monitor strictly*

If it is felt that the interests of both parties are best served by continuing the business, then formal arrangements will be made. Lending is usually made on a formula basis, related to balance sheet items like debtors, stock or current assets. There is no fixed rule to setting formulae but, during a crisis, it will be monitored very closely. Firm control based on a realistic plan will give the customer the best chance of survival.

### *8.18.5 Wind up the customer*

A last resort measure, taken when it is clear that further support is merely ploughing good money into bad, and increasing the debts of the ailing concern. The two main options taken in these cases is to appoint an administrative receiver or a liquidator, whose job will be to realise the maximum amount to repay the bank. This subject will be covered in greater detail in the next chapter.

## 8.19 Export credit risk management

The management techniques above can equally well be applied to both domestic and overseas customers. The obvious difference with exports are:

1 Shipments and accompanying documentation are more complicated.
2 The customer is further away, making it more difficult to get to know him as well as a domestic customer.
3 Trading customs and legal systems vary from country to country.

### *8.19.1 Shipping and documentation*

A most important though complex part of exporting, is making sure documentation is in order. To a developed country or EEC member this is not so big a problem. However, to less well developed nations, where payment is to be by letter of credit, correct documentation is essential. Payment delay is more likely as a result of failing to dot an 'i' in the bill of lading, than slow payment from a weak customer. It therefore follows that credit risk management begins at a much earlier stage with exporting.

### *8.19.2 Distance from customer*

Visits to overseas customers are less frequent, and additionally there will be language barriers to overcome. Therefore it is much less easy to get to know such a customer. Overseas status reports will give some information, but the depth and quality of it will depend on the country involved. Companies with overseas sales managers are at an advantage in this respect.

Often, however, overseas trading is done via an agent. Under these circumstances it is possible to build up a rapport with the agent, to the extent that he will be able to manage the credit risk on your behalf. A *del credere* agent does just this, by guaranteeing payment from the end customer.

### *8.19.3 Trading practices*

Export credit risk management involves getting to know a country, and the way its companies behave. In developed nations there are many similarities, though legal systems are on the whole different. This affects the exporter's position should a crisis occur. A good agent should know the system, and be able to take the most suitable action to protect his risk and yours. Because he is on the spot, he can speak to the customer or try to recover goods. In the last resort he can make sure your claim is registered with legal authorities responsible for winding up the customer. The latter point is very important – as an overseas unsecured creditor, you are at a distinct disadvantage in trying to uphold your rights if you have no representation in that country. If no agent can be used, then a reputable lawyer will have to do.

## CHAPTER SUMMARY

1 Definitions:
   (a) 'inevitable bad debt': a fact of life which it is often impractical to guard against;
   (b) 'unavoidable bad debt': despite all efforts to prevent this, there will always be some losses which cannot be avoided;
   (c) 'avoidable bad debt': is the result of an inefficient risk management system.

2 Methods of management: Risk management measures should be finely tuned so that they are not too intrusive, but very effective when they are brought into action. There is a tendency to be overcautious, which can be counterproductive to the objective.

   Banks are in a good position to manage credit risk, without some of the difficulties encountered by corporate credit managers. However they do have the delicate power of life or death over a customer. The methods of management are as follows:
   (a) controlling shipments: making sure that supplies can be effectively withheld when necessary;
   (b) setting credit levels which fall into the following categories:
      (i) the lowest figure, when assessing expected trade and creditworthiness;
      (ii) the highest figure geared to creditworthiness irrespective of expected trade;
      (iii) control credit limits, held deliberately low so that orders have to be individually cleared;
      (iv) quick-start: a small level set with little or no investigation, to get an account started;
      (v) none at all: credit levels replaced by a grading system which requires 'referral' before shipment.

3 Grading systems: used to easily identify risky customers. Can be based on two principles:
   (a) a mixture of customer type, and track record;
   (b) an assessment of creditworthiness and track record alone.

4 Responsibility for credit risk control: a skilled job requiring analytical abilities. Best done by specialists. Banks establish formal training and well defined levels of authority for those responsible for credit risk management.
5 All customers are monitored, but some should also be regularly reviewed by renewing customer information. These should be high-risk customers, and those who are of key importance to the company.
6 Computer assistance is an invaluable aid to spotting risk, in the form of printouts and exception reports:
   (a) aged receivables report;
   (b) overlimit report;
   (c) stop list;
   (d) DSO calculation;
   (e) cost of credit, based on DSO, measures profit erosion;
   (f) orders on hand, looks ahead at future credit problems.
   Banks look at the following features in the account balance statements:
   (a) turnover;
   (b) average balance and trends;
   (c) rounded amounts;
   (d) standing orders and direct debits.
7 Crisis customer visit. This is an effective way to take stock of a difficult situation, and discuss in person with the customer, how it can be resolved. With banks visits are likely to become more frequent during a crisis period, and a higher level of information will be required from the customer.
8 Crisis management. The main steps are:
   (a) notification to all parties concerned;
   (b) suspension of trade;
   (c) compile a neat report;
   (d) urgent bank report;
   (e) speak to the customer, by phone or visit;
   (f) put everything into writing which transpires after the crisis has begun;
   (g) exercise retention of title if used;
   (h) get extra security if customer wishes trade to continue;
   (i) consult other suppliers who may be keeping the customer afloat.
   For banks, the main steps are:
   (a) identify early warning signs;
   (b) ask questions;
   (c) assess the position, if necessary using independent advice, to arrive at a survival plan;
   (d) set strict limits and controls over the plan;
   (e) if plan fails, or position too bad, a last resort is winding up the customer.
9 Risk management of overseas customers follows the same principles as above. Pre-shipment control of documentation is as important as post-shipment monitoring. Due to distance and country differences, it is advisable to have an agent (preferably *del credere*) to protect your interests.

# CHAPTER 9

# COMPANY FAILURE

No company or bank is immune to one of its customers failing, even if the most sophisticated techniques for credit analysis and management were used. Systems should therefore be measured in terms of their success at minimising potential bad debts.

This chapter is devoted to insolvency, the reasons for its occurrence, and the legal framework which exists to handle it. This will necessarily include mention of the Insolvency Act of 1986, though it is reasonable to note that throughout the developed nations, similar ideas are used. Special attention will be paid to the main causes of insolvency, and once again they are applicable throughout the international trading community.

## 9.1 Bad debts and credit risk analysis in perspective

Even though insolvencies in the UK number on average ten thousand per year, to individual organisations customer failure is still a rare event. It is revealing to consider that on average each year, a company is likely to lose ten times more money in financing slow payments, than in bad debts. The message is clear – good cash collection has a higher priority than good credit risk analysis.

However, in no way should this be interpreted as a good excuse for relegating the important role of credit analysis. Bad debts can best be avoided by not trading with the customer in the first place. Failing this, many thousands of pounds can be saved each year by being alert enough to spot the potential insolvency and wind down trading accordingly. In addition the process of credit risk management can be used to good effect to target sales activity and market awareness. None of these activities is possible without an established credit assessment system.

The attention paid to credit analysis is to some extent linked to economic features. Periods of economic boom herald a relaxation of credit granting standards. This is particularly so in the consumer credit field. In the UK a credit card holder who can also produce a further document of identity, ideally a bill (electricity, rates etc), can purchase on credit almost any major domestic item. It has even been known for such an agreement to be offered when the bill presented was a final demand and threat of legal action! An extreme example perhaps, but suggestive of the attitude of the credit grantor – it was merely the existence of identity, rather than what it contained, that allowed the credit transaction.

This can be translated into corporate trading terms too. Larger companies with a high incidence of new customers often find it expedient to offer a standard credit account with the barest of credit checks. Assuming a boom period, and remembering the priority of cash collection, this approach is understandable.

However, there is much evidence at the time of writing this book that the economies of the western world are overheating. The debt burden of the US, a large balance of trading deficit in the UK, and the effects of Third World loan default, serve to undermine the stability of the international economy. Recent industrial growth rates, especially in the UK, are a clear suggestion of an increase in demand. There are more and more companies entering the field to capitalise on it. As competition increases profits need to be pared to the minimum in order to offer attractive prices. One possible result could be deflation and ultimately recession.

There are many pundits offering this view, and just as many who feel it is too alarmist. However, there is one feature which should increasingly concern the credit granting community. In a highly competitive environment one of the best ways of keeping ahead is not to beat the competition, but to buy it. So many companies, after successfully completing their 'three-year probationary period', end up being bought by larger concerns. A constant task of credit management is to keep track of group exposures as more and more customers lose their individual identity. There are two sides to this coin – larger companies are better able to fend for themselves, but the bigger they are the harder they fall. Should the boom end and some of the worst predictions even partially be realised, the repercussions could be most painful not at the small-company end of the scale, but with the medium to large sized company. Now is the time to gear up credit management systems to protect against this event.

## 9.2 Causes of insolvency

Most companies seem to get things right, or at least right enough to be able to continue in business. Yet some companies get things wrong, even though they may well be selling a broadly similar product under similar trading conditions to their many trading colleagues. There is one obvious characteristic individual to every company – its management. It therefore follows that the inability of management to cope with the intense pressure of trading is the root cause of every insolvency.

This is the view of those responsible for sorting out the affairs of failed companies, the insolvency practitioner. Company management is the first item to come under his scrutiny after being called into action. It is a sort of 'catch-all' which is bound to result in some criticism once all the facts are known.

As an underwriter of many years' experience, the author feels somewhat uncomfortable with this understandable attitude. The benefit of hindsight is a powerful weapon when looking at underwriting decisions which have gone wrong. Still more so in company failure. However, there is a thin dividing line between success and failure. For each failed company there could be one, or maybe five, or even ten companies with equally bad management, which for some reason have not failed. No-one can say for sure because those companies do not come under the scrutiny associated with insolvency. Even the largest companies can have management weaknesses which, because of their sheer size, power and the bureaucracy within them, go unnoticed.

What can be said is that all insolvency involves bad management, even though not all bad management leads to insolvency.

Because of this slight reservation on the role of bad management, it is perhaps appropriate to place it subjectively into two categories:

1 Prime weaknesses which singly or in combination place a company in an excessively vulnerable position which eventually leads to failure.
2 Secondary weaknesses which, due to circumstances beyond management control, or simple bad luck, caused a failure.

### *9.2.1 Prime management weaknesses*

This section looks solely at the causes. In the next section we will try to identify those features which are a sign of these weaknesses.

1 Lack of financial information and control: the motivation underlying all business activity is profit. To make profit depends on selling sufficient goods to cover all the costs and expenses in making or acquiring them. The most unforgivable management weakness is failure to apply this essential measurement on a frequent and regular basis.

There is no shortage of expertise in financial management, and there are many tools such as computers, which can be used to keep the books and report figures. Even the smallest of businesses must assume the cost of good financial management in order to control their activities. It is a discipline, like making VAT returns and paying National Insurance contributions, which is unavoidable.

2 Failure to act on financial information: compiling figures is one thing, but understanding what they mean and acting on them is another. It is the responsibility of the finance director to make sure the figures are properly presented and commented upon. It is also the duty of all directors to make sure they fully understand them.

3 Unbalanced management: companies managed on an autocratic or dictatorial basis are at a severe disadvantage. Unless the company is very small, no

one person could be reasonably expected to have the knowledge, expertise and time required to devote proper attention to the full range of corporate functions. The best managing directors are those with the ability to select a strong team, and then delegate. The opposite to this is a management team of demotivated 'puppets', who have a title but ultimately no power.

### *9.2.2 Secondary management weaknesses*

To a creditor owed a lot of money, or to an employee of many years' standing, it may seem a little pointless to make a distinction between one management weakness and another. However, under the current insolvency law in the UK, there is a difference. Directors *and* managers can be called to account for their actions and, if deemed wrongful, can be compelled to contribute their personal assets to the insolvent estate. It could be argued that any primary weaknesses might stand a better chance of qualifying under this rule. However, the ones which follow could perhaps be regarded more leniently.

One further observation on secondary weaknesses is that they are more likely to arise if any of the primary weaknesses are present. The correlation between the two may vary from case to case.

1 Overtrading: this is a failure to ensure sufficient working capital is generated or available to service production needs. It is characterised by an attractive increase in sales, possibly also profits, and a full order-book. Also there is a notable increase in the amounts owed to creditors, and collectable from debtors.

Take for example the computer manufacturer with hundreds of machines ready for delivery except that they have no keyboards. The reason is they are on stop with the keyboard supplier for not paying the bill. They cannot pay the bill, or any others for that matter, until they receive the cash from the units ready to sell. They cannot sell them without keyboards, however. Eventually they are liquidated by a creditor who was unable to get his money any other way.

Overtrading is a vicious cycle which can catch a company unawares, because in its early stages overtrading can be easily misinterpreted as business success. It happens to most companies at some stage, and requires careful financial management to avoid.

2 Poor planning and strategy: it is essential for all businesses to look ahead at likely changes in products, markets and the financing needed to achieve targets. The biggest danger is to be overtaken by the competition, left with an out of date product, or underfunded. Flexibility and an acknowledgement that the world will not stand still is required.

To use another computer example, the well known UK manufacturers Apricot faced a considerable dilemma in the mid-1980s. Though their micros were technically sound and well regarded, they did not conform to the emerging industry standard of IBM compatibility. Recognising a consequent decline in the balance sheet, which could have become terminal, they altered their product range to conform to the industry standard, and have never looked back.

A slightly different example is the DeLorean collapse. The strategy of producing a high quality sports car was probably sound, but the planning process went wrong. The cars were too heavy, which meant their performance suffered. Delivery costs were also much higher than planned because the 'gull-wing' door design reduced the number which could be parked side by side on board a ship.

3 Bad luck: fate can play a major part in business failure. Fires are a good example – despite taking prudent action to minimise the risk they do happen, and are a cause of failure of several insolvencies.

The Laker Airways crash is a good example. First delays in getting a transatlantic flight licence meant that 'Skytrain' had not started operations before the oil price rise of the early 1970s. Second a cartel of airlines, subsequently judged to be illegal, eventually contributed to the financial state which finally defeated Laker.

There are many other examples of types of bad luck which play a role in insolvency. These include: construction companies encountering unexpectedly adverse weather conditions which severely delay a project; responsible and hygenic egg producers suffering from a severe drop in demand caused by inaccurate rumours of health dangers; sheep farmers suffering from the after-effects of Chernobyl; fashion designers losing business opportunities because of the theft of patterns and subsequent cheap manufacture of the designs elsewhere.

4 Communications: effective management relies on everyone being aware of what the others are doing. This is especially important when dealing with trading problems or hurdles.

5 Marketing: profits cannot be made without sales, and sales cannot be made without marketing. Failure to target successfully and promote products and ideas can have an immediate influence on profit.

Companies producing unusual or innovative products are most prone to this. An example is the demise of the Sinclair C5 motorised three-wheeler. At first sight this was an enterprising way to provide the customer with a cheap form of transport, with the possible expectation that our streets could soon be similar to those in Far Eastern cities.

## 9.3 Signs of insolvency

The cause of insolvency is by definition discovered after the event. What outward signs can give us an insight into these causes? The review of customer and financial attributes (customer-speak) gives us a useful routine for picking up danger signals, and it is the responsibility of marketing, sales and the credit department to be constantly alert to them.

It is rare for an insolvency to occur completely 'out of the blue'. There can be a preceding period of months or even years during which time the signs are there to be seen. However, there is still the problem of timing and judging the extent to which the 'survival instinct' is present. None of the suggestions below can therefore be described as a one hundred per cent accurate sign of insolvency.

### *9.3.1 Worsening trading experience*

Assessing the implications of slow payments and poor trading experience is one of the most difficult in credit management. So many companies pay late almost as a matter of policy that this alone is not a reliable danger signal. The turning point is often linked to the level of customer disputes, or a clear change in the payment pattern. Specious or unfounded disputes used as an excuse for non-payment are the most obvious warning signs (it follows that deliveries should be made with extra care to slow payers to ensure they do not arise).

Sometimes a customer will admit to having cash flow difficulties, and request extra time to pay. This again is an obvious time to exercise extreme caution, and is a good moment to review and update customer information to see if other warning signs are present. Like overtrading, or even as a symptom of overtrading, cash flow problems may only be temporary in nature. For instance highly seasonal businesses often encounter shortages of cash during a trough in their trading cycle. The admission of cash flow difficulties soon after an account becomes overdue for the first time, could be a more honest reaction and less worrying sign than when made after overdues have existed for many months.

The failure to keep repayment promises is the next major sign. If the promise or arrangement was made formally, by someone in authority from the customer (repayment schedules must always be confirmed in writing) then later deviation should be regarded as very serious. It is an important part of cash collection to be able to record promises made, and measure performance against them.

If an account is placed in the hands of a solicitor or collection agency, this may still not be a totally accurate suggestion of potential failure. If an account reaches this stage, no further supplies should be made whatever the assessment of whether the customer will be paid. This act is a sign that the trading relationship has irrevocably broken down. By ceasing to trade there will be no increase in amounts owing and the task remains to recover what is owed by whatever means possible. This could involve winding up the company.

The need to petition for compulsory liquidation is the final straw which brings about the failure of the customer, unless the account is settled.

The position of banks is slightly different to that of the trade creditor. Borrowings may range from an agreed overdraft, to a secured loan, to an endorsed acceptance credit. However, current account activity is the best way to monitor the trading patterns of their customers. Many checks exist to spot instances where the overdraft limit has been exceeded without agreement, or round-valued cheques have been issued to suppliers, or a scheduled loan repayment missed. Normally discussions with the borrower will resolve the problem. If subsequently the problems recur, the sanction of refusing to honour cheques is a way of controlling the risk. This is used as a reluctant last resort because should the customer still be unable to meet his obligation to the bank, some form of insolvency procedure is almost inevitable.

### *9.3.2 Increasing reliance on borrowed funds*

The so-called gearing of a company can be closely correlated with its failure. Without plans for business expansion or purchase of capital items, increased borrowing is a possible sign of mismanaged cash flow and lack of profits.

During periods of high interest rates, highly geared companies are at their most vulnerable.

The attitude of bankers in the UK errs on the side of securitised lending. Provided security or collateral is available, which is acceptable to the bankers, loans are generally forthcoming. Coupled with the reluctance of banks to appear miserly, or be accused of causing company failure, many companies find it possible to get deeper and deeper into debt.

It is not possible to give a clear suggestion on what point the debt burden becomes unbearable, or where the gearing ratios are too high – these are better measured by comparison with industry norms. Debt servicing is a better sign – if insufficient cash prevents servicing the interest on debts, this is a clear sign of overborrowing.

Even these measurements are not conclusive. A company with a successful outlook, with justified expectations of sales and profits increasing, may be able to weather the storm. Banks are much more likely to continue support if they can see the customer going in the right direction.

So it can be seen that high gearing, with a heavy interest burden and declining performance, is a very useful danger signal.

### *9.3.3 Increased reliance on associated companies*

This is similar to 9.3.2 above, but with the funds being borrowed from within the group. It is reasonable to assume that a parent or holding company has a family interest in keeping its siblings in business. At the very least they have an equity stake in the business which could be lost if the subsidiary failed.

However, the existence of borrowed money from a parent, or from a bank under a parent company guarantee (usually stated in notes to the accounts), should be regarded with equal suspicion. Loss-making subsidiaries (and individual companies for that matter) can be closed down in an orderly fashion, with no loss to the creditors. But they can also be deliberately allowed to go into receivership. This usually happens as a result of the whole group collapsing.

If the parent is an overseas company, there can also be a greater danger of this phenomenon. For instance a company which is the sole UK subsidiary of an overseas parent may not necessarily be in a secure position. It can fall prey to the whims and fancies of its parent – should they decide their presence in a country is no longer required, or could be better served by an agent, then the tolerance and support level can be radically diminished.

For example, development agencies in the UK and Ireland, anxious to attract new business to their area, offer incentives for overseas companies to establish subsidiaries in the region. Some of these companies allowed the attraction of incentives to overrule their judgement on the long-term feasibility of the project. At the beginning of the 1980s there was a spate of insolvencies occurring as a result of the overseas parent losing faith in their newly created ventures, or being financially incapable of financing them.

### *9.3.4 Expansion through acquisition and/or capital expenditure*

This leads on from the point above. Always carefully monitor a company when it makes its first few acquisitions. Ambitious companies, or rather their ambitious owners, often find acquisition as the fastest route to expansion. Most of the time this strategy works, but sometimes it can create a millstone around their necks.

An example of this is Motorists Discount Centre (MDC). It became a very successful company, offering a reasonable alternative service to the longer established Halfords chain. However, another smaller spare parts chain was purchased in order to increase the distribution of outlets around the country – certainly a credible strategy. This acquisition, and the debt and marketing strain it placed on the new company, became untenable, and MDC failed. Incidentally another reason for failure was an autocratic management style.

Capital expenditure can create a similar problem. The building of a new factory, or extension of the existing one, is at face value a progressive sign. However, if it was done to meet higher demand and without careful financial management and planning, all the symptoms of overtrading can arise.

### *9.3.5 Board resignations*

The resignation of a director, especially if accompanied with acrimonious publicity, is a clear sign of problems. It can signal an autocratic leadership style. More pertinently if someone with close inside knowledge of a company sees fit to get out, it casts the finger of suspicion on that company.

However, this sign should not be confused with the power games played in major companies. The treatment of the event by the financial press is a good judge on whether this is so.

### 9.3.6 *Late figures*

Though lower down in the list of signs, this is in no way meant to imply lesser importance. There is a good saying – 'bad figures take longer to add up'. Time after time this is proved to be true.

A company showing a mediocre to poor balance sheet, which then neglects to lodge further figures when required, is a very likely candidate for insolvency.

Banks are in the front line when it comes to this aspect. A customer who finds it difficult to produce figures on time, or makes a poor job of presentation, is unlikely to find favour should extended borrowing be required.

## 9.4 Insolvency law

As we have seen, early examples of bankruptcy occurred in Roman times. The law has progressed somewhat since then. It has evolved to a state where considerable effort is placed in trying to keep a technically insolvent business alive. Two techniques for doing so can be used:

1 An informal or formal agreement between the company and its creditors to reschedule or reduce the amounts owing, so that the business can continue.
2 Enlisting the help of the court or professional insolvency practitioner, to take over management of the business, with a view to keeping it alive. This will involve an agreement among the creditors, and between the creditors and the insolvent. Debts can be rescheduled or compromised. The benefit to creditors will be that they will receive fuller or more prompt payment than on liquidation. Injection of funds or guarantees by third parties may be involved.

The new insolvency law encourages (2). Any procedure which preserves business will appear to favour insolvent debtors, and in some countries (notably the US) actually does so. A balance may be struck, however. What damages the biggest group of moneylenders, the unsecured creditors, far more is the extent of secured claims. Insolvency procedures must preserve the priorities of secured creditors.

In order to illustrate both business-rescuing and final procedures (the company doctor and the company undertaker functions) the UK Insolvency Act 1986 will be examined. As the date implies, this act has only comparatively recently come into effect and there are elements of it which have yet to be fully tested. It has been designed to give the greatest chance of keeping a business alive, and to encourage debtors to use it at an earlier stage, rather than stagger onwards into an even worse trading position. The management of insolvent companies must be placed in the hands of experienced people, that is a licensed insolvency practitioner. The various stages of liquidation are well publicised, and information on its causes is more readily available to creditors in general.

There follows a description of the main components of the UK Insolvency

Act 1986 (the Act). The intention is to explain the Act as it is now, rather than make any comparisons to its earlier version. Also the provisions which apply to individuals' bankruptcy are not discussed.

### *9.4.1 Voluntary Arrangements*

The insolvency of a company is naturally a catastrophic event to be avoided if possible. For this reason it is highly desirable to all affected parties that some form of arrangement, scheme or moratorium be agreed. It may involve some financial loss to the creditors, but it is also a route towards minimising that loss, and perhaps even keeping the business going.

The problem with a scheme of this nature is that it can be destroyed by the action of a single belligerent creditor.

Under the Act, a debtor may approach a licensed insolvency practitioner with a proposal explaining the circumstances, financial implications and benefits to creditors, that such a scheme entails. If the practitioner accepts the job, he assumes the title of nominee, and becomes responsible for presenting the proposal first to a court and then at a meeting of creditors. Creditors may oppose the proposal, in which case a liquidation is likely to ensue. However, the existence of a proposal, and the acceptance of it by a practitioner, adds credibility to the arrangement, and the incentive to cooperate is increased.

If accepted, the arrangement is supervised by the practitioner (now called the supervisor), who is responsible for keeping records and reporting regularly to the creditors on the progress of the arrangement.

How closely the supervisor will be involved in day-to-day administration of the company in the voluntary arrangement will depend on two things:

1 How much the supervisor and the creditors trust the company's management.
2 How sophisticated the arrangement is.

Closer involvement by the supervisor increases the costs. If the arrangement involves elements falling outside reasonable management expertise (such as conversion of unsecured claims to equity or loan stock), then close involvement by the supervisor will be necessary.

### *9.4.2 Administration*

The objectives of an administration are to reorganise the company back to profitability; and/or make proposals for the profitable realisation of assets; and/or achieving an agreement with creditors. A petition is made to the court, usually by the company directors, though it could be by a creditor or combination of both. If the petition is accepted, the court will appoint an administrator (nominated by the company or creditor).

The legal significance of this appointment is considerable. Individual enforcement action by creditors, under security, hire purchase, leasing or retention of title, is suspended. No receiver can be appointed to the company, nor can it be wound up. Administrators are given the power to run the insolvent company as they see fit, which includes hiring and firing; selling assets (except those under a fixed charge for which court permission is needed); taking legal action; borrowing money; authorising VAT bad debt relief (if there appears to be no prospect of any payment to unsecured creditors).

The administrator, throughout the duration of his appointment, will endeavour to act for all interested parties, including unsecured creditors. Before appointment however it is necessary to serve notice on debenture holders (usually a bank) who have the right to appoint an administrative receiver.

### *9.4.3 Administrative receivership*

Formerly this was known as 'receivership'. It occurs when a lender secured by a floating charge appoints what is now called an 'administrative receiver' to recover the indebtedness. The all-embracing nature of the charge means that the receiver can continue the company's trade. This procedure has often rescued businesses or parts of them, although far less often companies. In many ways the powers of an administrator are modelled on those of a receiver. However, because the receiver acts for one creditor rather than creditors generally, he has not the protection against individual creditor action enjoyed by the administrator.

A secured creditor who has the right to appoint an administrative receiver can, by doing so, block the making of an administrative order. After an administration order is made, however, the secured creditor can no longer appoint an administrative receiver. The creditor is almost always the company's banker, and knows something of his problems. Therefore an administrative receiver will often be appointed before there is any question of applying for an administration order. If this does not happen, a secured creditor faced with the choice of appointing an administrative receiver or accepting an administrative order will often appoint, to ensure the choice of practitioner.

### *9.4.4 Liquidation*

There are three types of liquidation:

1 Members' voluntary liquidation (MVL): strictly speaking this is not an insolvency at all. It is a course of action taken by the directors/owners of a company to cease trading, realise its assets and pay its liabilities. This includes an interest element calculated from the time the liquidation began. The directors must make a 'declaration of solvency' that the company can meet all its liabilities within 12 months, supported by a statement of affairs. The winding up is carried out by a liquidator, who must be a licensed

insolvency practitioner. Should it appear that debts will not be discharged in full within the allotted timescale, then the liquidator has the power to convene a creditors' meeting and (unless a dissatisfied creditor petitions for compulsory liquidation) the proceedings can be transformed into a creditors' voluntary liquidation.

2 Creditors' voluntary liquidation (CVL): initiated once again by the directors, they must convene a meeting of shareholders to wind the company up; and of creditors, at a reasonable time and place, to review the statement of affairs and appoint a liquidator. Thereafter the creditors may form a committee to monitor the progress of the liquidation. As the term suggests, the liquidator is restricted to liquidating the company in an orderly and legally correct manner, and settle debts in descending priority.

3 Compulsory liquidation: is often brought about by a creditor issuing a notice requiring repayment of the debt within twenty-one days. Failure to do so means the creditor can ask the court to wind the company up. The official receiver becomes liquidator. If it is clear that there is little or no money for distribution, the official receiver may take rapid and terminal action to liquidate the company. In a more complex case, an insolvency practitioner will be called in to undertake the liquidation, in a similar way to the CVL.

### *9.4.5 Wrongful trading/director's disqualification*

Clearly something has gone wrong if a company ceases trading. Creditors are naturally interested in finding out what it was. There are cases where the insolvent company may have committed some acts which directly contributed to the position, or gave unfair advantage to selected creditors.

The Company Directors Disqualification Act 1986 provides some powerful disciplinary measures which can disqualify a director for a period up to fifteen years from holding company office. The Insolvency Act 1986 also has provisions to force a director to contribute to the insolvent estate from his own funds for wrongful trading. This occurs when a director realises the company is hopelessly insolvent yet fails to take every step to protect creditors. It also applies to any director who should have realised it but did not. Both the actual abilities of the director and those to be expected of one in his job are taken into account.

At the time of writing only one case has come to judgment. It suggests that all directors will be expected to know at any time what the books and accounts of the company would have disclosed, had they been properly kept and up to date according to the Companies Act.

There are other examples of conduct which may enable a liquidator to recover funds for the benefit of creditors generally:

1 Transactions at under-value: where the company entered into a transaction for little or no return, within two years of the insolvency.

2 Preference: where the company placed a creditor or guarantor in a more favourable position than they would otherwise have held in the insolvency. The timescale here is six months before the event (or two years if the creditor or guarantor was 'connected with' the company).

If there is evidence of misconduct, a report is made by the insolvency practitioner, and is submitted to a government department whose job is to decide whether disqualification is appropriate. Within the first two years of this Act less than four per cent of referrals resulted in disqualification.

### *9.4.6 Retention of title (ROT)*

Ever since the *Romalpa* judgment, there has been considerable interest in establishing a retention of title claim on goods sold. Some have gone to considerable and elaborate lengths to retain ownership of goods until paid, to the extent that their claim assumes the legal characteristics of a charge on assets. Nevertheless ROT is a valid legal procedure which must be acknowledged in insolvency by the practitioner.
The golden rules are:

1 Keep it simple.
2 Make sure the customer has agreed to the ROT, if possible by written acknowledgement of sale conditions if they include ROT provisions.
3 Clearly mark the goods supplied, so they can be quickly and easily identified. Include reference to the identity on the invoice.
4 Be persistent. If the ROT is valid then it is in the interests of the practitioner to deal with your claim, and get it out of the way.

It should be noted that ROT cannot apply to services. It is also worth suggesting that an ROT clause on customised goods, or goods which cannot be easily resold, could rebound on the supplier if asked to take back goods he did not want.

### *9.4.7 VAT bad debt relief*

In the UK, where VAT is paid on sales, it is possible to obtain relief equal to that paid in connection with an insolvent company. To do so requires getting official acknowledgement that a debt is outstanding from the person handling the insolvency.

In liquidations, this is a routine matter whether or not there is an anticipated dividend for unsecured creditors. The position may not be so clear cut in an administration or administrative receivership. If there will be nothing for ordinary unsecured creditors the insolvency practitioner will certify this, and only then is the relief available.

### *9.4.8 Insolvent company restructuring*

By definition an insolvent company has more liabilities than assets. It is the duty of the insolvency practitioner to liquidate the assets at the best possible price. A common method of doing so is packaging the viable part of the business, and maybe transferring it to a wholly-owned subsidiary. This may then be purchased as a going concern, and much to the chagrin of unsecured creditors, the purchaser could even be the previous owners who end up continuing their business (providing there was no disqualification of directors).

### *9.4.9 Creditors' meetings*

These can be, and often are, stormy affairs. Also there are many legal aspects at play. An inexperienced creditor may therefore fail to exercise his rights effectively, if he does not know what they are. Since insolvencies are comparatively rare, this is highly likely to be the case.

An important service freely given by the larger UK insolvency practitioners is to attend such meetings, represent their clients' interests, and produce a report for the creditor. The benefit of doing so from the practitioner's point of view is that he may subsequently acquire the appointment to administer or liquidate the company.

### *9.4.10 Practitioner responsibility for debts incurred*

Creditors are often faced with a dilemma when they are asked to trade with a company in formal insolvency. It is very often necessary for the practitioner to purchase raw materials and services in order to maximise the sale of stock, or keep the business as a going concern. Who takes responsibility for honouring these debts?

The answer is that the insolvency practitioner is not personally liable, and a note to this effect will be included in any contract entered into. However, post-insolvency debts receive the highest priority from the insolvent estate. The credibility of a practitioner to do his job relies in part on his trustworthiness in this matter. Creditors are therefore safe in supplying under these conditions, though a separate account should be used, and orders carefully vetted to ensure that they are authorised by the practitioner.

## 9.5 A CASE STUDY

The following example is of an administration. It shows how the Act can be used to protect the interests of the unsecured creditor, by enabling the company to continue in business. The name of the company is Smallman Construction Ltd (SCL), and the insolvency practitioner involved is Stephen Adamson of Arthur Young (AY).

SCL was incorporated in 1977 and carried on business as an erector and fabricator of structural steelwork. The company is owned and run by the Smallman family and has an issued share capital of £10,000. Their turnover increased threefold from the year ended December 1986 (£3.5m) to December 1987 (£10m), and this was largely due to entering into several large contracts as a subcontractor on various phases of the Broadgate development in London. Financing of the company's expansion was done primarily through an increase in the overdraft facility and extended credit taken from suppliers.

Several phases of the Broadgate development encountered difficulties and monies which SCL claimed were disputed as being owed by the main contractor. The refusal to pay led to a projected overdraft requirement of £1.5m and the bank was not prepared to increase beyond £700,000. The directors of SCL then made extensive efforts to attract investors, but with no success.

A report prepared by AY for the bank concluded that under either an administrative receivership or a liquidation it was unlikely that the business would be continued. This would not have been in the interests of the unsecured creditors due to the weakening of SCL's position in respect of the dispute with the main contractor, and also the evaporation of any value the business may have had as a going concern. The report recommended that an administration order would have been in the best interests of the unsecured creditors, without prejudicing the bank's position.

Before petitioning the court it was first necessary to ensure that the bank was prepared to provide a facility to the proposed administrators and this in turn required a personal guarantee to be given by Mr and Mrs Smallman. On making the application to the court it was anticipated that, with the moratorium on the creditors and the company continuing to trade, a suitable investor would be found by the directors within three months.

The court granted the order in April 1988. At this date SCL had unsecured creditors of £1.1m and preferential creditors of £0.4m. The bank as a secured creditor was repaid during the first eight weeks of trading.

A large part of the planned future trading of the company, and its attraction to potential investors related to a further phase of the Broadgate development (phase eleven). SCL was anticipating entering into this contract as a joint venture along with two continental steel fabricators. At the date of the administration, negotiations had been entered into but no formal contract reached. SCL's portion of the proposed contract was to be for more than £4m.

The meeting of creditors was held in June 1988 and a summary of the nine proposals put forward was that the company would continue to trade and enter into phase eleven via a dormant subsidiary of SCL; the litigation against the main contractors (gross value £2m) would continue; the terms of a voluntary arrangement would be negotiated.

Trading was maintained during July and August 1988 while negotiations continued for the participation in phase eleven. These negotiations became exceedingly complex, due partly to the Continental involvement and also the complicated funding arrangements required due to the administration. At the end of August the other proposed parties to the joint venture decided that SCL was no longer to play a part, and a settlement was then negotiated for the withdrawal of SCL from the 'contract'. A settlement was finally offered but it was necessary due to the contract forming a significant part of the proposals to either call a meeting of creditors (for which there was insufficient time) or apply to the court. The latter approach was made and the court authorised the administrators to accept the offer but to call a meeting of creditors and put the revised proposals before them.

This was done at a meeting in September 1988. The main alteration was the removal of SCL's involvement in Broadgate phase eleven.

It was still considered that investment/sale would take place and the progress of the litigation against the main contractor had been satisfactory albeit slow. The creditors approved the revised proposals.

The loss of the phase eleven contract resulted in a slack three months trading for SCL; however, another major contract with an approximate value of £3.4m was obtained for a development at St. Thomas More Street. This, together with several smaller contracts, meant that the company's future trading appeared satisfactory, although unlikely to maintain the legal and professional costs of the administration. This heightened the urgency to find a purchaser/investor so that a continued reduction in SCL's assets could be prevented.

An advertisement in the *Financial Times* resulted in about fifty initial enquiries which reduced ultimately to two keenly interested parties who made offers for the business including all present staff and employees.

The sale was eventually completed in February 1989 and resulted in the purchaser buying the assets of SCL at book value together with a payment for the value of the new contracts which the company was to continue.

Having achieved the sale the administrators were then able to prepare proposals for a voluntary arrangement with the creditors. These proposals were for a dividend of between 30 and 40 per cent payable immediately. Should the litigation against the main contractor prove successful (still in progress at date of writing) then it is quite possible that unsecured creditors will ultimately receive 100 per cent of their debt.

There are several interesting points to arise from this study:

1 The warning signs of overtrading were present given the massive growth in turnover. Creditors were used to finance the expansion which would have reflected in trading experience.
2 SCL's problems were deepened by the dispute with the main contractor, an event that may not have been foreseeable when planning for the expansion.
3 The bank precipitated the crisis by refusing to increase the overdraft. However, subsequently they made the administration possible by not insisting on a receiver being appointed, and providing finance albeit under a guarantee.

4 The administrators, under the direction of the court, were able to exercise their powers in negotiating the phase eleven contract and obtaining a settlement, which was accepted *before* the creditors could be consulted.
5 Because of the administration, it was possible to keep the company in a sufficiently fit state for a purchaser to find it an attractive buy.
6 Unsecured creditors were able to minimise their loss by supporting the voluntary arrangement.

## Chapter summary

1 Insolvency is thankfully a rare event. The interest expense of supplementing cash flow because of slow payments, is on average ten times higher than the bad debt figure.
2 Current economic trends are adverse. Also there is an increasing frequency of small companies being bought by larger ones. This could result in the average size of individual bad debts becoming much higher.
3 The causes of insolvency are normally attributed to bad management. Some management weaknesses are more serious than others, and can be categorised as:
   (a) primary weaknesses:
      (i) lack of financial information and control;
      (ii) failure to act on financial information;
      (iii) unbalanced management;
   (b) secondary weaknesses:
      (i) overtrading;
      (ii) poor planning and strategy;
      (iii) bad luck;
      (iv) poor communications;
      (v) poor marketing.
4 Signs of insolvency:
   (a) worsening trading experience;
   (b) increased reliance on borrowed funds;
   (c) increased reliance on associated companies;
   (d) expansion through acquisition and/or capital expenditure;
   (e) board resignations;
   (f) late figures.
5 The main types of insolvency are:
   (a) voluntary arrangements, always supervised by a practitioner, designed to keep the business going and minimising creditor loss;
   (b) administrations, where the administrator is given considerable power to continue the business with a view to finding the best possible resolution of the insolvency, with the approval of all creditors;
   (c) administrative receiverships, similar to administrations, except that the appointment is for a secured creditor (debenture holder), whose debt is paramount;

   (d) members' voluntary liquidation, provides for the orderly winding up of a company, without loss to creditors;
   (e) creditors' voluntary liquidation, instigates the winding up of an insolvent company, with creditors receiving dividends according to priority;
   (f) compulsory liquidation, usually results from a creditors' petition following non-payment of debt.
6 The Act embodies powerful provisions for punishing directors (or senior managers) for failing to act responsibly in managing their companies. They can be asked to contribute to the insolvent estate out of their own assets, or even imprisoned.
7 Further powers under the Company Directors Disqualification Act 1986 can disqualify imprudent directors from holding office for a period up to fifteen years.
8 Provisions exist to penalise those involved in trading at undervalue or giving preferences which unfairly reduce the amounts available for distribution to creditors.

# CHAPTER 10

# CREDIT RISK PROTECTION

No matter how good your up-front credit vetting, or how effective the subsequent cash and credit risk management, losses still occur. Their impact can range from a pinprick to a gaping hole in the profit and loss account. Sometimes it is necessary to mention this latter loss in the annual accounts, to the acute embarrassment of the finance director (or more likely the ex-finance director).

The good news is that there are many ways to minimise the risks inherent in credit trading, whether domestic or overseas. However, effective credit protection costs money. In the long term this expense is very likely to pay for itself.

Choosing the most suitable credit safeguards is difficult. It depends very much on past experience, and a perception of trading conditions in the future. The idea of time is very important to bad debt costing. In any one period it is advisable to look back three or four years, and look forward for two. In a good year, the cost of protection may exceed the actual losses suffered. Averaging it out over a longer period gives a better perspective.

Over a period of time, the typical bad debt curve will be more or less flat, with perhaps one peak in every five years. To many this represents a controllable problem which can be handled by prudent bad debt reserving.

This chapter will examine credit protection methods, looking at their effectiveness and cost. They are:

1 Retention of title.
2 Security.
3 Bad debt reserves.
4 Cash flow support for domestic and export trade.
5 Domestic credit insurance.
6 Export credit insurance.
7 The credit insurance marketplace.

Attitudes to credit risk protection vary widely. Smaller companies are much more heavily concerned with creating sales opportunities than minimising bad debts – that is until they suffer a huge loss, which can sometimes be a major contributory factor to failure. Larger companies learn by experience that more attention is needed to protect the profit margin. In banking, it is a central activity which plays a crucial role in the amounts and types of lending.

Two aspects of trading have a significant, if perhaps subconscious part to play on attitudes to credit losses.

1 It is by no means unusual for a company to lose up to seventy per cent of sales! This staggering statement is a little inaccurate, but it serves to emphasise the point. To better define it, take the example of a company with a turnover of £30 million. During the course of a year, it is quite possible for them to have generated selling opportunities, and issued quotes, for business amounting to £100 million. Such is the effect of competition, only thirty per cent of those quotes were successful.

   An often-used argument for quantifying the result of a bad debt is that sales of up to ten times its value are needed to replace the profit lost. While a reasonable comparison to make, its impact can diminish when put in wider perspective. Even the best and most efficient salesforce will continually see sales and profit opportunities vanishing. A bad debt is just like one of those opportunities lost. The credit department is totally unaware of these events.
2 As already mentioned insolvency is a rare event, and bad debt losses tend to occur in a relatively static proportion to sales. A loss of 0.15 per cent of sales is a rough average for bad debts incurred each year. Profit erosion caused by slow payment can cost ten times more.

## 10.1 Retention of title (ROT)

A most elegant way of eliminating credit risk, at no cost, is to retain ownership of goods until they are paid for. In theory this gives the supplier the right to recover goods which have not been paid for.

Retention of title agreements fall into two broad categories:

### *10.1.1 Simple Agreements*

These seek only to retain ownership of identifiable goods. The advantage of this form is that it is more easily enforceable, especially if a receiver has been appointed to the customer. If any stock can be easily traced as being the subject of an unpaid invoice, the receiver has little choice other than to return those goods. To strengthen the position, goods should be clearly marked, and a reference to that mark included on the invoice.

The disadvantage is that only goods in their original form stand any chance of being recovered. Suppliers of basic raw materials or basic products will find that usually their goods have been converted into a finished item, or resold, thus rendering the ROT ineffective.

### *10.1.2 Complex Agreements*

These tackle the problems of conversion, by 'tracing' the value of goods into the finished item. This means the proceeds of the sale of any goods incorporating your product should be made available to settle the outstanding invoice. A variant on this is to require the customer to establish a separate bank account into which these proceeds are lodged.

The advantage of the complex agreement is that it can increase the value of recovery, by including unconverted goods and the proceeds of the sale of converted goods.

The disadvantage is its complexity. The tracing element of the agreement, if worded too widely, can be interpreted as a charge over assets, which requires formal registration under the Companies Act.

Simple agreements can be easily incorporated into standard terms and conditions of sale, which the customer should at some time have formally acknowledged. Complex agreements are more suited to individual contracts, acknowledged as such by the customer.

Despite the apparent elegance of this method, it is unwise to regard an ROT as an adequate form of risk protection. Though goods may remain your property, the fact they are not in your possession means you have no control over them.

## 10.2 Security

A way to achieve a degree of 'peace of mind' when giving credit, is to request some form of security. Given customer default or insolvency, the security can be realised to offset or completely repay any debt. There are several types of security:

### *10.2.1 Debentures*

This is a loan, normally over a period of years, with a fixed repayment time. Debenture holders receive annual interest at a fixed rate, this being paid before dividends. As secured lenders, debenture holders have a high priority if the company fails. Debentures are often charged against assets of the borrower. This could be a fixed charge (over property, in which case the debenture may be called a mortgage debenture) or a floating charge over the general assets of the business.

### *10.2.2 Mortgages*

A long-term loan issued on the security of land. The title deeds to the land stay with the lender, who will also receive regular repayments over the term.

### *10.2.3 Guarantees*

The use and availability of guarantees and security depends on the type of credit being offered. In the UK, bank lending tends to be securitised whereas in corporate credit instances are very rate. Natural market forces and practices have made this so. A bank borrower is conditioned to supplying security, which will be requested whichever outlet is approached.

To ask for a guarantee in corporate trading is a totally different matter. Many customers will simply take their business to a supplier who does not insist on it. A cynical but realistic conclusion is that a customer who is prepared to give a guarantee has no other option if he is to get the goods. Such trading can be categorised as high risk.

The onus is on the customer to provide either a guarantee or security concerning credit trading. As such it is another no-cost option for the supplier.

Guarantees can be given by individuals or associated companies. They are individual signed agreements where the guarantor will agree to honour outstanding debts. The extent of the guarantee can be limited to a fixed or variable amount and time. However, the security afforded by such an agreement is itself dependent on the creditworthiness of a guarantor. It is therefore necessary to vet the guarantor in the same way as the customer.

Guarantees made by individuals are the least secure. It is difficult to find out the true extent of their assets, or the existence of any other personal guarantees.

### *10.2.4 Irrevocable letters of credit (ILCs)*

This is a payment term used in exporting. It is a means of transferring the final responsibility for payment from the customer to a bank. As such it differs from the other types of security above, where the arrangement is made directly with the customer. With an ILC, a third party is involved.

LOCs come in two forms:

1 Unconfirmed irrevocable letter of credit: the customer arranges with a local bank for them to assume the responsibility of payment for goods, provided the shipping conditions set by the customer are honoured by the supplier. The bank will recover its money from the customer, with the addition of commission and interest charges. The risk to the supplier is theoretically reduced since banks tend to be creditworthy. Apart from the solvency of the bank, this security depends on two other features. First the supplier must conform to the letter with the shipping conditions. Second if the bank is prevented from transferring money to the supplier's account, either because of a shortage of foreign currency, or regulations are brought into force preventing transfer, then payment will not be forthcoming.
2 Confirmed irrevocable letter of credit (CILC): this is basically the same as an ILC except that the confirming bank accepting responsibility for payment will be in the supplier's country. The transfer risk is effectively removed, though the security does depend on the solvency of the confirming bank. Confirming banks will usually have a relationship with the local bank (they may indeed be associated). Care must be taken not to confuse

the role of the confirming bank. Both the ILC and CILC will in practice be honoured by the confirming bank, who will note the letter of credit as being 'confirmed' for payment. However, this does not necessarily mean that the bank assumes responsibility for payment come what may. If this is the case it will be specifically noted on the CILC.

## 10.3 Bad debt reserves

Every lending organisation or credit provider will set a reserve against bad debts, before the next financial year.

The simplest way to allocate this reserve is to analyse past bad debts as a percentage of sales. This percentage can then be applied to the sales forecast for the following year. However, there are other considerations which must be taken into account.

First, what if any reserves already exist? If losses have been below expectation in the past, there may be sufficient reserves to carry forward into the next financial year, without having to make any further allocation.

Second, how will trading conditions influence the level of bad debts? In this respect there is a time lag between movements in the economy and bad debts. For instance, in a period of high interest rates it takes time for the effects to materialise. Bad debts due to high gearing will begin to occur some twelve months after the trend began. With an upturn in the economy, and lowering of interest rates bad debts are likely to continue unabated for a year after its onset.

Third, what bad debts can reasonably be expected, based on current experience? Close analysis of risky customers is required at least once a year, to assess the likelihood of failure. This is a good moment to renew customer information and seek the opinions of everyone involved with those customers. Careful credit assessment assumes an important role in this instance, though even this is incapable of predicting the timing of an insolvency.

There is a limit to how scientific an approach can be made to bad debt reserving. Over- or under-estimation are equally undesirable, both representing a cost to the organisation. For a recent example, many major banks underestimated the level of Third World loan default. This not only affected their profitability, but has sometimes put their continued existence in jeopardy.

So it can be seen that even in the most sophisticated of environments the uncertainty of bad debts can expose shortcomings in the careful planning of reserves. This leaves management with a difficult decision to make – should reserves be made to minimise the cost, or the uncertainty of bad debts?

In an attempt to answer this question, it is worth repeating the equation mentioned at the beginning of the chapter. The cost of a bad debt must be measured not only in terms the loss incurred, but the costs of generating sufficient sales to recover that loss. The lower your profit margin, the higher the cost will be. It therefore follows that businesses with a low margin need to think carefully about minimising uncertainty. The same applies to those with high credit exposures. For this reason, serious consideration of the next two types of credit protection is required.

## 10.4 Cash flow support for domestic and export trade

While bad debts have an adverse effect on profit margins, shortage of working funds (as we have already discussed) can be a much more serious problem. This is especially the case with smaller companies, who have less capital and assets, making it more difficult to borrow from their bank.

One of the largest assets in any company is its customers, which often represent as much as forty per cent of total assets. There are several ways to obtain finance, using this asset as security.

### *10.4.1 Factoring*

In its traditional form, factoring solves two problems at once. First the factor will buy your invoices. Second he will assume the risk of customer non-payment. The form of a typical factoring agreement is:

1 Each sales invoice is sent to the factor, who will immediately advance most of its value (eighty per cent is around the norm). The balance can be drawn after the goods have been paid for.
2 The factor undertakes to collect the money from the customer, issue statements and reminders and perform normal collection action.
3 The factor keeps accurate records of open items and credit notes. He also keeps the client informed about the balance of sales factored and total payments made.
4 If the factoring agreement is 'non-recourse', the factor will sustain any bad debt loss for his own account.

Factoring of this sort can be of enormous benefit to the user. It is most attractive to smaller companies, who have less credit and collection experience, and a greater need for predictable cash flow. Nevertheless companies need to consider carefully the cost of this service.

Factoring charges come in two forms. There is a payment charge on invoices factored, comparable to overdraft charges. Then there is a service charge of around one to two per cent of sales factored. This charge varies according to the volume factored and whether it is recourse or non-recourse. It can be equated with the cost of a credit department plus credit insurance. The growth of factoring in the last decade suggests these costs are acceptable to more and more companies.

There are two other benefits of note:

1 Factoring is perhaps the most effective way of combating overtrading. Since regular cash flow is guaranteed, there is no problem in paying creditors.
2 If using a non-recourse agreement, and a customer ceases trading, the factored client gets paid one hundred per cent of invoices outstanding.

As mentioned above, factoring is a costly form of credit protection, but then it also offers many benefits to its users. Most important of all, factors are continually looking at new ways to be of service, and are therefore prepared to be more flexible if the circumstances merit.

### *10.4.2 Invoice discounting*

Another service offered by factors is invoice discounting. It differs from full factoring in that the client maintains his own collection system, while instructing his customers to make payment to the factor. The factor guarantees payment for each invoice raised. The payment charge will be similar, but a lower service charge (0.5–1.0 per cent of factored sales) is rendered to reflect the reduced service. The client normally sustains his own losses, though non-recourse invoice discounting can sometimes be arranged, at extra cost.

Companies concerned with protecting cash flow may find this a useful means to raise cash without surrendering equity or losing control of their business.

### *10.4.3 Confidential factoring*

Similar to invoice discounting in that collection is done by the client. Payments received from customers are paid into a special bank account accessible by the factor, but made out to your name. By doing so the customer does not realise that a factor is involved. Once again the agreement is subject to a payment charge equivalent to an overdraft, and a lower service charge (0.25–0.75 per cent of factored sales).

Larger companies with established credit systems, but who wish to keep their financial arrangements confidential, will find this service of benefit.

### *10.4.4 Finance and credit protection facilities*

A variation on the factoring and invoice discounting theme is operated by London Bridge Finance (LBF). This company becomes an 'undisclosed principal' to your contracts of sale, whereby they undertake to purchase the full value of invoices, leaving you to collect the money on their behalf. The only charge made on this service is a discount for early payment, which works out to be roughly equivalent to an overdraft charge. Apart from getting one hundred per cent of the value of invoices, a major benefit of this scheme is that you can choose whether to utilise these services.

A similar scheme exists for invoice discounting. The legal basis is different but the mechanics similar.

LBF also offer a form of credit protection bound into their discounting services. In return for a commitment fee based on sales to customers approved by LBF, they will purchase outstanding debts at any time. The client can choose when to sell invoices to LBF in this way, even after the customer has ceased trading.

### *10.4.5 Export factoring, financing and protection*

There are several cash flow support and protection schemes available to exporters:

1 Export factoring, as its title suggests, is an exporting version of domestic factoring. Since overseas customers are involved, the factor (most probably using an associated company in the country of the customer) will carefully vet the customer, and cover is dependent on this being satisfactory. The overseas factor will collect on the invoice and transfer funds to the domestic factor.

The factored client has the choice of a non-recourse arrangement, in which case the costs are lower. Alternatively he can hypothecate an existing export credit policy to the factor, or even ask the factor to provide cover himself.

2 Export financing is provided by several companies, such as Exfinco (The Export Finance Company Ltd), CADEX (C.A.D. Consultants), MIDFES (an export financing subsidiary of the Midland Bank plc) and the confirming houses.

Exfinco act as 'undisclosed principle' on whose behalf the exporter trades. Invoices are purchased on presentation and the exporter is responsible for collection. Overseas customers should be covered under an approved export credit policy. Exfinco also buy foreign currency invoices at the sterling equivalent, enabling the exporter to avoid the uncertainties of exchange rate fluctuations.

CADEX is a service attractive to smaller exporters. Using their ECGD export credit policy, they offer financing and credit protection for their clients. This cuts down the exporter's administrative work.

MIDFES offer financing for exporters with an approved Export Credit policy.

Confirming houses are long-established specialists in export financing and credit protection. Over time they have built up contacts and relationships with overseas companies. This means they can act for an exporter or an overseas buyer, assuming the responsibility of paying the exporter.

### *10.4.6 Discount houses and forfeiting*

Exports which are invoiced on short term (180 days or less) bills of exchange payment terms can be discounted. Specialist discounters may be prepared to advance the value of the bill, for a fee. Their willingness to do so is influenced by the size of the bill and the standing of the export customer. Bill discounting is done with recourse, and is effectively limited to larger transactions on creditworthy customers.

Another form of bill discounting is forfeiting. This differs from bill discounting in that it is without recourse to the exporter, and over a longer period.

## 10.5 Domestic credit insurance

All companies use insurance, sometimes because it is a legal requirement, or else as a matter of prudence. For instance car insurance is a legal requirement. A large company will expect to make use of this policy on a regular basis, hopefully only to cover minor accidents. It makes sense to insure premises against fire, to the extent of installing expensive fire fighting precautions such as sprinkler systems. Hopefully this insurance is never used.

The credit insurance market, which originated just after the First World War, is dedicated to insuring the debtor asset. It protects the insured against loss through customer bad debt or non-payment. As with car insurance, it is a policy likely to be in regular use. Yet the total number of credit insured companies (for domestic risk) in the UK is less than ten thousand. Export credit insurance is better used, since the range of risks is expanded to cover the so-called transfer and political risks.

There are many reasons that this form of insurance has not attracted more users. It is less well understood; can appear to infringe on the autonomy of business management decisions; requires a certain amount of time-consuming administration; is regarded by many as being more expensive than self-insurance.

Until the early 1980s these drawbacks might have been valid. Some companies willing to put up with them did so because they knew full well they were especially vulnerable to customer insolvency. Premiums needed to reflect this higher risk so that the insurer could balance his books.

Since then, however, there has been a major reshaping of the services offered. A wider range of policies is now available, and the insured can avoid many of the drawbacks above.

Credit insurance should be seen as a way to share credit risk. It is not a replacement for good credit management. Companies with proper expertise in this area will get a better level of cover at a lower premium. Such a policy is also well regarded by banks and finance companies because of the security it provides on the debtor asset.

The cost of credit insurance will vary according to circumstances. Features the underwriter will examine most closely are:

1 Credit management systems.
2 Bad debt history.
3 Creditworthiness of the larger customers.
4 Industry, and types of goods being covered.
5 Spread of debtors.
6 Payment terms.
7 Any current problem cases causing concern (the underwriter is not interested in picking up bad debts in the early part of the policy).

The number of companies offering credit insurance are few, and there is a broad similarity in the types of policies on offer. Largest and longest established in this sector is Trade Indemnity plc, and the descriptions which follow are based on their product range.

### *10.5.1 Types of credit insurance*

1 The whole turnover policy

This is the most common form of credit insurance. It covers customer insolvency and protracted default (normally payments not received ninety days after invoice due date or extended due date). Business is not covered on no-risk customers, such as nationalised industries, government departments and associated companies. The insured will also be asked to sustain a small proportion of any loss (not less than ten per cent).

The cost of the policy is linked to the actual level of insured sales (excluding sales to non-insured customers and VAT). Premium charges are payable in quarterly instalments according to declared sales to date, with an adjustment at the end of the period to take account of the actual sales value covered.

Also required are regular declarations of invoices seriously overdue, and any customers giving cause for concern. This enables the insurer to monitor trading experience, and advise other policyholders that problems are being experienced with the customer.

The insurer controls his risk by issuing 'approved limits' on customers. The insured can exceed this limit if he wants, but the excess will not be covered. If a limit becomes insufficient to cover trade, an increase can be requested. To the insured, an approved limit is a valuable piece of customer information. There are several variables to take account of the individual needs of the insured:

(a) The discretionary limit: not all customers covered under the policy will have an 'approved limit', especially so if there are many thousands. Using guidelines laid down in the policy document, the insurer will be allowed discretion to set his own limits, up to a certain amount. This amount will depend on the size of the business and the expertise of the insured.

(b) Thresholds: an insured can choose not to have his smaller bad debts covered, thus reducing the cost and administration of the policy. A threshold is the amount below which any loss or default will not be covered.

(c) Datum lines: an option available to the insured is to limit cover to customers whose sales currently exceed, or have exceeded in the past, a stated amount. Called the datum line, it is again a technique for reducing the number of customers covered, and therefore the cost.

(d) Goods sold or losses arising: a bad debt is easily quantified as the value of invoices unpaid, or goods sold. However there are occasions where this is not the only loss.

Goods ordered by the customer may still be in a state of preparation. Worse still they may be non-standard or specially designed for the customer. Under these circumstances it is possible to insure for the full loss arising, including work-in-progress, though at extra cost.

(e) Waiting periods: already mentioned is the ninety-day period before a claim for protracted default can be made. There is a waiting period of up to six months before a claim is paid. This is to give time to take further legal or winding-up action to collect the debt. With insolvency the waiting period is thirty days from the date of confirmation of debt. A duty of the insured is to obtain confirmation of the amount outstanding from the receiver, liquidator or administrator. It can take some time to do so, especially if the insolvency is complex.

(f) Credit control procedures: these are bound in the policy, and the insured is expected to observe them always. Since they are specified by the insured in the first place this should be no problem. It does mean the insurer should be consulted if on-standard action is taken with an approved customer.

(g) First loss: another cost reduction option is for the insured to accept for his own account a small sum (usually in the region of £1,000) besides his ten per cent retention.

2 Small company whole turnover policy.

Small companies, defined for insurance purposes as having a turnover of less than £1 million, can also benefit from credit insurance. They may not have credit management systems, or the manpower to handle the administration of a standard policy. Any bad debt can significantly influence their cash flow, and they may still be maturing in terms of managing credit risk.

An almost 'off-the-shelf' policy is available for these companies. It has a fixed discretionary limit and first loss figure, regular declarations are simplified and minimised, and there is a standard premium charge.

3 Single risk or specific account policy

There are occasions when an exceptional business relationship is developed, with a single or small number of customers. Insolvency in these circumstances would have very serious repercussions. It is possible to obtain credit insurance for this risk. Cover is up to ninety per cent of the approved level, and premium is charged either as a percentage of turnover or as a fixed sum in advance.

It is not unusual for these situations to exist. Perhaps the customer base consists of one or two large exposures totally out of proportion to the rest. Whole turnover insurance would be possible, but more expensive because of the sales to smaller customers. However, specific account cover is not designed to convert a bad risk into a good one.

### 4 Excess of loss policy

The excel policy (to use its abbreviated name) is a long established type of insurance. Not until 1982 was a serious attempt made to market the excel principle, by a company now called PanFinancial Insurance Co. Ltd.

It is aimed at the larger company with well-established credit management systems. Usually a turnover in excess of £20 million qualifies, but smaller companies may be considered if they can show very good credit management systems. The policy works as follows:

(a) The insured continues to bear his normal annual bad debt losses. This is called the annual aggregate. Protracted default is not covered, but buyer risks on overseas companies can be included.
(b) If the annual bad debt losses exceed the norm, or aggregate, the insurer will cover one hundred per cent of the excess up to an agreed maximum.
(c) A fixed annual premium is payable, at inception of the policy.
(d) The insured has total discretion over customer trading levels, without reference to the insurer (though other credit insurers offer an excel policy giving the option on whether approved limits are used).
(e) Smaller losses (called non-qualifying losses) do not contribute towards the aggregate. This further reduces the amount of policy administration and the price.

These simple features have several attractions. The policy is much simpler to operate. Should a catastrophic loss be incurred (the policy is sometimes called 'catastrophe cover'), its impact will be cushioned by insurance. Because the annual aggregate and premium are set in advance, so the cost of the policy can be easily budgeted for.

A typical excel policy may have the following terms:

| | |
|---|---|
| Maximum liability | £1,000,000 |
| Annual aggregate | £100,000 |
| Non-qualifying loss level | £2,500 |
| Premium | £50,000 |

The premium is determined by the quality of credit management, industry and customer base, and can be further adjusted according to levels of the aggregate, maximum liability and non-qualifying losses.

Larger companies benefit even more by using an excel policy. Premium is not linked to turnover, so that a £500 million company could conceivably pay the same as a £50 million one. Another major advantage is that export cover can be easily included in the same policy (Trade Indemnity offer a version covering political and buyer risk).

## 10.6 Export credit insurance

Exporting is well recognised as being riskier than domestic trading. As a result export credit insurance is more widely used than its domestic counterpart, although its origins date back to about the same time. The key difference between the two is the range of risks covered which, with export insurance typically include:

1 Buyer risks
   (a) insolvency;
   (b) protracted default;
   (c) failure or refusal to accept goods dispatched which comply with the contract.
2 Transfer (political) risk
   (a) difficulties or delays in transferring money from the buyer's country;
   (b) political events, legislative or administrative measures occurring outside the UK which prevent or delay payment.
3 Political risk
   (a) government action which wholly or partly prevents performance of the contract:
   (b) war or civil war outside the UK which prevents performance of the contract;
   (c) cancellation or non-renewal of an export licence, or the imposition of new restrictions on export after the date of contract;
   (d) failure of government buyer to fulfil any terms of the contract.

For a standard sale on short credit terms (up to one hundred and eighty days) these are the main risks that are likely to be encountered. For more complex trading and large single contracts, with credit terms over a longer period of time, there are even more risks. These transactions fall outside the scope of the book.

Export credit and domestic insurance policies are similar, except for the risks covered. Here is a review of the different types, based on the services provided by ECGD:

### *10.6.1 The comprehensive short term policy*

Covers sales to trade customers and public buyers with payment terms no greater than six months. Associated companies may also be covered for political risk, such as transfer difficulties, but this does not include buyer risk. Sales sourced in a third country can be included.

A discretionary limit is set, above which all customers will be given an approved limit by the insurer. The major credit insurers have large amounts of overseas information to call upon, and are often able to agree a new or revised limit within twenty-four hours. Also included in the approval are the payment terms acceptable to the insurer, which the policyholder must make sure trading falls within.

Waiting periods before claims can be paid vary according to circumstances:

1 Insolvency: immediately on proof of the buyer's insolvency.
2 Protracted default: six months after due date.
3 Refusal to accept goods: one month after resale if the original buyer failed to take up the order.
4 Other causes of loss: four months after due date.

Export insurers will cover between ninety and ninety-five per cent of each risk, the higher percentage being applicable to political risk.

As part of the insurers' own risk control system, they decide the maximum levels of trade they can insure in any one country. This is reflected in their policies, where a maximum exposure limit for certain countries may be stipulated. The same applies to customers.

### *10.6.2 The excess of loss policy*

Again this is available to larger companies only. The annual aggregate, maximum liability, non-qualifying level and premium are set in advance. Also endorsed in the policy will be the approved terms and maximum exposure permitted on a country by country basis. Larger risk may have to be specifically approved by the insurer.

An important characteristic of an excel policy, noted in the last section, is the way it can be adapted to include domestic and export risks.

## 10.7 The credit insurance marketplace

A wider choice of credit insurance products is now available. Considerable flexibility can be built into the policy, which can reduce its cost, in terms of price and administration. Therefore it is no longer possible to assume that credit insurance is an unbearable expense.

Credit managers need to be constantly alert to new developments. Credit insurers are very willing to react quickly with a policy quote, and to flex their policy if appropriate. Tailor-made policies are becoming more widely available. This is where the specialist credit brokers provide a valuable service in joining the two.

Most credit insurance policies are sold via a specialist broker. Because they concentrate solely in this area, their knowledge of the various products is high. They build up good relationships with credit insurance underwriters, and are very capable at getting a good deal for their client. Their services are free, income being made on commission from the insurer.

Credit brokers can be contacted direct. Very often the broker for the general portfolios of insurance have a department specialising in credit. If not then they will know a broker who does. There is nothing to be lost in regularly seeing them for advice on credit insurance.

The main credit insurers are:

1 Trade Indemnity plc: the longest established private credit insurer, offering a complete range of whole turnover, excel and specific account policies. Policies are available to cover domestic, export or a combination of the two risks.
2 Export Credit Guarantee Department: the longest established export credit insurer. At present it is a self-financing government department, but plans are being considered to privatising them. Policies for short-term credit include whole turnover and excel.
3 PanFinancial Insurance Co. Ltd: a company specialising in excel policies and many kinds of political risk. Excel policies can include domestic and export sales. No whole turnover policies are written.
4 American International Underwriters (UK) Ltd: the UK subsidiary of a large US insurance company, they offer whole turnover and excel policies covering domestic and export risk.
5 Credit and Guarantee Insurance Company plc: a long established credit underwriter, who now specialise in the bonds and guarantee markets. They continue to consider specific account policies.
6 The Insurances of Credit Company: a UK branch of a major Belgian credit insurer, offering whole turnover policies covering domestic and export risk.
7 London Bridge Finance Ltd: a part of the Hill Samuel Group, offering a special form of non-recourse financing, explained above.

## Chapter summary

There are many forms of credit protection, which vary in effectiveness and cost:

1 Retention of title: can be a simple agreement, part of conditions of sale, retaining ownership of goods which can be easily identified, until paid. More complex agreements include tracing the value of goods into other products, and setting aside special funds to account for these proceeds. Generally it is not a reliable form of protection.

2 Security:
   (a) debenture: loans, usually over a long fixed period, specifying interest which is payable and often guaranteed by security such as fixed or floating assets. If insolvency occurs, high priority is given to repayment of the debenture;
   (b) mortgage: long-term loan secured on property. High priority in insolvency;
   (c) guarantees: personal or corporate. Can be for a fixed or floating amount, open-ended or limited in duration. Value very much dependent on the creditworthiness of the guarantor;
   (d) letters of credit: payment method of export trade, where confirming bank, either in customer's or supplier's country, undertakes to honour payment.
3 Bad debt reserves: standard accounting practice for setting aside funds to cover bad debts over a financial year. Can be based on experience or expectation. The most common form of credit protection.
4 Cash flow support: financing of the debtor asset, with or without recourse in the event of bad debts.
   (a) factoring: factor purchases invoices and collects money for his own account. Costs equivalent to an overdraft, and additional service charge to cover collection service and credit protection, if used;
   (b) invoice discounting: factor purchases invoices but does not provide a collection service. Smaller service charge made, in addition to the discounting charge;
   (c) confidential factoring: factor purchases invoices, but no collection service. Client maintains his own collection but proceeds paid into a special account for the factor. A way of getting the benefits of factoring without the customer knowing;
   (d) finance and credit protection: London Bridge facility, which is very flexible, and includes non-recourse finance;
   (e) export factoring and financing: similar to domestic factoring but for exports. Other forms of financing provide protection against exchange fluctuations. Normally provided where client has existing ECGD cover, though also available from the financier;
   (f) discounting and forfeiting: non-recourse financing on the back of bills of exchange. Normally reserved for large sums, often over long credit periods.
5 Credit insurance: a means of sharing most of the credit risk (90 per cent) with a credit insurer. Can be used for domestic, export or a combination of trade. The main forms of policy are:
   (a) whole turnover policy: all trading to standard customers covered against loss through insolvency or protracted default. On export customers political and transfer risks also covered. Premium based on total insured sales during a year. Approved limits given by insurer on

larger customers. Simplified versions of this policy can be used by smaller companies;

(b) excess of loss policy: for larger companies with established credit management systems. One hundred per cent of losses (up to an agreed maximum) in excess of the average annual bad debt figure are covered. No limits set by insurer, and policy can be flexibly tailored;

(c) specific account policies: cover arranged for a single, or small group of customers.

# CHAPTER 11

# COMPUTERS AND CREDIT ANALYSIS

In the late 1960s and early 1970s a new device appeared, capable of rapidly performing mathematical calculations – the calculator. In the beginning it was a relatively bulky and very expensive item, but in the intervening years it has drastically shrunk in price and size, and is now an ever-present feature of the desktop.

The same progression can be seen with the microcomputer. The first desktop versions appeared in the late 1970s. Ten years later their price has reduced to a tenth of those first machines. There are many full functioning examples which are small enough to be carried around like a briefcase.

The calculator embodied obvious benefits to the credit analyst. In particular the analysis of numbers in a balance sheet became far easier and quicker to process. Also there was no learning curve required on how to use the calculator.

However, this is not the case with a micro. It is a very much more complex and powerful machine, whose capabilities can only be explored by taking some time to learn how to use it. To compound the problem, an abundance of software can confuse as much as help this learning process.

This chapter unravels some of the mysteries surrounding the machine, and describes how micros can be used to positive benefit in the credit granting environment.

## 11.1 Computing in perspective

The popular image of the computer is perhaps a little sensationalised. In the film world computers tend to be portrayed as being capable of herculean feats on the one hand, and drastic infallibility on the other. In one film the world plummeted to the brink of world war because of difficulties in preventing a supercomputer from automatically launching a lethal nuclear arsenal. In another a mysterious space mission into 'the beyond' was ruined by a computer which tried to annihilate the crew. There are many other examples of this nature.

Moving into the real world, computing was a contributory factor to the 1987 stock market crash. Massive 'mainframes' had been programmed to automatically buy and sell shares according to predetermined formulae, and this automated process did nothing to stabilise the volatility of the market situation.

Even closer to home, the familiar sales ledger is now totally computerised in most companies. Capable of storing millions of transaction details, and producing forests of print-outs, the computer has become an integral part of the credit department. Along with it have come problems; like 'downtime' which can lose a day's worth of input, or the long wait for the DP department to action a special request for apparently simple *ad hoc* reports, or screen changes.

Perhaps the most interesting current topic is the science of 'artificial intelligence' (AI). This purports to emulate the process of human thought by applying of a set of rules programmed into the computer. An example of an application of AI is facial recognition. To a human, the recognition of a person by looking at his face is instantaneous and instinctive. To a computer it is necessary to apply thousands of rules, one by one, before an attempt is made to put a name to the face.

The credit industry has been slow to make full use of the computer, though this is a position which is rapidly being put right. Credit agencies now recognise the value of a full customer database in terms of the products they can provide.

## 11.2 MICROCOMPUTING IN THE CREDIT DEPARTMENT

Given the mixed image of the computer, it is understandable that micros have received an equally mixed response. The scientific and engineering and design communities have embraced them with alacrity. In the credit world their emergence as a valuable management tool has been slow. Now micros are used in the credit department in three main ways:

1 'On-line information gathering: sees the micro being used as a glorified postman. Credit information is requested direct from the credit agency database, then sent down the phone line to the micro, where the information can be printed or stored.
2 Financial spreadsheets: where balance sheet numbers can be analysed in the form of ratios. Other types of 'spread' can also be developed to help budgeting and calculating bad debt reserves.
3 Word processing: micros are quickly replacing the typewriter as the most effective means of preparing letters and reports. They are especially useful for preparing standard letters.

In this chapter the following additional uses will be examined:

1 Constructing models: Bathory's model, working worth and attribute analysis models can be easily operated on a micro.
2 Establishing customer databases: much valuable information gets hidden away in credit files. By using a computer, it can be easily retrieved and used to promote consistent underwriting.
3 Downloading financial information: it is now possible to cut out much laborious manual input by 'downloading' information direct from 'on-line' credit agency databases.

## 11.3 THE MICROCOMPUTER

Before looking at ways of using the micro, it is worth spending a little time examining how it works.

The micro has three basic characteristics:

1 It is incredibly stupid – incapable of doing anything without being given specific instructions.
2 It is absolutely literal. It acts precisely on every instruction it is given. It cannot question or choose to ignore an instruction. Program a computer to blow up, and it would do so unhesitatingly (though I should hastily add that no such instruction exists in any computer language).
3 It is incredibly fast. The more powerful micros are able to perform three million or more instructions every second (the equivalent human process of counting from one to three million would take days).

The six basic components of a micro are:

1 Central processor unit (CPU). This small component acts like a filing clerk who picks up bits of information and files it in a cabinet for future recall. The number of actions which can be done every second, depends on the speed of the CPU. The CPU in the modern IBM and compatible micros is known by the manufacturer's reference number (8088, 80286, 80386).
2 Memory. The amount of information that can be handled by the CPU 'filing clerk' at any one time depends on how much memory can be randomly allocated to accommodate it. So-called random-access memory (RAM), it is used to store programming instructions and current work files. It varies in size from 256,000 'bits' (binary digits – the language the computer uses internally all the time) to 16 million bits (often called 256K and 16MB). For example spreadsheet software can use as much as 350,000 (350K) 'bits'. If the micro has a memory capacity of 640K, then this leaves 240K for workfiles (the balance of 50K being used for the micro's operating system). The most modern 'user-friendly' software devotes much programming to making it easy to learn and use. These programs use up many more bits of memory. When the computer is switched off, all the information stored in RAM is lost.
3 Storage. This could be likened to archive files which can permanently store information for recall as often as required. The most basic way of storing information is on a 'floppy disk'. This is like a record with tracks of information, though, unlike the record, the information can be altered if required. Floppies can be removed from the micro and stored in a separate safe place. Another form of storage is the hard disk, which is like a series of floppies stacked on top of each other, and permanently positioned in the computer. Hard disks are capable of storing huge volumes of information

(20MB–300MB is the most common size range), and they also read and write information on the disks much quicker than with a floppy. Other forms of storage media are emerging all the time, including compact disks (called CDROM) and DAT (digital audio tape).

4 Input. The micro reacts to input from several sources. The most obvious is the keyboard. Other devices include joysticks (for games software), the mouse, digitiser tablets, and an input of the future – voice activation.

5 Output. The screen is the prime output method, followed by printouts and communications using a modem.

6 Software. Though not necessarily part of the computer, a micro is incapable of doing anything without instructions in the form of software. The most important software is the 'operating system'. This provides the micro with a protocol on how to do its tasks, and must be present before any other software can be used. There follows a myriad of software dedicated to performing a huge range of functions, from handling spreadsheets, on-line communications, information storage and many more. An examination of the most appropriate types of software for credit analysis will be made later.

## 11.4 Databases and computer languages

These elements of computing are worthy of special note. Computers spend most of their time storing and retrieving information which has been written to disk. They can perform these operations at lightning speed. An example of a database is the sales ledger. It consists of:

1 Records. These are held on each customer, normally referred to by their name. Each record holds parcels of information on the customer.

2 Fields. Each item of information is stored in a field. It can vary in nature, from a name and address, to an invoice reference number and amount.

3 Indexes. The computer stores records wherever an available bit of unused disk space can be found. However, the user will want the information in some sensible order, either alphabetical, or by value, location, division etc. Indexing is a way of ensuring the computer finds the right information and displays it in the right order.

4 Keys. The selection of an index is done by specifying a field on which the records are sorted. This field becomes known as the index key. Keys are an important part of database management, and they serve several functions. A search key is the name of a field that has been selected to find a record – a typical search key is the name. Relational keys are fields which are common to more than one database. For instance the sales ledger may only hold fields of invoice data. However, in order to print out an invoice the name and address, the information may need to be obtained from a different customer file. The name can once again be used as the relational key which links the two databases.

Unfortunately, the information in a database tends only to be accessible by the software which was used to create it. This is because software packages use many different types of computer language to process and store data. Large mainframe systems often use a language called COBOL (Common Business-Oriented Language), whereas the most popular micro database language today is called DBase. The two are not compatible. There are however three ways that information can be exchanged between different languages:

1 Conversion utilities: which have the ability of reading information in one language, and converting it to another. This is a complex process which requires full knowledge of both the systems being used.
2 Text files: this is a common protocol used by all computers. Whereas software may not be able to understand the language of another, all software is able to recognise simple characters. A COBOL database record can be easily converted into a series of characters which can be read into DBase and then converted into this different language. The process must be carefully managed so that both systems know exactly which information has been earmarked for conversion, and the exact order of the characters. The most common technique for on-line communication is by this method, where the host database record is converted into a text file which can be stored on the micro.
3 Structured query language (SQL): this is a dedicated and very powerful database language which is becoming increasingly popular. Records stored in SQL format can be accessed by any software using any language, provided it has the built-in ability to handle SQL. Many of the most modern micro database software packages have this capability.

Effective and easy connection between a mainframe and a micro is one of the most important issues in computing. The former is very good at storing huge volumes of information, and handling the many terminals which may be networked to it. The latter is very good at manipulating information. Connectivity between the two, in credit management terms, would give the analyst an opportunity to view all available customer information – financial/customer data and full payment experience, in one simple session using a micro. Gone will be the need to make a special request every time information is required in a form not covered by standard tabulations.

The future of credit analysis is likely to be significantly influenced by databases. All manner of information, customer, financial, press and market will be accessible on a database, allowing the analyst to compile a very thorough customer profile – quickly and cheaply. The information can be stored and further combined with internal trading experience records by the micro. 'Information is power', is a term often used in connection with credit management. There is no doubt that the use of databases will add considerably to the power of the credit manager.

*Table 11.1* Suppliers of main on-line credit information

| Supplier | Database |
|---|---|
| Telecom Gold | Infocheck<br>ICC<br>Finsbury Data<br>Jordans<br>Kompass |
| Data-Star | Dun & Bradstreet |

## 11.5 'ON-LINE' INFORMATION GATHERING

The quickest way to get customer information from a credit agency is to use their on-line facilities. The equipment needed besides the micro is:

1 Modem. This device converts the digital pulses generated by the micro into a series of sound pulses which are transmitted across an ordinary phone line, also converting them back again into digital pulses. Modems are available in two forms – as a standalone device placed near to the micro, or as a 'card' which can be slotted inside the micro (assuming there is an available slot; micros vary in the number they have available for use).
2 Communications software. The operation of the modem; procedures for entering an on-line database and searching for information; the processing of information generated as a result of the enquiry, are all functions of the communications software. Sometimes it is sold along with the modem, otherwise there are many software packages either dedicated to communications, or with such facilities among their many features.
3 Telephone point. The modem must be connected into the phone system by this means. A direct line is preferable since this cuts out ay interference from a switchboard, though this is by no means essential, and the communications software can ensure that a line is obtained before starting to attempt to contact the on-line database.

To access an on-line database, the subscriber must first enter a public network. Prestel, Telecom Gold, PSS, Micronet, Data-Star are all examples of networks which act as a gateway to the various companies offering database information. Table 11.1 lists the main networks providing credit information.

Communications software will automatically ensure the correct instructions are used by the micro to access these networks. It may take a few attempts to do so, since during some periods of the day, the host may be in contact with many subscribers as well. Once connected, the next step is to 'log on' to the host database, which requires the use of a password unique to each subscriber. Finally the user is placed under the control of the host database, which gives on-screen instruction on how to select the required information.

Information can be sought in several ways. Most obvious is the selection by name. It is important to ensure the correct name is entered, otherwise an existing record may not be found. Often the host has sophisticated software capable of finding records which exactly or nearly match your request, giving the opportunity to select the appropriate one. With some databases it is possible to be selective in the information required. This is especially important if, for instance, you are looking for press information on a particular subject over a short period of time.

Once you have found the required information, there are two ways of capturing it. Instructing the printer attached to your micro to print out the report is the least useful way. Although the result is achieved, and a report obtained, all the character information is lost the moment it has been printed out. A better way of obtaining information is to save it to disk. Your communication software will include instructions on how to do so. The advantage of this is that the information can be retrieved much more easily, without having to refer to a credit file. It can be printed out, using a simple word processing package or viewed using just the screen.

The costs of using on-line information vary. There is a fixed cost associated with using a public network, and the normal phone charge. Information cost varies according to the agency used. Some charge a fixed sum for each report requested, others charge a fee based on the amount of time spent using the database. This latter method is probably the most economical, and it pays to be fully prepared with the information necessary to request a credit report. This cuts down the amount of time spent using the database. Another cautionary point – make sure the on-line session is terminated properly, otherwise a phone bill can mount up without anyone noticing.

Figure 11.1A-E shows an example of a standard credit report obtained using Dun & Bradstreet's DunsPrint on-line facility.

## 11.6 Spreadsheets and models

By far the most popular use of micros at the moment is for spreadsheets. A spreadsheet is actually a database of 'cells', which are presented on screen in grid fashion. Each has the ability to hold a number, a word, or a formula and number. The procedures for using a spreadsheet are relatively straightforward, and it is possible to begin using them for constructive purposes within a very short space of time.

### *11.6.1 Hints on constructing spreadsheets*

Before looking in more detail at some spreadsheet examples, it is worth dwelling on techniques for getting the best out of them. There are seven points to remember:

```
CONFIDENTIAL......THIS REPORT IS FURNISHED BY DUN & BRADSTREET LTD.
IN STRICT CONFIDENCE, AT YOUR REQUEST UNDER YOUR SUBSCRIPTION
CONTRACT NO.--------------, AND IS NOT TO BE DISCLOSED.

          ATTN: TEST

       *IN DATE*

DUNS: 21-456-7885          STANDARD REPORT          DATE PRINTED  3 MAY 1988

PALMER DISTRIBUTION LTD                                     RATING R
SUB OF: PALMER HOLDINGS INTERNATIONAL
        LTD,
        SUTTON,
        U.K.

'ROMFORD STAPLE REMOVERS'
'WYCOMBE REMOVERS'

LAMBOURNE HOUSE
WESTERN ROAD
ROMFORD
ESSEX RM1 3ND
UK

TEL. 0708-567879                           STAPLE REMOVER MFRS, EXPTRS &
TELEX 4423791                              MFRS AGTS & CARDBOARD BOX MFRS
                                           SIC(S):    3579    5112    2652

    ANY AMOUNTS HEREAFTER ARE IN POUNDS STERLING UNLESS OTHERWISE STATED

SUMMARY

STARTED          1932          SALES         (EST) 23,000,000
DATE INC         1952          NET WORTH              2,198,413
LEGAL FORM       SEE BELOW     EMPLOYS                282
REG NO           434567                                (261 HERE)
CONDITION        UNBALANCED    NOM CAP                2,000,000
TREND            DOWN          ISS CAP                500,000
FINANCING        SECURED

PRINCIPALS
         Frederick R Palmer, chairman.
         Joseph H Palmer, managing director.
         Alan Palmer, sales director.
         Henry Ralston-Smith, company secretary.

PAYMENT SUMMARY

DATE RANGE: 08.87 - 12.87   HI CREDIT:    30000  AVG HI CREDIT:     12525

         ANTIC/DISC   PROMPT   SLOW TO 30   SLOW 31 TO 60   SLOW 61+   TOTAL
```

*Figure 11.1A* DunsPrint standard report

PALMER DISTRIBUTION LTD 03 MAY 1988 PAGE 002

| | | | | | | |
|---|---|---|---|---|---|---|
| ALL SOURCES: | 0 | 3 | 3 | 0 | 0 | 4 |
| HIGHEST CR: | 0 | 15000 | 30000 | 0 | 0 | |

PLACED FOR COLLECTION: 0

In some instances, payments beyond terms can be the result of overlooked invoices or disputed accounts.

PUBLIC RECORD INFORMATION

Registered 15.6.86 a county court judgment for 345 against Palmer Distribution Ltd of R/O 14 Staple Ho 114 High St Romford. (Plaint number: 8754634 Court: Plaistow).
Registered 20.9.85 a county court judgment for 2470 against Palmer Distribution Ltd of R/O 14 Staple Ho 114 High St Romford. (Plaint number: 8347135 Court: Walthamstow).

On 12.12.86 a petition for the winding up of subject was presented by Sticks Ltd of Throwley Way Sutton. At a hearing on 25.01.87 the petition was dismissed by consent

BANKERS

National Westminster Bank PLC 1 Long Acre London WC2E 9LJ (50-30-21)

Barclays Bank PLC PO Box 2 Town Square Stevenage Herts SG1 1BB (20-81-86)

FINANCES

* A FINANCIAL SPREAD SHEET OF COMPARATIVES, RATIOS AND INDUSTRY AVERAGES MAY
* BE AVAILABLE. ORDER A DUNS FINANCIAL PROFILE VIA YOUR DUNSPRINT TERMINAL
* OR LOCAL DUNSTEL CENTRE.

| | Fiscal Group 31.12.84 | Fiscal Group 31.12.85 | Fiscal Group 31.12.86 |
|---|---|---|---|
| Turnover | 26,425,210 | 27,746,470 | 23,584,499 |
| Pre-tax profit(Loss) | 2,166,867 | 199,434 | (586,681) |
| Net Worth | 4,703,000 | 4,248,275 | 2,198,413 |
| Fixed Assets | 2,951,498 | 2,825,503 | 2,331,793 |
| Total Assets | 15,638,409 | 16,040,679 | 15,413,308 |
| Current Assets | 11,541,911 | 12,322,676 | 12,189,015 |
| Current Liabs. | 10,008,035 | 10,931,454 | 12,383,440 |
| Working Capital(Deficit) | 1,533,876 | 1,391,222 | (194,425) |
| Long Term Debt | 927,374 | 860,950 | 831,455 |
| Employees | 325 | 357 | 282 |
| investments | 420,000 | 167,500 | 167,500 |
| Intangibles | 84,320 | 75,888 | 68,299 |

*Figure 11.1B* DunsPrint standard report (cont.)

PALMER DISTRIBUTION LTD 03 MAY 1988 PAGE 003

| | | | |
|---|---|---|---|
| Capital | 500,000 | Land & Bldgs | 1,224,428 |
| Share Premium A/C | 125,000 | Fixtures & Equipment | 1,107,365 |
| Reserves | 20,000 | Goodwill/Intangibles | 68,299 |
| Retained Earnings | 1,621,712 | Investments | 167,500 |
| Deferred Taxation | 25,750 | Deposits | 725,000 |
| Mortgages/Loans | 802,755 | | |
| Hire purchase | 2,950 | | |
| Current Liabilities: | | Current Assets: | |
| Trade Creditors | 10,910,092 | Stock & Work in Prog | 7,825,183 |
| Accruals | 111,273 | Debtors | 4,102,022 |
| Bank Overdraft/Loans | 572,179 | Prepaid Expenses | 71,366 |
| Other Loans Payable | 100,000 | Other | 146,376 |
| Directors Accounts | 65,750 | Cash | 3,276 |
| Taxation | 325,425 | Due from Group Co's | 1,420 |
| Due to Group Co's | 227,500 | Other Current Assets | 39,372 |
| Other Current Liabs. | 71,221 | | |
| Total Current Liabs. | 12,383,440 | Total Current Assets | 12,189,015 |
| Total Liabilities | 15,481,607 | Total Assets | 15,481,607 |

Profit and Loss Account: Annual from 1.1.86 to 31.12.86.

| | |
|---|---|
| Sales | 23,584,499 |
| Cost of Goods Sold | 20,754,359 |
| Gross Profit | 2,830,140 |
| Selling/Admin. Exp. | 3,517,756 |
| Deprec./Amortisation | 293,710 |
| Payroll | 2,784,327 |
| Operating Income (Loss) | (687,616) |
| Income Tax | 89,745 |
| Profit After Tax | (676,426) |
| Extraordinary Items | (1,381,025) |
| Net Loss | 2,057,451 |

| | |
|---|---|
| Retained earnings at start | 3,679,163 |
| Net Loss | 2,057,451 |
| Dividends | 0 |
| Retained earnings at end | 1,621,712 |

The notes to the accounts give the number of employees as 282.
Balance sheet above was prepared from an accountants statement by White, Marwick & Co, London.
Statement obtained from Companies Registry 05.08.87.
Accountants opinion: We have audited the financial condition in accordance with approved auditing standards.
In our Opinion the Financial statements five a true and fair view of the condition of the company at 31.12.85 and of the loss and source and application of funds of the company for the year then ended and comply with the Companies Act 1985.

*Figure 11.1 C* DunsPrint standard report (cont.)

PALMER DISTRIBUTION LTD 03 MAY 1988 PAGE 004

Contingent debt: 1,300,000 represented by Cross Guarantees.
Stocks valued at lower of cost or market.
Debtors shown as a net value, less 65,000 allowance for doubtful accounts.
Fixed assets shown as a net value, less 4,275,355 accumulated depreciation.
Tangible net worth is computed after deducting intangibles consisting of: Trade Patents (68299).
Investments consist of: Listed (124000) & unlisted (43500) investment stocks.
'Other income' represents rents receivable & income from listed/Unlisted investments. 'Extraordinary items' represents redundancy payments made to staff employees. 'Deposits' represent fixed term Government Bills.
Charges have been registered including: Registered in 1978 a general charge to National Westminster Bank PLC.
Registered in 1978 a general charge to Barclays Bank PLC.
Registered in 1985 a debenture to Barclays Bank PLC.
Registered indebtedness at annual return date was shown as 275450.
On 7.8.87 Joseph H Palmer submitted the following partial estimates.

Turnover for 311287: 23,000,000.
Profit for 311287: 420,000.
Projected annual turnover: 25,000,000

He stated that the losses for 1986 were due to a slump in the industry and a Price Cutting War between competitors. A rationalisation programme has been undertaken which has reduced staff levels by approximately 75 and subjects branch in Milton Keynes has been closed. Forecasts for 1987 show an improved position.
Subject has plans for expansion which involve increasing export sales by 15% to Europe. An overdraft facility of 20000 is currently maintained of which 10000 is currently utilised
In view of the trading and balance sheet figures, suppliers may wish to seek suitable assurances or guarantees.

HISTORY

Frederick R Palmer (born 1920) - work history: over 40 yrs experience in the industry. Appointed as director: 01.11.52 - appointed as chairman: 06.07.82 - also associated with Lime Regis Ltd & Stevenage Staple Removers Ltd.

Joseph H Palmer (born 1921) - work history: Former Managing Director of Stevenage Staple Removers Ltd. Appointed as director: 01.11.52 - appointed as managing director: 10.12.66. - also associated with Lime Regis Ltd, Staple Removers (South East) Ltd, Aberdeen Staple Removers Ltd, Stevenage Staple Removers Ltd & Universal Contractors.

Alan Palmer (born 1945) - work history: Former Sales Manager of United Tupperware (UK) Ltd. Appointed as sales director: 20.03.76 - also associated with Staple Removers (South East) Ltd, & Aberdeen Staple Removers Ltd.

*Figure 11.1D* DunsPrint standard report (cont.)

```
PALMER DISTRIBUTION LTD                    03 MAY 1988              PAGE 005

          Henry Ralston- Smith FCCA, MICM - work history: Appointed as Company
          Secretary 01.01.71. No other recorded directorships.
          Business started 1932 by Rodney A Palmer under the style 'Romford
          Staple Removers'
          Registered as a private limited company 01.11.1952.
          Name changed from Romford Staple Removers Ltd on 31.12.71.
          Nominal Capital 2,000,000 in 2,400,000 shares of 50p each.  Issued
          Capital 500,000.
          Search at Companies Registry 050887 showed annual return made up to
          010587

          The following are related through principal(s) and/or financial
          interest(s).
          Lime Regis Ltd (50%)
          Universal Contractors Ltd (25%)

PARENT/
SUBSIDIARIES
          The company is a subsidiary of PALMER HOLDINGS INTERNATIONAL LTD,
          SUTTON RM12 7HH, U.K. (Duns: 22-537-1442) , which holds 60% interest.
          - year started: 1971 - operates as: Holding company
          The ultimate parent is United Kingdom Staple Removing Co Ltd.
          Balance of shares are held by the Trustees of R A Palmer.

          Subject has 2 subsidiaries.
          Staple Removers (South East) Ltd, % of ownership: 100 - year
          started: 1971
          Aberdeen Staple Removers Ltd, % of ownership: 100 - year started:
          1971

OPERATIONS
          Manufacturers, importers and exporters of staple removers and other
          stationary accessories, including cardboard boxes.
          EMPLOYEES: 282 including 4 principal(s).   261 are employed here.
          Sells to: Wholesale/distribution companies principally. Price range:
          1.00 - 30.00. Terms are: Net 30 days (UK) & letter of credit
          (overseas). Number of accounts: 400. Territory: 70% National.
          Exports 30% of sales to Europe, Sweden & Norway.
          Imports 25% of sales from Far East & U S A.
          Product Names: 'Easilift' & 'Coribox'.
          Seasonal business peaking Summer
          Owns offices, factory, warehouses covering 123000 sq.ft.
          Registered office: 14 Staple House 114 High St Chadwell Heath
          Romford

BRANCHES
          15 High St High Wycombe Bucks HP3 5UT, branch. Operates as: staple
          remover importers.


          A DUNSP.A.R. MAY BE AVAILABLE ON THIS BUSINESS. TO FIND OUT WHEN YOU
          ARE LIKELY TO GET PAID USE DUNSP.A.R.

          PRINT IT ON-LINE USING DUNSPRINT OR PHONE YOUR DUNSTEL HOTLINE
          NUMBER.

                       - STANDARD DISPLAY COMPLETE -


F=COMPREHENSIVE REPORT   P=PAR REPORT                I=BUSINESS INVESTIGATION
                         A=ACCOUNTS ORDER            CAN=MOVE TO NEXT ENQUIRY
                         C=CREDIT APPRAISAL          M=MAIL OPTIONS
                         D=DUNS FINANCIAL PROFILE
```

*Figure 11.1E* DunsPrint standard report (cont.)

1 Forward planning: before putting finger to keyboard, spend some time in thinking through exactly what you want to achieve.

2 Clarity: simplicity is the key. Underline titles and group together any related numbers or calculations. In the initial design phase leave plenty of space for additions – spreads have a habit of evolving over time to include new items or formulae.

3 Accuracy: it is very easy to program a formula incorrectly. The inadvertent omission of a bracket, for instance, can completely throw a formula:

Quick ratio calculation:

| Cell coordinate | Value | Comment |
|---|---|---|
| B18 | 1200 | Total current assets |
| B15 | 200 | Stock |
| B27 | 900 | Total current liabs |

One spread formula for calculating this ratio is:

$$B18 - B15 / B27 = 1199.78$$

Though this formula is mathematically correct, the answer is incorrect. This is because the micro has a fixed order (described in the software manual) of priority for calculations. It has started by dividing B15 by B27 and then subtracting the result from B18. The correct spread formula is:

$$(B18 - B15) / B27 = 1.11$$

Always crosscheck formulae by duplicating the calculation on a calculator during the design phase. It is very good practice to put comments in the formula to explain its function. It also helps other people who may subsequently have to use the spread to understand it better. Comments are normally made by use of the semicolon as follows:

(B18 – B15) / B27 ; Quick ratio curr assts less
stock divided by curr liabs

4 Validation: where possible try to check the validity of the figures and formulae. With balance sheet analysis this is easy. Subtracting total liabilities from total assets should always produce the same figure as the total equity. Any difference suggests an incorrect figure has been input somewhere.

5 Protection: accidental input of a number into a formula field can erase that formula, which could be a great pity if it was a particularly long and complex one. A way to avoid this is to 'protect' the cell, a spreadsheet function which prevents any entry in the designated cell without first 'unprotecting' it.

6 Back-ups: the total loss of a complex spread, perhaps because of computer failure or a simple matter of spilt coffee, can destroy hours of work. Regularly save the spread during design, and always take a back-up copy to store in a safe place.

7 Documentation: once the design is completed, make brief but comprehensive notes on its purpose and construction.

### *11.6.2 An Example Analysis Spreadsheet*

Figure 11.2 shows a financial spread of the balance sheet of Coms (Northern) Ltd, our commercial vehicle parts dealer. Let us examine in detail the main features of this spread. By the way, readers with absolutely no previous experience of spreadsheets should not be put off by some of the details below. The following contains some useful tips on how to make the spreadsheet work for you, which hopefully you will have an opportunity to practise.

1 Layout: the spread fits neatly on an A4 sheet of paper, and has clear dividers round its four main sections. (NB all printers have a capability of using A4 paper, which, to give my personal opinion, is preferable to the more familiar wide and lined computer printout paper).

2 Balance sheet items and general information: looking first at the top left section, this contains the main financial figures. General details like the name, credit limit, industrial sector, year end date and denomination (000's or millions etc.) appear at the top. The number of months covered by the statement is included, just in case the figures are for a shorter or longer period than normal.

Two performance figures are shown – the sales and pre-tax profit. With modified accounts, you are lucky even to get these two figures. They are sufficient to cover most of the ratios shown below.

The main balance sheet items appear in groups, with a prefix (FA, CA, FL, CL and EQ). They denote whether it is fixed or current asset or liability, or equity.

Below this are some totalled figures. Note the NASSTS figure (net assets) is the same as the total equity. NASSTS has been calculated by subtracting total assets from liabilities, and confirms the validity of the figures shown.

3 Ratios: the first nine ratios are described in Chapter 4, except for real liquidity (REAL_LIQ). This is a hybrid ratio which measures how much cash can be generated in a thirty-day period to meet a hypothetical scenario where the bank withdraws its overdraft giving thirty days' notice, and half of the creditors exceptionally request full repayment of outstanding invoices. A figure above 1.0 suggests good liquidity and the ability to cope in this scenario.

| NAME | Coms (Northern) Ltd | | | COMMON-SIZE ANALYSIS | | |
|---|---|---|---|---|---|---|
| C/L | 60000 | | | | | |
| SECT | CVM | | | | | |
| YEAR | 31/03/85 | 31/03/86 | 31/03/87 | | | |
| MONTHS | 12 | 12 | 12 | | | |
| DENOM | | | | | | |
| SALES | 1808825 | 2359703 | 2951896 | | | |
| PTPROF | 22820 | 0 | 0 | | | |
| FA_FIXED | 243726 | 224182 | 208587 | 17 | 14 | 11 |
| FA_OTHRS | 0 | 0 | 0 | 0 | 0 | 0 |
| TOTAL | 243726 | 224182 | 208587 | 17 | 14 | 11 |
| CA_STOCK | 558512 | 628539 | 351357 | 39 | 40 | 19 |
| CA_DETRS | 214360 | 728039 | 1301436 | 15 | 46 | 70 |
| CA_OTHRS | 403358 | 0 | 626 | 28 | 0 | 0 |
| TOTAL | 1176230 | 1356578 | 1653419 | 83 | 86 | 89 |
| FL_LOANS | 0 | 0 | 0 | 0 | 0 | 0 |
| FL_OTHRS | 0 | 0 | 0 | 0 | 0 | 0 |
| TOTAL | 0 | 0 | 0 | 0 | 0 | 0 |
| CL_CREDS | 408185 | 351806 | 560633 | 45 | 35 | 39 |
| CL_BANK | 55579 | 86962 | 58920 | 6 | 9 | 4 |
| CL_OTHRS | 449595 | 579934 | 813582 | 49 | 57 | 57 |
| TOTAL | 913359 | 1018702 | 1433135 | 100 | 100 | 100 |
| EQ_SHRS | 50000 | 50000 | 50000 | | | |
| EQ_OTHRS | 456597 | 512058 | 378871 | | | |
| TOTAL | 506597 | 562058 | 428871 | | | |
| WCAP | 262871 | 337876 | 220284 | | | |
| NASSTS | 506597 | 562058 | 428871 | | | |
| WWORTH | 384734 | 449967 | 324578 | | | |
| TOTASSTS | 1419956 | 1580760 | 1862006 | | | |
| TOTLIABS | 913359 | 1018702 | 1433135 | | | |

| RATIOS | | | |
|---|---|---|---|
| CURRENT | 1.3 | 1.3 | 1.2 |
| QUICK | .7 | .7 | .9 |
| GEARING1 | 1.8 | 1.8 | 3.3 |
| GEARING2 | 1.8 | 1.8 | 3.3 |
| DSO | 44 | 115 | 164 |
| ROS | 1.3 | .0 | .0 |
| REAL_LIQ | 2.91 | 1.64 | 3.54 |
| EFFICIENT | 159 | 214 | 208 |
| STOCK T/O | 115 | 99 | 44 |
| CSH/CDEBT | .05 | .00 | .00 |
| ROCE | .05 | .00 | .00 |
| EQ/CL | .55 | .55 | .30 |
| TNW/TL | .55 | .55 | .30 |
| WC/TA | .19 | .21 | .12 |
| BATMODSCR | .28 | .26 | .14 |

| LOOKUP TABLE | | | |
|---|---|---|---|
| SCORE | -1.64 | -1.58 | -4.62 |
| C/L REC | 48092 | 56246 | 0 |
| RISK | 11908 | 3754 | 60000 |

| RATING | PERCENT |
|---|---|
| -4.60 | 2.50 |
| -3.90 | 5.00 |
| -3.20 | 7.50 |
| -2.50 | 10.00 |
| -1.80 | 12.50 |
| -1.10 | 15.00 |
| -.40 | 17.50 |
| .30 | 20.00 |
| 1.00 | 25.00 |

*Figure 11.2* Balance sheet spreadsheet

The last six ratios are those needed to calculate Bathory's model. The cashflow/current debt ratio is not strictly accurate according to the formula, which requires a profit figure after tax, depreciation and increase in company's deferred taxation account. In the spread no such figure is available (such figures are not available in modified accounts anyway). The model score (BATMOD-SCR) shows a worsening position.

With ratios the number of decimal points shown is a matter of personal preference. Large numbers, like the DSO, are best as integers (whole numbers), smaller numbers showing either one or two decimal places.

4 Common size analysis: each item is shown as a percentage of either total assets or liabilities, in three columns to the right of the items themselves.

5 Lookup table: this final area includes several advanced spreadsheet techniques, to calculate a 'preferred' credit limit (see Chapter 5).

The SCORE is the sum of liquidity ratios (first two in the ratio list) less the sum of the gearing ratios.

In the lookup table, the SCORE has been compared to the RATING scale of 1 down to −4.6. Using the working worth analysis model the spread has identified the appropriate PERCENT figure (for the first year the SCORE of −1.64 falls in the 12.5 per cent band) and applied this percentage multiple to the working worth on the left (WWORTH). The formula used to do so is:

```
@if(D31 < 0, 0,
@if(I41 < −4.6, 0,
D35 / 100 × @VLookUp(I41, $H$46 : $I$54, 1)))
```

The first two lines test whether the total equity (D31) is less than 0 (i.e. technically insolvent) or the rating (I41) is worse than −4.6. If either of these conditions is true, then the cell value will default to 0. The third line divides the working worth by 100 in preparation for multiplying it by the percentage figure according to the rating scale.

The @VLookUp function is a powerful tool in this spread. It takes as its range the group of cells H46 to I54 (headed RATING and PERCENT) and uses the second column (offset by one column) to provide the value of I41 (in the example 12.50 for the year ending 1985). This is multiplied by the working worth to arrive at a figure of 48092, which becomes the 'preferred' credit level or C/L REC.

The lookup function is common to all powerful spreadsheet software, though its syntax may vary from one to another (details would appear in the manual). Note how, in the formula above, each main instruction is put on a separate line. This is a sensible programming technique which makes it easier to understand and debug (correct) if it does not work properly first time. Again the ability to do this depends on the software used.

The last figure requiring explanation is the RISK. This subtracts the C/L

REC from the C/L at top left. If the result is positive, implying the 'preferred' level is below the actual credit limit, then there is a notional 'risk'. The formula has been designed so that if there is no risk, then a message in the cell 'NO RISK' will appear:

@if($D$3 – I42 < 0, "NO RISK", $D$3 – I42)

By the way, the '$' appears in some of the cell references to denote an 'absolute value'. When copying formulae to different cells on adjacent rows, spreadsheet software automatically adjusts any formulae to show the adjacent cell reference. However, D3 (the C/L) is fixed in a single position and no adjustment should be made in copying. This is done using the '$' sign.

## 11.7 Word processing

I do not propose to delve too much into this area of microcomputer use, except to say that no credit department should be without such software. It is most useful for standard documents with standard formats, like for instance monthly reports. A 'template' of the report can be designed so that, rather than retyping it each month, just the new details need be overwritten on the template, significantly reducing the preparation time.

Since micros are an increasingly popular management tool, many people are acquiring better typing skills simply by practising on the machine on their desks. It does not take long to reach a stage where typing a visit report for instance, can be done as quickly as a handwritten or dictated version.

Sometimes the presentation of information is as important as its content, and this is where word processing comes into its own.

## 11.8 Establishing customer databases

A customer database is an alternative storage method for underwriting information. Table 11.2 lists credit analytical and management functions where the micro can be of great help.

There is much to be gained in harnessing the power of the micro. To do so takes a little time, and a lot of planning. In this section are some hints on how to construct a customer database successfully. They assume also that dedicated database software is available complete with manuals on how to construct and manage a database.

### *11.8.1 Choosing information to store*

Storage space is at a premium in a micro. A neat and streamlined design will save space and increase the speed of the micro. Only save information that has some value to the underwriting process or later management. The idea is to complement the traditional credit file, not replace it. Information on directors,

*Table 11.2* Credit functions useful to perform by micro computer

| Function | Micro facilities |
|---|---|
| Accurate and thorough analysis | Spreadsheets, using models, and storing results in a database |
| Industry comparison | Variance reports based on industry norm database |
| Customer comparison | Variance reports based on customer information database |
| Consideration of non-financial features | Spreadsheets, using models, and storing results in a database |
| Targeting potential failures and successes | Review of financial database |
| 'Intelligence source' for other depts. (sales, marketing, production) | Customer and industry norm database |

names of referees, description of operations, number of employees are all useful background items. However they do not play so significant a part, and are thus best kept in the file.

Figure 11.3 lists 85 fields of useful information, along with their field type (A = alphanumeric, N = number only, D = date) and length. They are arranged into three groups, the purpose of which is explained below.

### *11.8.2 Database design*

This is a 'relational' design which links the three together by use of the index/relational key SHORTNAME. For this reason no duplicate shortnames should be allowed under any circumstances.

The strength of this design is that it minimises wasted space. If all the fields were put in a single database then, should no financial or attribute details be available, up to 65 fields would be wasted – each one consuming computer memory and storage space (even if the field is left empty) for no purpose.

As time goes on, the general information database will have occasional amendments made to it as circumstances and dates change. Records in the other two databases will completely change once a year, requiring a new record to be made on an annual basis. Taking a three-year period, and assuming full information is available, this means the number of records associated with a single customer will increase from three to seven.

### *11.8.3 Indexing*

Indexing determines the order in which information can be displayed, and also how it can be retrieved. All records should be displayed in alphabetical order, but it is useful to order it into the following groups:

| Financial figures | | Financial figures (cont.) | |
|---|---|---|---|
| Financial year | D | Reserves retained | N 10 |
| Months | N 2 | Total equity | N 10 |
| Denomination | A 5 | Working capital | N 10 |
| Sales | N 10 | Net worth | N 10 |
| Pre-tax profits | N 10 | Capital employed | N 10 |
| Plant and equipment | N 10 | Total assets | N 10 |
| Other fixed assets | N 10 | Total liabs | N 10 |
| Total fixed assets | N 10 | Working worth | N 10 |
| Stocks | N 10 | Current ratio | N 7 |
| Debtors | N 10 | Quick ratio | N 7 |
| Other curr. assets | N 10 | Gearing 1 ratio | N 7 |
| Total curr. assets | N 10 | Gearing 2 ratio | N 7 |
| Long-term loans | N 10 | DSO | N 7 |
| Other fixed liabs | N 10 | Stock turnover | N 7 |
| Total fixed liabs | N 10 | ROS | N 7 |
| Creditors | N 10 | ROCE | N 7 |
| Overdraft/ST loans | N 10 | Rating | N 7 |
| Other curr. liabs | N 10 | Sales growth | N 7 |
| Total curr. liabs | N 10 | Equity growth | N 7 |
| Shares paid and issued | N 10 | Pre-tax prof growth | N 7 |

*Figure 11.3* Suggested fields for a customer database

| General information | | Attributes | Question | |
|---|---|---|---|---|
| Short name | A 10 | Year | | N 2 |
| Full name | A 30 | Att. analysis | Q 1 | N 2 |
| Address | A 100 | Att. analysis | Q 2 | N 2 |
| Phone number | A 12 | Att. analysis | Q 3 | N 2 |
| Telex number | A 15 | Att. analysis | Q 4 | N 2 |
| Contact name | A 20 | Att. analysis | Q 5 | N 2 |
| Account number | A 10 | Att. analysis | Q 6 | N 2 |
| Credit limit | N 10 | Att. analysis | Q 7 | N 2 |
| Credit rating | A 5 | Att. analysis | Q 8 | N 2 |
| Review date | D | Att. analysis | Q 9 | N 2 |
| Registered no. | A 10 | Att. analysis | Q 10 | N 2 |
| Date registered | D | Att. analysis | Q 11 | N 2 |
| Date started | D | Att. analysis | Q 12 | N 2 |
| Activities | A 30 | Att. analysis | Q 13 | N 2 |
| Industry sect | A 5 | Att. analysis | Q 14 | N 2 |
| SIC code | N 4 | Att. analysis | Q 15 | N 2 |
| Remarks | A 60 | Att. analysis | Q 16 | N 2 |
| No of 'stops' | N 2 | Att. analysis | Q 17 | N 2 |
| Highest credit | N 10 | Att. analysis | Q 18 | N 2 |
| Salesman | A 20 | Cust. att. score | | N 2 |
| Collector | A 20 | Prty. att. score | | N 2 |
| | | Fin. att. score 2 | | N |
| | | Overall score 2 | | N |

*Figure 11.3* Suggested fields for a customer database (cont.)

1 Credit limit: it is useful to look at records in this order, or search for groups with a similar limit.

2 Review date: this is the microcomputer version of a brought forward diary, where once a month the database is searched for records with a specific current review date.

3 Industry sector: customer characteristics can depend largely on their industrial sector, which is why it is useful to be able to search on this criterion.

The principle of an index system is that a designated field (such as the ones shown above) becomes an INDEX and SEARCH KEY. The software will then be able to search quickly and accurately sort all available records according to a single index. Most database software will also be able to keep its indexes up to date automatically and in good condition, even if changes are made to index keys.

The latest generation of database software allows for more sophisticated searches to be made, using a technique called 'query by example'. The idea is for an empty record to be displayed into which you enter details in some of the fields. These are used to search for other records matching those fields. The benefit of this system is that it makes searching for information easier, and all the fields (not just index fields/keys) can be used in the search.

### *11.8.4 Reporting*

Following on from indexing, database software usually has sophisticated ways of preparing reports. Report generation involves selecting the index/search key, specifying a search criteria (e.g. all customers with credit limit above 100,000; all with a review date of 31.12.89, etc.), and then specifying the content of the report by naming the appropriate fields.

Reports extracted from a database, can be invaluable to good credit management. Let us take a few examples of what I mean:

**Example 1:**
*Problem*
- Because of high interest rates over a long period, evidence is now appearing of an increase in corporate insolvency caused by excessive gearing.

*Solution*
- Identify customers who are most vulnerable by using the database to search for those with gearing ratios above 3.0, and whose sales and profit are declining.

**Example 2:**

*Problem*

- Marketing wish to identify which markets represent the best potential, based on the actual performance of your customers.

*Solution*

- Get an alphabetical listing in sector order, to identify some of the best and worst growth rates, and profit levels.

**Example 3:**

*Problem*

- Even though all reasonable effort has been made to get overdues down, disputes resolved and customers chased, you still need to collect more money to meet monthly target. Which customers should you now concentrate on?

*Solution*

- Get a listing of those customers with the best liquidity ratios, and who are therefore most likely to be able to pay if chased. Concentrate on any who have not already been subjected to intensive collection activity.

The greatest strength of micro databases is the considerable flexibility in reporting. New formats can be designed in minutes rather than months. They can be printed at will on the office printer. It is no longer necessary to cram as much information into a report as possible since it can be extracted in smaller logical chunks.

### *11.8.5 Input and screens*

There are two ways of entering information into a database – manual input, and downloading (explained in the next section). Manual input needs to be made as quick and easy as possible. Arrange fields into logical groups and try not to squeeze too much on a screen. The balance sheet spread is a good example of this. By arranging fields in more or less the same order they appear in annual accounts, it is quite possible with practice to be able to fill in three years of figures in less than ten minutes.

Depending on the use of the micro, it is sometimes important to use an input form, which has to be signed after input and put away in a file. Customer details like the credit limit need to be recorded properly for obvious reasons, so that it can be seen that the right person authorised it and that the correct figure was put in the database.

### *11.8.6 Downloading*

This is a means of entering information into the database without having to do any manual input. At the time of writing the only available downloading facilities are offered by ICC Company Information Services Ltd. However, downloading is a type of service which is likely to become more widely available as micro use in the credit department increases.

The principle behind it is that information from a host database is transmitted as a rigid format text file to the micro. The purpose of the rigid format is to ensure that each item is put in its correct place in the spreadsheet. Using specially designed software, the text file is broken down into individual items which can be copied one after the other into a spreadsheet or ultimately a database. ICC have designed a software package called Access to do this. Instead of taking ten minutes or so to do a spread of a balance sheet, it can be done in ten seconds (assuming a powerful micro is used).

### *11.8.7 Transfer of Information*

Storing information in a spreadsheet is an inefficient use of computing power. Spreadsheets cannot be made available for database actions like searching and reporting; they use up a lot of memory to reproduce their design and formulae and it is a waste to use up storage space with this information. A better way of storing balance sheet numbers is to extract them and put them in a database, using the spreadsheet merely as a template display area.

The more sophisticated spreadsheet and database software allows this to be done by in effect reassigning a spreadsheet cell as a database field. If this is not possible then another technique is to assign a 'macro' (a series of keystrokes which is recorded and then repeated by pressing a single key) to transfer spreadsheet numbers directly to a database field. The operation is sometimes called 'cutting and pasting'.

## Chapter Summary

1 Despite a sometimes mixed image of the benefits of computers, they do have many useful qualities, as evidenced by the profusion of software for sales ledger management available on mainframes and micros.
2 Microcomputers are now powerful enough, simple to use and relatively inexpensive. Their use in all spheres of business, including credit analysis, will increase.
3 Current uses of micros include:
   (a) 'on-line' information gathering;
   (b) spreadsheet analysis of balance sheets;
   (c) letter and report preparation using word processing software.
4 Future use of micros will be:
   (a) model based underwriting;
   (b) customer and industry information storage;
   (c) establishment of databases for use in comparative analysis.

# BIBLIOGRAPHY


Adamson, S., *Practical Financial Management*, Arthur Young McClelland Moores & Co, 1983, pp. B7/1–B7/17.

Andrews, D., 'Factoring Sharpens its Image', *Credit Management*, October 1988, pp. 40–2.

Archer, G., 'Taking the Risks from Trading', *Credit Management*, March 1989, pp. 30–3.

Bathory, Alexander, *The Analysis of Credit*, McGraw-Hill Book Company (UK) Ltd., 1st Edition, 1987.

Coleshaw, J., 'A Simple Approach to Balance Sheet Rating', *Credit Management*, mid-June 1984, pp. 21–3.

Dun & Bradstreet International, *International Risk & Payment Review*, April 1989.

Edwards, H., *Export Credit, The Effective and Profitable Management of Export Credit and Finance*, Shaws Linton Publications Ltd., 1st Edition, 1980.

ICC Business Ratios, *Industrial Performance Analysis*, ICC Business Publications Ltd, 1988/89 Edition.

*Quarterly Economic Review*, Trade Indemnity PLC, Winter 1988 Edition.

Wilson, R.M.S. and McHugh, G., *Financial Analysis: A managerial introduction*, Cassell Educational Ltd, 1st Edition, 1987.

# INDEX